Singing

Personal and performance values in training

By the same author and published by Dunedin Academic Press:

The Human Nature of the Singing Voice: Exploring a holistic basis for sound teaching and learning

For details of this and other Dunedin Academic Press titles see www.dunedinacademicpress.co.uk

Singing

Personal and performance values in training

by

Peter T Harrison

DUNEDIN

EDINBURGH ◆ LONDON

Published by
Dunedin Academic Press Ltd

Head Office:
Hudson House, 8 Albany Street,
Edinburgh, EH1 3QB

London Office:
The Towers, 54 Vartry Road,
London, N15 6PU

ISBN 978-1-78046-006-2

British Library Cataloguing in Publication Data
A catalogue record for this book is available from the British Library

Typeset by Makar Publishing Production, Edinburgh

Printed by CPI Group (UK) Ltd., Croydon, CR0 4YY

DEDICATION

To the memory of my mother, Dorothea,
and my father, Raymond, who taught me to consider the
true value of things.

To what I have understood of a lost tradition.

Contents

Foreword

by
Malcolm Martineau

I am very happy and flattered to have been asked to write the foreword to Peter Harrison's new book. In doing my job, I have observed singers and singing all my professional life, and this book deals with subjects which have not been aired in this way before.

It is definitely not a manual on How to Sing, and in fact Peter points out that there is not one single vocal exercise in the book! It makes me very glad that his first premise is that the human being was designed to sing as well as to speak.

In the first section he deals with the physicality of singing with diagrams and very clear explanations of the throat and the respiratory system, but then goes on to talk about the very important issue of a singer finding their own true voice and individuality. I remember hearing an interval discussion from Live at the Met on a Saturday afternoon with Joan Sutherland, Birgit Nilsson and Marilyn Horne, who all said that their voices would be too idiosyncratic and individual to get jobs in opera houses today! Peter states rightly that the unique sound is so important and conveys emotion on its own. His work on the history of singing, and particularly *Bel Canto,* shows that sometimes we have lost our priorities.

An exploration of the means of communication and projection, touching on the thorny topic of support, leads on to a section devoted to all aspects of studying to become a professional singer. It is much more than just developing a vocal technique, but in his wonderfully wide scope includes dancing, clowning, Alexander Technique as well as acting skills and, of course, the knowledge of languages which every working singer now has to have.

In the final two sections we hear about the physical, emotional and psychological conditions which are vital to the development of a singing talent and the educational system, including a curriculum, in which it should all be implemented.

I have learnt many things from reading the book and will frequently refer to it to stimulate ideas – physical, philosophical and practical.

Note to the Reader

Singing attempts to share a personal vision. I hope it will make sense to you as it unfolds.

Chapter 2 sets out the holistic paradigm that I consider essential to the full comprehension of our subject. Readers may also be interested in my earlier book, *The Human Nature of the Singing Voice*, which explores this topic in depth.

Chapters 3 to 6 present defining guidelines for both Parts III and IV, and are therefore crucial to the argument. The values implied in the subtitle – 'Personal and Performance Values in Training' – are developed gradually through Parts III and IV, until they reach their final shape in Chapter 27, Ethical Matters.

Preface

My passion for music was born in the chapel of King's College, Cambridge. If Sir David Willcocks, a kindly and encouraging disciplinarian, was my 'musical father', that supreme example of late gothic architecture was my glorious, inspiring 'mother'. The chapel and its music, especially that of the Tudors, were spiritually and aesthetically uplifting.

It was not until several years later, however, that I began to understand what it was about singing that really excited me. For in retrospect it was neither singing in the choir, as sweet as that was, nor the later prospect of participating in opera, however grand. It was not the voice of the chorister or the voice of the professional soloist, for all the wonderful music that they were capable of producing.

What truly grabbed me in my mid-teens and intrigues me to this day was the human voice. My fascination was captured the moment I first heard the singing of the great Swedish tenor Jussi Björling. It touched me in a way that no singing had touched me before. At the time I would have been hard put to explain my experience, but the discrepancy between what I had been used to hearing and what I now heard was stark.

It was not that Björling was singing opera – a genre with which I was barely acquainted and for which I had no preference. It was not that his was a better voice or a differently produced one. It was not simply exceptional singing or the faithful portrayal of an operatic character. Rather, it seemed to lie in what the voice itself conveyed. In that voice I heard the humanity of the singer.

It was hearing that human being in Björling's voice that struck the chord that resounds in my curiosity and wonder to this day. And my quest to discover what was behind the vocalisation of such depths of feeling dates from that experience.

Hitherto, I had thought of the voice as something with which to sing great music, especially in the context of worship. I had thought that singers were more or less good at this, and that it was largely a matter of being musical. Lessons were to help you articulate words and music – instrumentally. Björling's singing disturbed this somewhat academic notion. My own desire to sing, which had not yet been fully investigated, let alone satisfied in any significant way, took on a new urgency!

That is my story, and perhaps all it means is that I had a strong desire to express myself. Whatever the reason, I experienced the teaching of five or six different teachers before coming across an approach that began to feel vocally liberating. My problems lay not so much in physical ability or musicality, but in emotional uptightness. I was a difficult pupil, not for want of curiosity or willing, but because for years I had unconsciously practised protecting myself. I owe the patience I have with my own pupils to the example of my first genuine voice trainer, Joy Mammen.

Joy had been a pupil of Frederick Husler and Yvonne Rodd-Marling, and a first class singer. Her teaching derived from what can be called the Husler School. Contrary to the belief of many who teach under its banner, there is no such thing as the 'Husler technique'. Rather, it is an approach to singing or a school of thought. Any technical work deriving from it is based fairly and squarely in physiological principles. The teaching is an individual matter.

Joy Mammen's own interpretation of Husler's philosophy and practice was for me a revelation. It completely transformed my thinking about singing and teaching. For a start, it looked for the 'good' rather than the 'bad', acknowledging that the voice, if somewhat locked up, was there to be discovered. 'Bad', I discovered, was a misnomer for false tension caused by – and intended to compensate for – structural or physiological weakness, and nothing to do with my grasp of the teaching. With this understanding there was no way that anything could be imposed or that the work would amount merely to the treatment of symptoms. The work was well grounded, positive and systematic – and demanding!

This initial experience, later reinforced by Pieter van der Stölk and Yvonne Rodd-Marling, was for me a steep but exciting learning curve. I very soon got hooked on teaching, and began directing my focus and my ears to that end. I consider myself most fortunate to have been given such a solid start.

Preface

I wrote *The Human Nature of the Singing Voice* more than six years ago for 'anyone who deals directly or indirectly with singers'. Exploring a holistic basis for sound teaching and learning, it attempts to answer the critical question 'what are we actually dealing with?' Partly philosophical, partly theoretical and partly practical, it forms a backcloth and sets the stage for action. *Singing,* while advocating specific and wide-ranging improvements in the training and education of singers, suggests what form such improvements might take.

While I don't pretend to be either a scientist or a scholar, the content, conjectures and conclusions of this book derive from my conversations with pupils and teachers from all over the world, as well as my observations working closely with singers for more than forty years.

I consider being in a position to help a person to find his or her singing voice a great privilege. You get to know your pupils in a unique and highly personal way – through their sound. It has been with an awareness of the responsibility that this work carries that I have written this book.

Acknowledgements

Many of the ideas expressed in this book have already appeared in print. I have done my best to make all relevant attributions. Anyone who has reason for concern may contact the publishers so that inadvertent omissions or misattributions can be righted in any future editions.

Being a writer can be a lonely and preoccupying affair. The most valuable assistance therefore is the encouragement and patience of those who most matter to you.

Over the four or so years it has taken me to research and write *Singing* this type of support from friends, family and pupils alike has been generous and heart-warming, morale-boosting and constant. While it would be impractical to mention by name everyone who has helped to sustain me I am particularly grateful to those who it has been my pleasure to teach during this period.

As for help of a more academic or technical nature, almost every idea expressed in this book has been discussed with colleagues, singers and students, and digested over many years of personal and professional development.

In addition, I am indebted to Peter Nickol for his down-to-earth, sensitive and painstaking editing.

Finally, it would be less than fair if I omitted to renew my thanks to Kate Hopkins, the editor of the book I cut my author's teeth on, *The Human Nature of the Singing Voice*, for continuing, albeit silently, to advise and challenge me.

Introduction

Singing is addressed to all those who have responsibility for singers' voices, not least singers themselves. While it focuses on training and education at the highest level, it will benefit anyone who wishes to make the most of their singing voice and its wonderful music.

Throughout my teaching career, among the very fine singers at the top of the profession I have frequently observed voices that are tantalisingly incomplete or masked – enough to convince me that many singers could make a quantum leap towards excellence with a minimum of detailed work.

In my teaching I have come across numerous young singers who, from what they have told me of their training experiences, and from what I could tell from the results so far, have suffered greatly from the hands of misguided, uncaring or self-serving teachers. I am not referring to would-be singers with no talent, but to young people who have recently graduated. A strong motivation for this book is the fact that there continues to be an alarming supply of these victims of incompetence or indifference.

Other singers I have worked with have pursued a career for a number of years but found the going hard, not because of the toughness of the profession as such, but because their instrument couldn't cope. Again, it has not been for want of talent, but because they have been poorly served early on, when the foundations of their singing should have been securely laid and the necessary savoir-faire instilled. The majority had been pressed to run before they could walk. For others the 'technique' they were first taught made no physiological sense.

Vocal imbalance assiduously cultivated over even a few years can, alas, be impossible fully to right. I guess it was my half-successful attempts to get those singers back onto the performing road that earned me, in London at least, the unflattering reputation of being a 'voice mechanic'! But singing is not about mechanics. Singers are not robots! Singing is about being human and expressing our humanity.

Since the invention of the laryngoscope by Manuel Garcia in 1854, and more concertedly during the past 50 or 60 years, there has been a gradual increase in valuable scientific research into voice, and a corresponding accumulation of information. At the same time, traditional knowledge, as exemplified by the Italian Bel Canto School, has been irretrievably lost.

Consequently, the teaching of singing has become at one extreme vague or muddled and at the other awash with unhelpful or incoherent jargon. In between there is much pedagogic confusion, disagreement and malpractice. To date, no science or methodology has been able to prevent a growing existential crisis regarding declining standards and values in both training and performance generally.

Devising ways and means of achieving specified objectives – the approach for decades now – has so far merely perpetuated contradictory, inadequate, inflexible or inhibiting methodologies. The faults in these approaches are commonly exacerbated by premature end-gaining. With such goal-orientation everyone loses out – singers and their creativity, composers and the faithful (not to say accurate) rendering of their music, and audiences in the fullness of their experience.

A fresh look at so-called 'classical singing' is urgently needed. What constitutes excellence, and what is required to achieve it, both call for clarification. There needs to be a coherent basis for training which neither emulates a lost, sometimes imagined, pedagogical tradition, nor leans too heavily on as yet incomplete and fragmented science.

Albert Einstein said, 'We cannot solve problems by using the same kind of thinking (or from the same level of consciousness) we used when we created them'. I would like to see the training and education of singers based in human values – inner objectives rather than outer ones. The singing, with all its myriad facets, must, after all, come from within the singer.

If the nature of the singing voice is fully comprehended, it becomes clear that fundamental to singing of any excellence is the liberation of the singer's instrument, which is the same as saying the liberation of the singer him- or herself.

A broader, deeper and more reverential approach to singers' training and education is long overdue; a caring approach which is fully mindful of its purpose, individually appropriate, soundly constructive and manifestly sufficient.

PART I

The Singing Voice

CHAPTER 1

Defining and Identifying the Singing Voice

More than ever before in the history of voice pedagogy it is necessary to define the words 'singing voice' and to have foolproof ways of identifying it. The illusion that as far as the word 'singing' goes, anything goes, has never been greater; witness the spawning in recent years of 'talent shows', the proliferation of YouTube video clips (both of singing and how to teach it), singers with minimal vocal talent or training being hyped as 'opera singers', and celebrities from other fields jumping on the commercial singing bandwagon.

To appreciate the true nature and possibilities of the singing voice I believe we need to distance ourselves from styles and stereotypes, fashions and shows, and take a fresh look at the 'basics'. How else can we judge objectively whether singing is good or bad? How else can we ensure that aspiring young singers receive a truly progressive and meaningful education?

In this book, for the sake of simplicity, I distinguish between three voices: (1) the various configurations of parts of the singing voice used in genres such as jazz, rock and music theatre, which, with no disrespect to the many great performers in these fields, I will call collectively 'popular' or 'pop'; (2) the normal speaking voice; and (3) the voice that is commonly called 'classical'.

Unfortunately, the wide range of musical styles (and corresponding voice *types*) that are heaped together under the word 'classical' make nonsense of the single term 'classical voice'. While 'classical music' no longer refers just to the Classical *period* (1750 to 1830) which historically succeeded the 'Baroque' and preceded the 'Romantic' eras, we can rarely point to a 'classical voice' which is capable of singing (or at least doing justice to) all 'classical' music from the medieval to the 21st century. In fact, so differently is the voice generally configured for (say) early music, lieder, romantic opera and contemporary music that we might be drawn into believing that, as in popular usage, the singing voice is merely a question of style or a preferred sound. That might indeed make sense of the term 'modern' which is sometimes used to denote a 'more up to date' way of singing. But if we look further into the matter we come to realise, on the one hand, that the true singing voice is the most versatile and adaptable (some classical singers, given a sense of style, are capable of singing almost anything convincingly), and on the other, that a so-called *early music* singer's voice, a *romantic opera* singer's voice, or that of a *contemporary music* singer often cannot adapt to a genre outside its practised specialisation. On the contrary, it is often specialisation that *limits* vocal versatility.

Some might maintain that the 'singing voice', whether limited to one genre or several, is 'whatever serves', and that in any case some voices are more suited to one genre than to another. This is a superficial and misguided view. If there is such a thing as the 'singing voice', why should one person's singing voice be less adaptable than another's?

In this book I use the term 'singing voice' not as a vocal configuration that is suitable for classical or 'lyrical' music, thereby engendering unhelpful associations, but as a natural phenomenon which is both clearly definable and *not limited in its capacity to any particular genre.*[1]

For various reasons, which I explored in *The Human Nature of the Singing Voice,* this innate voice becomes, during childhood and teens, at least in the great majority of cases, more or less unbalanced or debilitated: thus the need for so-called 'voice training' (as distinct from learning to sing music).

My subtitle, 'personal and performance values in training', acknowledges that each singer's voice is unique, while its various musical and expressive skills are inherent and universal. A definition of the singing voice based on these truths points the way towards honest and potent performance as well as sound and responsible ways of teaching and learning.

In order fully to appreciate the above assertions and the 'four definitions' that follow in Chapters 3, 4, 5 and 6, the reader is asked to adopt a holistic perspective. This perspective and its various characteristics and qualities will later inform the approach to singers' general training and education that I propose in Part II.

CHAPTER 2

The Holistic (or 'Whole') Paradigm

We seek wholeness not for any capricious reason but because it is the foundation of our being.[1]

'Wholeness is not only a descriptive term, showing how parts are united within a pattern, it is also an epistemological term'[2] – a term of *knowing*. For those of us used to seeing and studying things compartmentally or in easily delineated units, the holistic perspective may demand a radical shift in our thinking and a broader, deeper, approach to our work which, like waking up to reality, can be both confusing and revelatory. The implications of a 'whole' view present us (individually and collectively) with an unprecedented challenge – nothing short of a fresh way of seeing life and of being in it.

The holistic paradigm is sometimes mistakenly pitted against that of *reductionism* – the Cartesian model of analysis by which a problem or subject is broken down into its constituent parts. The parts are measured and studied separately then rearranged in a logical order as though they were parts of a machine. Thus the modern Western mind divides and categorises – and 'mechanises'.

Newton considered that if something could not be touched or seen or described or calculated it could not exist. But I don't suppose he would have been any the wiser about the meaning of time, for example, by taking a watch to pieces!

Separation of parts from the whole, divisions into discrete units in order to see how they fit together, is foreign to organic nature. It can be alienating. 'Dissecting the fabric of reality into a multitude of component parts spawns the notions of separation and division'.[3] In 1994 Henryk Skolimowski, the creator of eco-philosophy, wrote:

> The growing esotericism of modern science, its remoteness from life and from culture, has been a cause of alarm among scientists themselves. So writes Erwin Schrödinger, one of the most distinguished of them all: '... there is a tendency to forget that all science is bound up with human culture in general, and that scientific findings, even those which at the moment appear the most advanced and esoteric and difficult to grasp, are meaningless outside their cultural context'.[4]

In the same book Skolimowski says,

> The piecemeal, atomistic, analytical approach, which so often goes in conjunction with the 'technical fix', does not work in relation to complex wholes such as the human being, society, the ecological habitat. What is needed is a new conceptual framework, a new cosmology from which a broadened and more enlightened rationality would follow.[5]

To his examples of complex wholes I would add 'the singing voice' and 'the art of singing'.

There is no doubt that, despite its subsequently discovered limitations, reductionism has accelerated scientific knowledge and development in countless life-enhancing (as well as life-destroying) and awe-inspiring ways; it held sway, albeit dogmatically, for about 300 years until the advent of quantum theory in physics. Einstein then observed, 'The results of scientific research very often force a change in the philosophical view of problems which extend far beyond the restricted domain of science itself.'[6]

> Quantum theory has abolished the notion of fundamentally separated objects ... and has come to see the universe as an interconnected web of relations whose parts are only defined through their connections to the whole.[7]

> Wholeness means that all parts belong together, and that means that they partake in each other. Thus from the central idea that all is connected, that each is a part of the whole, comes the idea that each participates in the whole. *Thus participation is an implicit aspect of wholeness* ... The idea of participation is among the most complex and beautiful in the history of the universe ... The degree, depth and richness of our participation determine the richness and meaningfulness of our life.[8]

In the activity we call singing, and in the educational sphere, we shall see just how crucial participation can be.

'Wholeness and holistic thinking are modes of understanding'.[9] They are modes of recognising, weighing up and realising properties, qualities, values and even experiences that emerge from complex systems such as the environment, management, education, medicine and the human body. Not only do these modes of understanding help us to see that all aspects of life impact on one another, but they take into account meaning, purpose and the spiritual. Thus they enable and encourage practices which are harmonious and creative.

On the health front we are told that,

> This indivisible entity we call a human being physically, emotionally, socially and spiritually extends out to, and interacts with, the rest of the universe in ways not yet fully explored within the profession. (Dossey, 1990, and San Francisco Cardiology Study, 1988)[10]

In the singing world – of teaching, learning and performing – the implications of connectedness and health are wide-ranging and far-reaching. They too are not yet fully explored.

Writing about the holistic paradigm

A difficulty when writing and reading about the interconnected and interdependent aspects of anything is that one is obliged to write and read in a linear fashion as though one topic followed another sequentially. Talking holistically of one aspect of singing, such as the voice or performance or the teaching-learning dynamic, one must assume constant linking with or referencing to all the other aspects upon which it has a bearing or of which it is an integral part.

To prepare the ground for my four singing voice definitions, let me focus briefly on some of the areas of concern that we have as singers and teachers, tentatively exploring some connections.

Health and Physical Structure

Promoting the term 'healthy behaviour', in preference to the relatively static 'health behaviour', Read and Stoll say, 'Healthy is defined as a state of *being* and, as such, is a dynamic and ever-changing state of bodymind'.[11]

Healthiness can also be described in terms of balanced, energetic function. Like patients in doctors' surgeries, singers come to the studio when their voices are out of kilter, out of balance and lacking energetic flow. In this condition their music suffers and so does their performance generally. But of course, considering our body is our instrument, we cannot expect something of our voice that we don't expect of our body. Consider the spine – upon which the rib-cage, throat and head depend for their true alignment – and our relation to gravity. 'Verticality allows for bodily surrender. Surrender in turn leads to flowering … To surrender to gravity is to surrender deeply into the experience of the body.'[12] Grounded but buoyant we are ready for creative work!

Structure and Emotion

The various interrelated zones of the body form a design of vital mutual dependency. This in turn maximises our ability to be emotionally expressive. 'The emotion and its physical expression coexist with each other…'[13]

> A body that has strayed from optimal alignment experiences gravity as a negative force against which it must brace itself to stand up … A body that holds itself rigidly to stand up must also hold itself rigidly in the face of strong feeling.[14]

The singing voice is a dynamic instrument through which strong as well as subtle emotions can be expressed without force or distortion.

Technique, Dynamics of Breathing and Aural Perception

It may be because singers lay so much store on technique that it is such a contentious and confused subject, and, instead of being a means (a process of work) to an end (a liberated voice) has become an end in itself. The great teachers and pioneers, Frederick Husler and Yvonne Rodd-Marling say,

> The voice trainer must realize that nothing extraneous can be added to the organ of song; that all the qualities needed in singing exist already within it. He must also realise that nothing can release these qualities except the proper functioning of the organ itself.[15]

This is both cautionary and reassuring. Substitute 'organ of song' with 'body and mind' (which is in fact what it is) and 'singing' with 'healthy being' (which is what the singing voice epitomises), and any physician or healer would endorse this attitude towards the natural qualities and proper functioning of the human being. It would guide his or her practice.

Healthy dynamic posture makes for healthy breathing, 'the coordinated interaction of the musculature of the entire body',[16] which in turn helps to maintain postural resilience.

It is generally recognised that healthy vocalisation demands a strong, flexible breathing system, but what tends to be overlooked is that muscular events that happen in the throat (both intrinsic and extrinsic to the larynx) influence how the breathing system itself operates. Many voices suffer from imbalance between these two main spheres of activity.

Just like the adverse effects of poor body alignment on emotional expression, muscular imbalance in the throat can lead to the perceived necessity to devise special breathing techniques (of support and control) which impede the natural coordination of the vocal system as a whole. This imbalance causes unnecessary muscular struggle. In other words the *perceived need for support comes through imbalance between what should be mutually dependent and supportive spheres.* If we can view the voice, and work with it, as a *natural balance of forces* we can avoid misplaced effort and instead realise and experience the voice (muscularly at least) as *self-supporting.* It follows that the more precise and efficient the work done within and around the larynx, the more precise and efficient will be the body's response.

The intrinsic musculature of the larynx cannot be felt. Precision in this sphere is therefore, first and last, a matter of aural perception. So crucial is our ability to hear (both as singers and teachers) that, in discussing basic principles at the beginning of their book, Husler and Rodd-Marling advise teachers that,

> Our first task, therefore, is to reawaken the sense of hearing, to revitalize and re-educate it, until it is able to hear the various physiological processes as they occur in the throat and organ of breathing. *It is the starting-point* for all work on the singing voice.[17] (my italics)

Hearing with regard to the voice is generally misunderstood. For this reason it is a theme throughout my first book.[18] While it is true that many singers get by on their physical sensations, their voices have not yet attained full freedom or refinement, and their concern with how it feels distracts them from the matter in hand: performance.

Learning to use and trust our ears as an accurate guide in training procedures we can:

- question our assumptions about the sound, confident that our ears will eventually recognise the natural
- feel comfortable pursuing a multi-layered, unpredictable, continuously evolving process of training
- detect, 'read' and weigh up important details of sound as and when they occur
- be tuned in to how things are actually progressing, as distinct from looking for what we want or expect
- detect and appreciate the qualities emerging from complex relationships between components
- weigh up 'parts' within and against the 'whole', thereby attaining homoeostasis by logical degrees
- check that all exercising is purposive and progressive
- liberate and enjoy the creativity of our intuition
- take due care of and delight in an individual's true and special qualities.

That may sound like a lot of listening – and I have mentioned only some of the benefits. When the voice is primarily an aural experience we are less inclined to struggle. We stop trying to produce it, control it or 'improve' it. Not only does the extraordinary capacity of our ears enable us to feel free and continuously constructive in our approach, but it makes way for the emergence of an as-yet-unknown 'sound picture' of the voice, which becomes more and more distinct and exciting as it takes shape.

While training a voice is a highly analytical process, visualising and hearing the voice as a dynamic working unity will help us to avoid mindless, formulaic vocal routines, which at best have a mechanising effect. Aural acuity will help us to move beyond 'solutions' or 'strategies' that treat only symptoms.

Muscle systems that contribute to the singing voice can be, and often need to be, temporarily 'worked' or emphasised in relative isolation. However, hearing with 'open, all-embracing ears' will help us to deal with the fact that *every* sound is necessarily a *composite* of muscle movements.

Whether we give a sound a label such as *falsetto*, 'chest voice' or 'head voice', or a description such as dark, light, covered or open, *every sound reflects faithfully what's behind it*. The label is not important. The sound *is*.

Wherever (in the throat or in the body) the emphasis of our work is placed, we can also stay aware of its relation to the rest of the organism. Instead of dealing with *a, b, c* and *d* – as though they were parts to be fitted together on an assembly line, we can recognise them through how they relate. We can determine how and to what extent they contribute to one another's efficacy, and how each component is defined by its relation to the whole. In this way too our diagnoses can become deeper and more accurate.

Self – within and without

Naturally, of all the elements that create the 'whole' in singing, the singer him- or herself is at the centre of the activity. But of what does this activity consist? To what, and to whom, do we bring our singing voice? Clearly we ourselves influence and connect, from within ourselves, to those things which appear to be outside us (music and text for example). At the same time *they* motivate and affect *us*. Through our agency the various inner and outer elements potentialise each other, giving us a sense of our own reality, illuminating our lives. Our listeners are similarly affected, as though by proxy.

The 'embodied meaning' to which performers aspire is multi-textured and associative. The meaning emerges with the coalescence of these various layers. With such thoughts in mind consider the mind map in illustration 2.1. This 'map' was done quickly, with little thought to organisation, but however far we extend it we realise how all the singer's skills and concerns might be mutually influencing and beneficial. Discover how easy it is to make such connections between seemingly disparate subjects. It is only with an awareness of the bigger picture that we can avoid missing crucial links, and give sufficient attention or weight to components which actually affect current progress or are integral to the building and shaping of our eventual performance. (More about systems and organisation in Chapter 19.)

Notice that a sizeable set of components – those that comprise the singing voice itself – is missing from the map. While all the subjects of

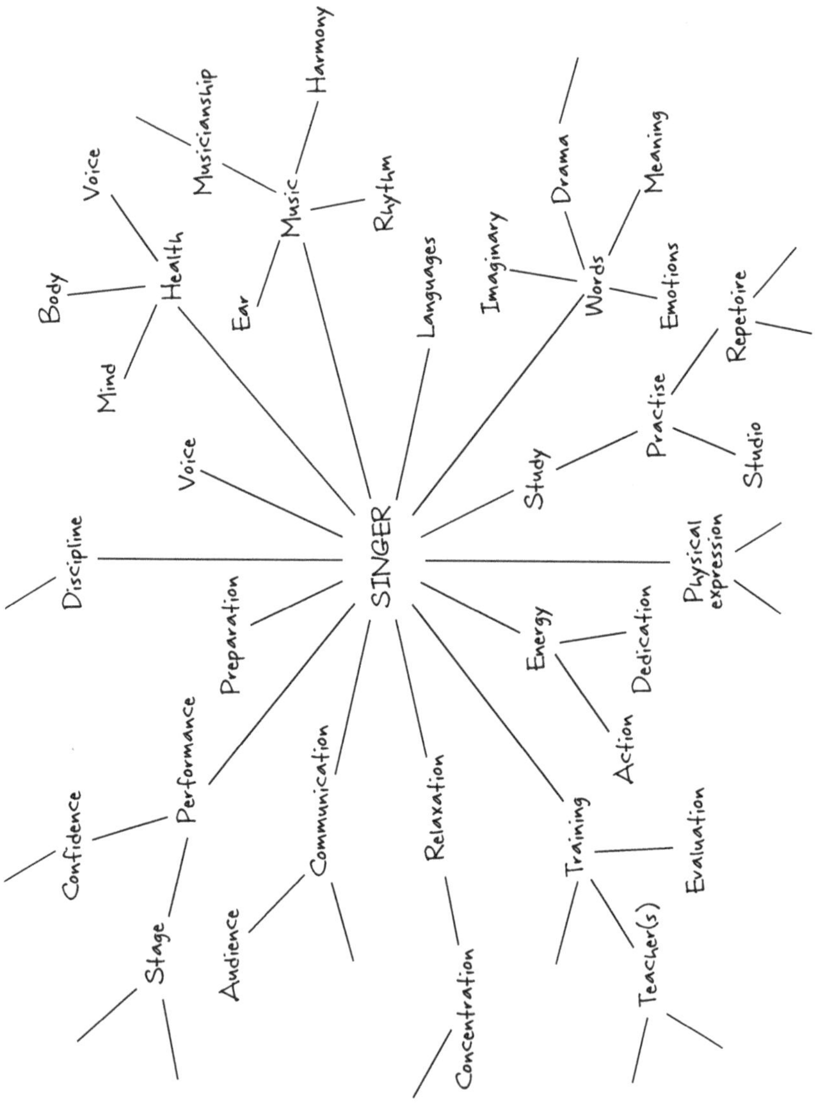

2.1 Mind Map centred on the singer: internal and external connections and influences.

the map are bound to have a bearing on a singer's voice and how it is employed, the voice and its condition affects in turn all the other subjects. At any given stage of training the voice tells us *how and when* and *in what proportion* to deal with them. In other words, *how effective the subjects eventually become depends on the condition of the instrument as and when those subjects are being dealt with.*

It is beginning to be understood, in various fields, how and to what extent our body can affect our thinking. It is easy to see in the singing context how adversely an unbalanced or inhibited voice can affect our *sense of self* and therefore our ability to express ourselves. Restoring our voice to its healthy, natural condition is a kind of self-actualisation. In his book *A Way of Being* Carl R. Rogers, founder of the human potential movement, describes 'an actualizing tendency' as 'a characteristic of organic life'.[19] And of further relevance to our particular field, Abraham Maslow says,

> My feeling is that the concept of creativeness and the concept of the healthy, self-actualizing, fully human person seem to be coming closer and closer together and may perhaps turn out to be the same thing.[20]

Communication

This is a vast subject – the reason I believe why we have a singing voice in the first place. Communication has to do with *relationships* – that with our audience, that with our subject matter (music, text, drama) and that with the instrument (ourselves) with which we convey or share it. Respect for our audience, for example, can ensure that we take due care of our material, how we present it and how we conduct ourselves on stage. Appearing indifferent, or dishing up something half-baked, is an insult as well as a potential turn-off. Egoism can destroy the integrity of our performance. The meaning and depths of feelings conveyed and the directness of our message depend not only on our attitude to performance and our experience of life, but on the health and precision of our vocal instrument.

Employing the full extent of our voice, we figuratively and literally sound our whole self – mind, body and spirit. We sing from our head, our heart and our life. Such profound and all-embracing activity can resonate equally deeply and extensively with those who listen. They participate (albeit silently) in their own mind, body and spirit.

In his book on leadership Deepak Chopra, talking about authenticity, quotes what Italo Magni said about public speaking,

> If you're talking with your head, you're going to speak to their heads. If you're talking with your heart, you're going to reach their hearts. If you talk with your life, you're going to reach their lives.[21]

Substitute 'talk' with 'sing' and nothing could be more true of the act of singing.

In the following four chapters I examine angles from which the true singing voice might be defined and identified as such. These will form basic guidelines throughout the remainder of this book.

CHAPTER 3

Physical Structure (Anatomy and Physiology)[1]

A structure is a totality; that is, it is a system subject to laws which apply to the whole system and not merely to some element or other within the system.

Jean Piaget[2]

Books and papers on the anatomy and physiology of the human voice by erudite, highly experienced, passionately committed voice scientists abound. And yet, while it is generally understood that there is much more to the human voice than the larynx, there seems to be an unwillingness – or inability – to perceive connections between analyses and practice: for example, between the detailed analysis of the marvellous complex structure of the vocal folds which gives us so many clues (more of this in Chapter 4) and what makes the difference practically between the so-called 'normal' voice and what is described as the 'exceptional' voice. Possible reasons for this are:

a) invasive experimentation or measuring techniques which necessarily prevent optimal functioning of the subject's voice. Natural connections can be made only in natural conditions.
b) a reductionist approach. We will get the picture only when *all* aspects are seen to be related.
c) an unwillingness to acknowledge the singing voice as *the healthy voice,* as against the normal voice which is not.
d) insufficient examples of vocally healthy singing available for research. If we want to know what constitutes good health we must examine healthy, whole voices.

As a result, there is little in the research so far that is of direct practical use for the singer and singing teacher – no *coherent theoretical basis* for the creation and development of integrated training procedures.

In the following brief survey I highlight various aspects of structure and physical operation which, taken together, and through the eyes and ears of a singing teacher with a holistic view, I see as crucial to our work.

Examining the singing voice as a musical instrument we see that, like any other, it has a recognisable structure of interrelated parts. Take a part or two away, or neglect them, and it will no longer play as easily as it did when it was whole. The more parts fail to work, or to work fully, the less recognisable the singing voice is as the instrument it was supposed to be. In my book *The Human Nature of the Singing Voice* I describe how, from the start of life, most singing voices become diminished not only because of neglect or on account of misguided teaching, but also by what I call 'civilising processes', in particular the *repression of vocalised emotion, speech acquisition* and *a sedentary lifestyle.*[3] We are left with a weak and wobbly structure.

The physiology of the singing voice is intimately bound up with our human emotions, the expression of which is its primary motivation. Apart from words and music and the singer's personal commitment, this is what is responsible for moving the listener. The 'moving' can be shallow or deep depending on the freedom (by which I mean wholeness) of the singer's instrument.

When people point to an infant's voice as proof that we are born with a singing voice, they are not pointing to a fully formed voice. The vocal ligament develops slowly, and the three-layer structure of the lamina propria within it is not clearly delineated until early teens. What can be observed in the infant, however, is an instrument (a fully animated body), which naturally coordinates in response to feelings – cries of discomfort or discontent on the one hand, happiness and wonder expressed with infantile lyricism on the other. It is from this 'lyrical-emotional' voice with all its expressive potential that the singing voice develops if it is allowed to and encouraged to.

The development of speaking, although it serves the developing intellect, can be seen as a superimposition upon, or a diminution of, the singing structure. Words adopt the budding and already adaptable singing mechanism and shape it to their own important purpose. Speech patterns vary of course from language to language, but all languages use only a small part of the potentially vast singing instrument. In other words, speech reduces the singing mechanism (with effects on the whole vocal tract) to the bare minimum required for forming words and conveying them at short range. The 'emotional message' is either excluded or comes out minimised, obscure or distorted. Technically, the finer parts of the vocal folds are under-used, and the larynx as a whole is left with minimal support from its extrinsic musculature – the 'suspensory mechanism' (See illustrations 3.1a and 3.1b). In the course of developing spoken words, unlike in singing, the glottis assumes a different shape and amount of opening or closing for each vowel. Likewise, the vocal folds gain or lose tension according to cultural (or familial) speaking habits. With this 'competition' the singing voice, with its potential for various musical skills and powers of expression normally has little chance of developing fully.

Undeveloped singing voices, fragmented as they are by a variety of consonantal mechanisms, and restricted in mobility as they are by at least a partially collapsed or inefficient 'suspensory mechanism', are unable to spin a tuneful line, let alone a meaningful one. Their vocal tone is inconsistent, with a short, speech-level range. They suffer from varying degrees of breathiness or tightness. Pitches attempted outside the normal speaking range (except in spontaneous exclamations) reflect the lack of operational integrity and usually prove unduly effortful. Emotion tends to be forced or weakly expressed. In the worst cases the sound is husky, 'swallowed' or congested. In short, we can tell very little about singing from normal speaking! The singing structure as such has collapsed.

When we look at or hear a healthy voice singing we get a completely different picture. First we notice a refreshing absence of the above negatives. To all intents and purposes, the glottis behaves in a continuously uniform manner regardless of the vowel (or 'threat' of disrupting consonants), so the tone and the 'message' it carries are consistent over a much wider range. The larynx is secure but free to move due to the *elastic support* provided by its extrinsic musculature. The tone is concentrated, neither breathy nor tight, so it carries well without effort and a long line is managed with ease. The voice is charged with emotion since this is its energy source.

So here, I think, we are faced with the first cause for misconstruing the task ahead – perhaps with our first procedural dilemma. What ought by nature to work spontaneously normally responds weakly or incompletely. Apparently our voice needs conscious help or coercion to sing. Unless we recognise the differences between this normal, uncooperative state and the fully fledged, natural state, we will easily be led into assuming that singing can *only* be achieved by devising and employing some kind of technique.

Our task may seem more onerous when we consider that the singing voice is not in fact a discrete entity. Not only has it been 'taken over' and (normally) restricted by our intellect but, as Husler and Rodd-Marling put it,

> Breathing organ, larynx and the network of muscles in which the larynx is suspended – these parts of a large and complex whole – constantly serve a wide variety of purposes. That is to say, they connect up into different mechanisms according to the purpose required: for instance, in breathing or performing certain vigorous physical acts, or in swallowing, coughing, sneezing, yawning and other such processes in the economy of the body ... for affective expressions such as laughing, crying, sobbing, screaming, etc. and for interjections and exclamations; while for singing a further mechanism originates (into which other mechanisms, or parts of them, are incorporated).[4]

They go on to point out that none of these has a fixed form. Each is temporarily erected on impulse:

> The fact that a voice-giving mechanism can be erected, unthinkingly, by an indwelling disposition, can only mean that it is just as innate as the mechanisms serving the other functional processes described above, which equally are formed out of an extremely mobile and modifiable mass of organs and musculatures. What else can explain the emergence, rare though it is, of the so-called 'natural singer', who sings perfectly from the very beginning, who has never had to 'learn'? ... In singing there is a physiological *right,* and therefore a physiological *wrong*; a manifest impossibility were singing not one of nature's designs.[5]

However we describe the singing voice – one of nature's most marvellous 'temporary arrangements' – we can but conclude that any treatment designed to liberate it *must accord with its nature*. In other words the natural, the innate, must be vigorously excited and stimulated back to life with appropriate non-mechanising, unforced, un-thought-out, spontaneous vocal gestures, for fear of inappropriate conscious 'interference' or fixing.

And since, as the cliché goes, 'you are your voice', there needs to be a way to be objective without being side-tracked by singers' particular problems. Since the workings of the singing voice are audible, we can use our ears to recognise it as it emerges, all the while underpinning our work as far as we can with the relevant anatomical and physiological knowledge.

In *The Human Nature of the Singing Voice* I describe and explore four spheres of physical activity which combine in the act of singing. This follows Husler and Rodd-Marling, who describe in an exceptionally clear, simple and detailed manner *The Larynx, The Suspensory Mechanism* and *The Organ of Breathing*.[6] In the latter sphere they cite 'body stretching' muscles. I refer to these as 'postural', making of them a fourth sphere. This is because I consider that, in our stressful times, it is more necessary than ever to emphasise posture's bearing on the singing instrument.

Husler and Rodd-Marling's *Diagram showing totality of movement* indicates the direction of the antagonistic forces at play at the instant of singing. It is of paramount importance to recognise and work with these antagonisms if we want to gain balance throughout the instrument. It is with balancing work that the 'self-supporting' I mentioned in Chapter 2 is achieved (see Figure 3.2).

Talking about the 'elementary cyclical movement in the organ of breathing', Husler and Rodd-Marling say,

> The body ... is capable of producing an elementary pattern of movement, one that is able to fashion the mechanism of singing by fusing its many parts together at one 'stroke' ... The various organic parts (always providing the *laryngeal* muscles are in fairly good condition) almost immediately slip of their own accord into the mechanism's 'predetermined' functional form.[7]

Here we are reminded of the dependence of the organ of breathing on the operational efficiency of the larynx. In singing, if the various intrinsic and extrinsic muscles of the larynx are in poor operational shape, the breathing system works overtime to compensate. In doing so it causes resistance at the throat instead of cooperating with it. Put simply, so that the breathing apparatus coordinates naturally and *reflexively* with the throat,

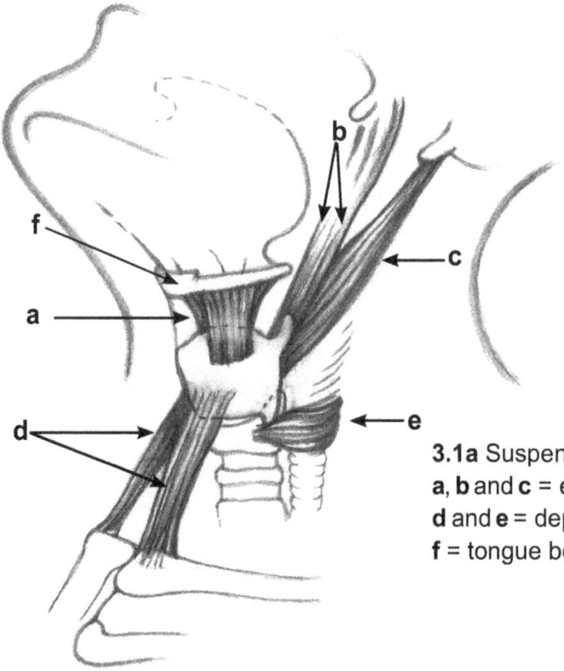

3.1a Suspensory mechanism:
a, **b** and **c** = elevators,
d and **e** = depressors,
f = tongue bone

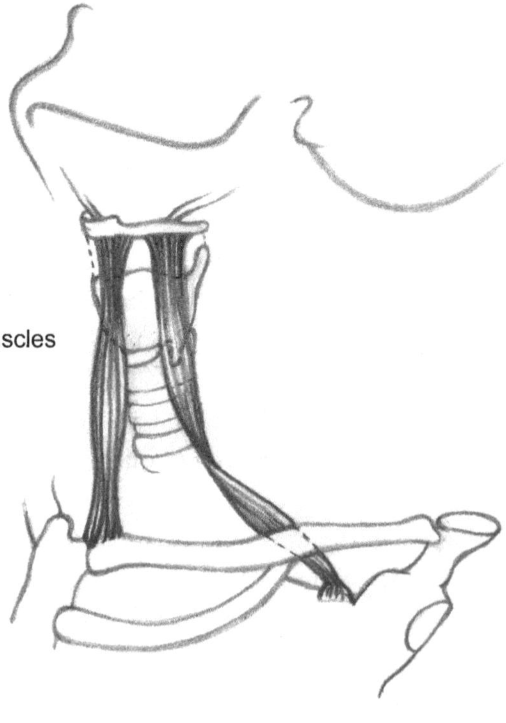

3.1b Indirect inspanning muscles

(After Husler and Rodd-Marling)

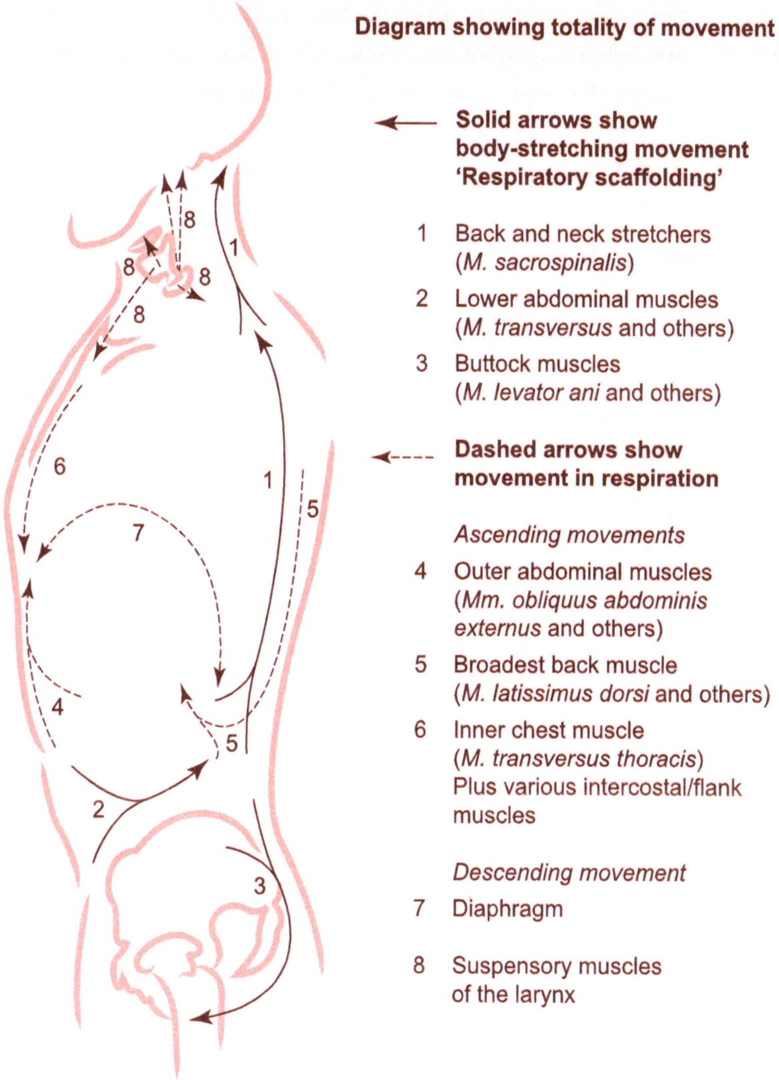

3.2 The large movement responsible for erecting the mechanism of singing is directed mainly from the back; from the powerful origins of the diaphragm and the body-stretching muscles. The most subtle influences in singing, however, take place at the front where diaphragm, abdominal wall and inner muscles of the chest, converge. Being extrelmely sensitive, the functioniung of this region is easily disturbed; it should never be fixed and immobilised (by permission of Phyllis Rodd)

> the epiglottis is raised, the larynx inspanned from above, below and behind ... while the larynx itself effects a series of movements, the most important of which are: the vocal folds are stretched, tensed (contracted), brought into apposition and caused to vibrate.[8]

Suspensory mechanism (1)

The muscles that in-span the larynx are nowadays usually referred to as 'strap muscles', owing to their shape. However, because the term suggests something tight or tightened, I prefer 'suspensory mechanism' or 'elastic scaffolding' as used in illustration 3.2.

It is the contraction and balanced interaction of these muscles that provides the larynx with both its *stability* and its *mobility* as it negotiates a sung phrase. It is by way of this system that the muscles of breathing are effectively united with the larynx – a crucial link which is normally very weak or out of balance. It is the suspensory mechanism that ensures the absence of resistance at or constriction of the throat.

Vocal folds

It is the vocal folds' 'vibratory action which ... is most directly responsible for the production of voice'.[9] Perhaps this is why whole techniques concentrate on arousing the 'chest register' (actually the thickest part of the folds) by singing 'in the mask'. All technical 'specialisations', however, eventually unbalance the voice. We are unlikely to misjudge or overemphasise the role of the chest register if we understand how the vocal folds are constituted.

> The inner, compact muscular bodies of the vocal folds are described as vocal *lips* (Labia vocalia), and the margins of the vocal folds, formed by the longitudinal strands of the elastic membrane that covers the vocal folds (Conus elasticus), are termed 'vocal *bands*' (Ligamenta vocalia).[10]

While singing *dans la masque*, or 'placing' the voice at the bridge of the nose, the muscular lips are active – referred to as 'tensors' because they contract – the longitudinal *bands* are passive. That is, unless they are *stretched*. It is the stretching of these *bands* that renders the lips 'effective' in singing terms. The stretching process is primarily brought about by the

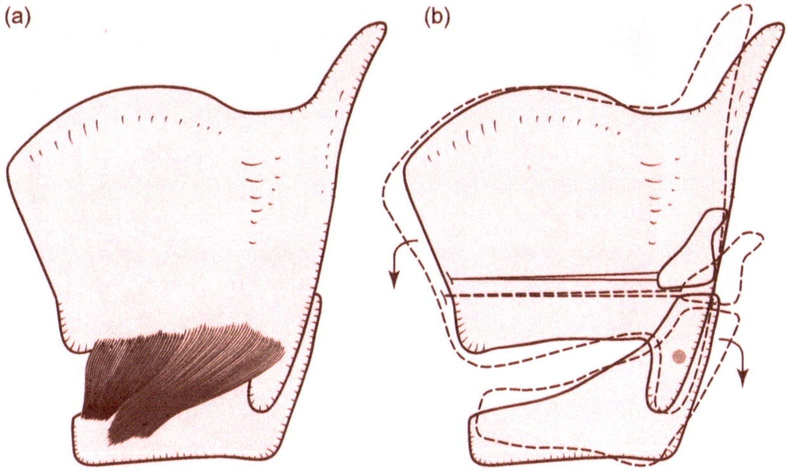

3.3a Ring-shield muscle (M. cricothyreoideus); **3.3b** Contraction of the ring-shield muscle stretches the vocal folds (after Husler and Rodd-Marling).

muscles that contract between the thyroid and cricoid cartilages, bringing them closer together (see illustration 3.3).

This action lengthens and thins the vocal folds (or lips) by stretching the mucous membrane that lines them. But, so long as the folds themselves remain inactive, the resulting sound is the 'disembodied' one that we call *falsetto.*

For the true singing voice to come about these two so-called 'registers' (the chest and the *falsetto*) must be a match for each other; they must be able to coordinate. Put another way, the lengthening and thinning of the folds is a pre-condition for effectively tensing them and thereby producing the core of the sung tone.

However, the *falsetto* on its own has insufficient strength to take more than a certain amount of vocal fold tension. The primary stretching process (*falsetto*) is therefore reinforced by the pull of the paired posticus muscle, which connects the cricoid and arytenoid (or pyramid) cartilages (see illustration 3.4).

This latter action, while stretching the vocal folds *en masse,* also opens the glottis (its *primary* task – for inhaling). When executed on its own, this stretching/opening process gives us the 'head voice' sound – more voluminous than the *falsetto.* Naturally, for singing purposes this opening

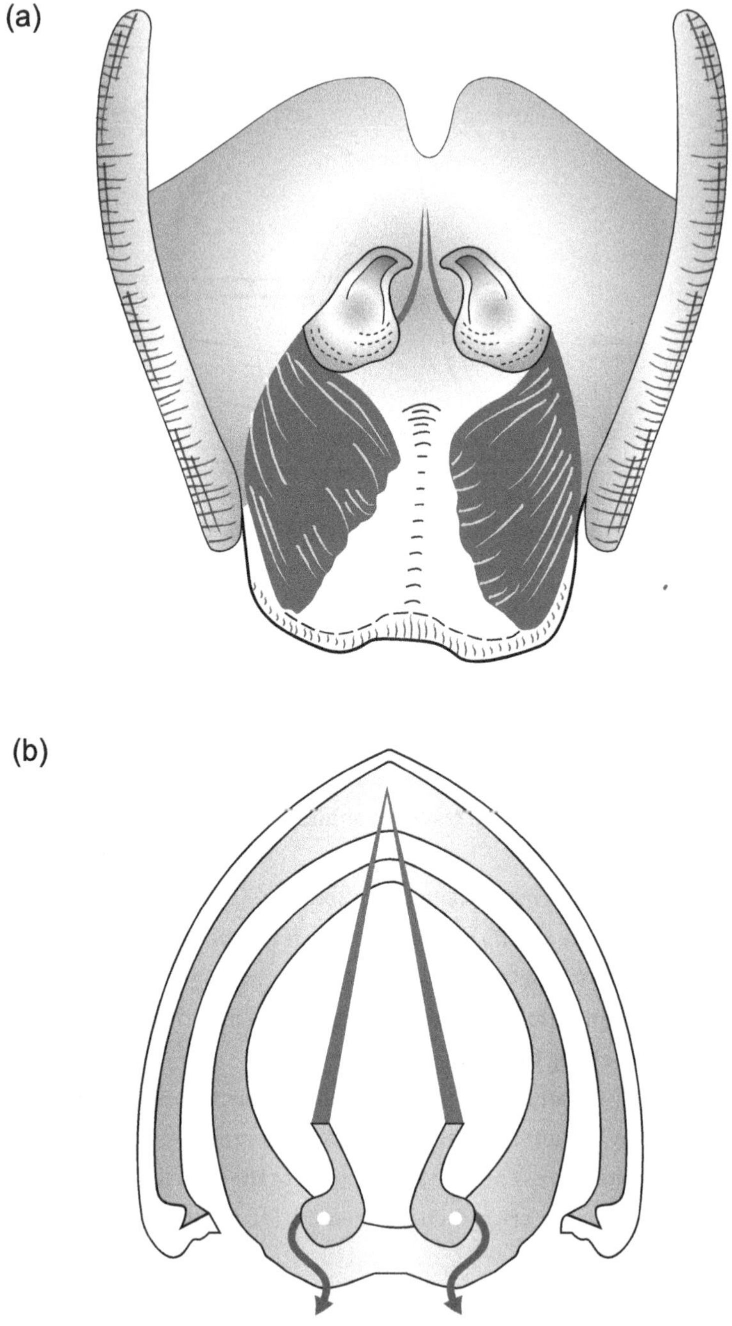

3.4a M. posticus in repose; **3.4b** The posticus muscle. Diagram of movement (after Husler and Rodd-Marling).

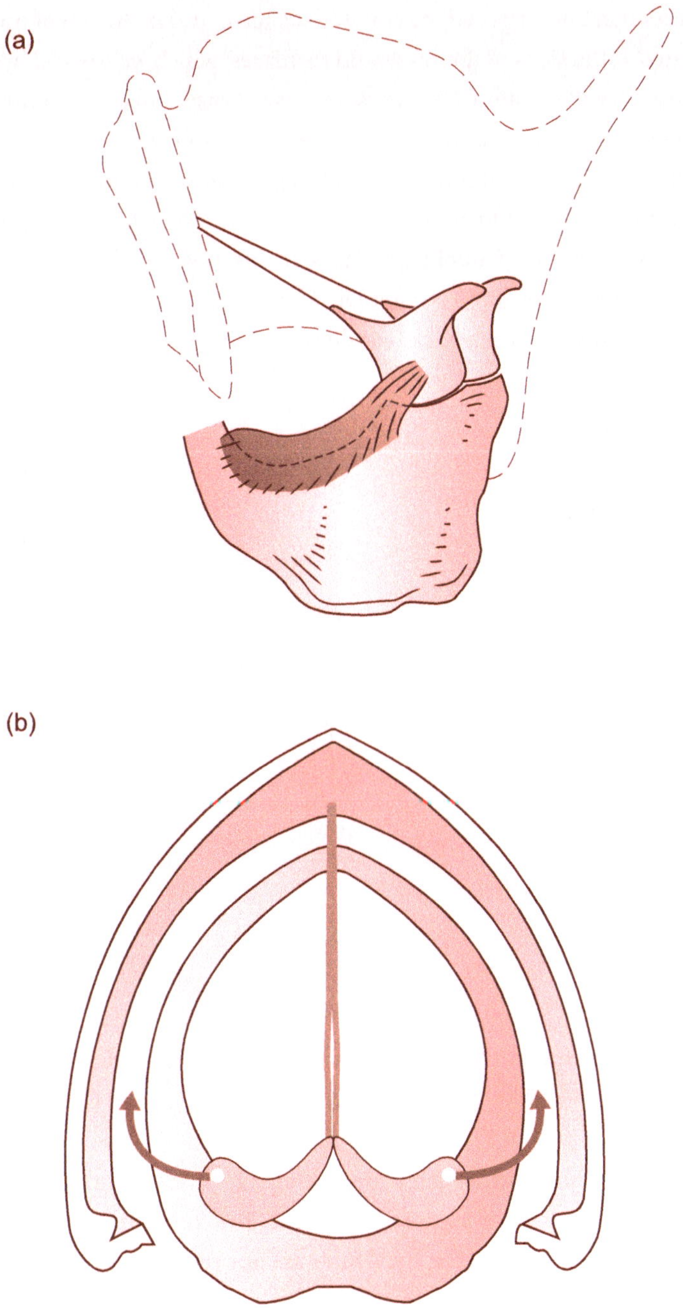

3.5a M. lateralis. Semi-diagrammatic. In repose; **3.5b** M. lateralis. Diagram of movement (after Husler and Rodd-Marling).

process must be 'opposed' or counterbalanced. This is the job of muscles situated at the sides of the arytenoid cartilages, which we can call 'specific closers' (see illustration 3.5). Thus, we have *openers* and *closers* acting simultaneously as antagonists. The folds are neither exaggeratedly nor weakly adducted. The tone acquires concentration – in the jargon it brings the voice 'forward' (see illustration 3.5a). Since in the 'specific closing process' just described the pyramid cartilages themselves are drawn apart, the whole complex operation is completed by the contraction of muscles situated transversely at their back (see illustration 3.6).

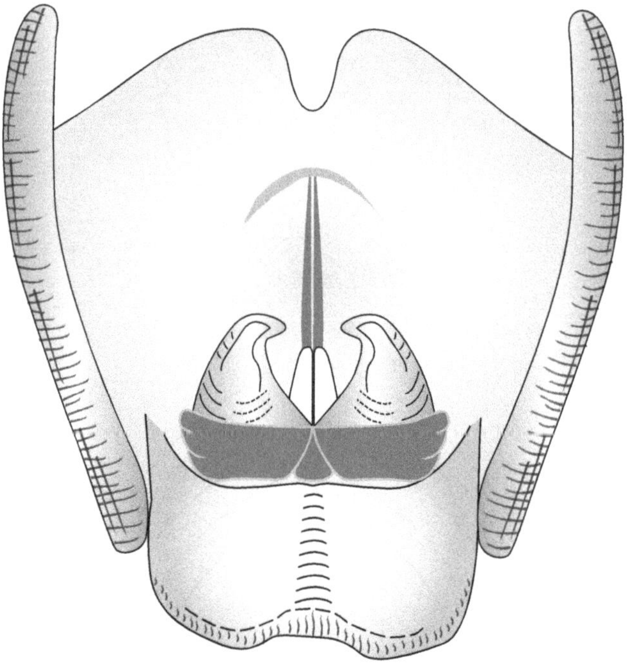

3.6 M. transversus. In action. Its contraction pulls the pyramids closer together (after Husler and Rodd-Marling).

The combination of stretching/thinning, tensing and closing still leaves a weakness at the centre of the glottis. The concentration of the tone is not complete because the vocal folds are not yet *fully taut* at their upper edges or margins.

We come therefore to the very heart and soul of the *singing* voice, the *coup de grâce,* if you like. I refer to fine muscle-bundles and fibres that Husler and Rodd-Marling call the *edge mechanism*:

> The fibres ... radiate into the outermost edges of the vocal *bands* (and thus into the elastic membrane that covers the vocal *lips*). It is these fibres that control in a remarkable way the margins of the vocal folds ... The manner in which the muscle-strands are placed, the fact that they consist of longer and shorter strands, that these traverse each other in their course, that they can act separately or jointly, that even single fibres are capable of acting alone, all this means that the possibilities of varying the quality and substance of the tone are almost unlimited ... Because these marginal muscle-bundles are, on the one hand, extensions of the main body of the vocal lip and, on the other, provide a connection with the elastic tissue from which the vocal *band* is formed, they also constitute the necessary bridge between the 'chest' and the 'head and falsetto registers'; in other words they make a *unity* of the two 'main registers'.[11]

The dynamic coordination of these various laryngeal activities constitutes the 'mixed voice' (*voix mixte*) or, if you like, the *complete voice* which is *capable of maintaining its integrity throughout the singer's range.*

While the various processes described above are audible as such when emphasised, we should always bear in mind that they are designed to work as a whole.

> A properly functioning singing organ consists of one vast interplay, a widespread cyclical process, in which all parts co-operate to support and help each other. In short: '*each muscle, as antagonist, regulates the action of another*'.[12]

Suspensory mechanism (2)

The muscles that serve to 'suspend' and support the larynx as a whole also serve in specific ways to facilitate and reinforce actions *within* the larynx. The main antagonist to the 'stretchers' (in addition to the aforementioned posticus) is the paired 'chest bone-shield cartilage' muscle (m. sterno-thyreoideus – see **d** in illustration 3.1a).

To avoid fixing the larynx down, it is important to remember that *this muscle works by reflex.* It responds to the *correct elevation* of the larynx. This partnership gives us the 'pure head voice'. Add the action of the crico-pharyngeus muscle and we obtain the fullest possible stretch of the folds ('full head voice'). In anchoring the cricoid cartilage backwards and downwards (in an 'elastic' manner), this vitally important muscle facilitates movement of the shield cartilage where it is hinged on the ring cartilage (see **e** in illustration 3.1a).

In most people the crico-pharyngeus muscle is very weak – it is little used in speaking and is often impeded in its action by contraction of the spine. On its own the 'head voice', and by extension the 'full head voice', gives a 'core-less' sound. This is because of the relative quantity of air present when the folds are stretched and opened. It has a strong, warm, in-breathing quality in which the diaphragm (the main *in-breathing* muscle) can be heard to be very much *alive* (best activated on 'oo' or 'ü').

When the normal person attempts to sing, the lack of innervation of the suspensory mechanism gives rise to tightening above the hyoid (tongue) bone: thus the term '*false* elevators' (see illustration 3.7 and compare with illustration 3.1a).

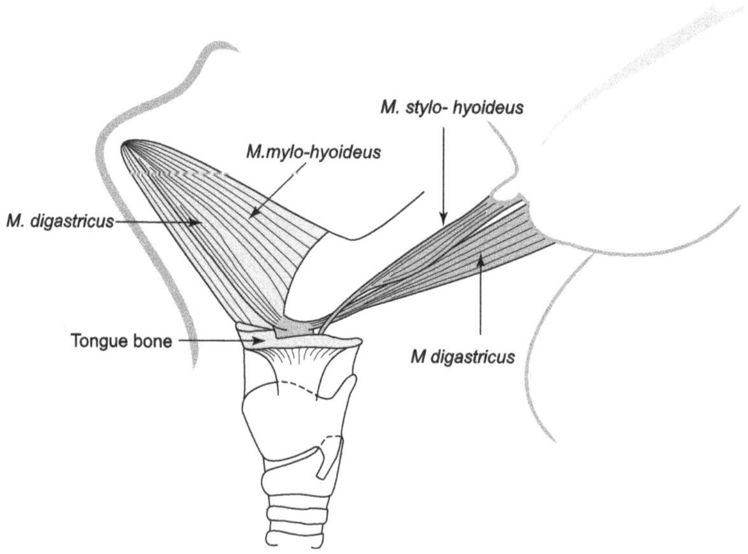

3.7 False elevators. Upper muscles of the tongue bone.

The anchoring down of the larynx obviates this 'compensatory' tension which would otherwise hamper the *true* anterior 'elevator' (m. thyreo-hyoideus – see **a** in illustration 3.1a) that links the shield cartilage to the tongue bone, as well as the tongue's ability to form words.

The Breathing organ (1)

As I have already indicated, how efficiently the breathing organ works in the process of singing depends on what is happening in the throat. It is also true that the vitality and efficiency of the throat is dependent on the natural vitality of the organ of breathing. If the work between the body and the throat is truly reciprocal there is no need for special breathing for singing. The primary impulse for the natural singing voice is neither conscious manipulation of muscles nor 'breath support'.

The Emotional Element

We hear so much false or forced emotion in singing – not only in the pop and music theatre world where, for lack of the relevant physical-physiological freedoms, it is *necessary* to simulate emotion, but also in classical singing, especially so-called 'operatic' singing – that it is no wonder many people try to avoid the very spark that fires the singer's voice into life.

Some singers get carried away and perhaps are not aware when (by attempting to be emotionally expressive) they are spoiling their singing instead of enhancing or enlivening it. Others have to overcome timidity or reticence about expressing emotions; conventionally, away from the stage, it is just 'not done' to voice feelings in anything like a free or whole-hearted, whole-voiced manner.

My experience tells me that the problem with emotion in singing is two-fold. Firstly, the process of unlocking the voice invariably releases emotional feelings which have been safely stowed away in muscular tension – a kind of visceral holding oneself together. This release can be deeply disturbing and is therefore avoided. Secondly, singers and teachers often misconstrue how emotion works at the 'technical' level, failing to see that the *physiology* of emotional expression in sound and the physiology of singing per se are virtually the same. If this were properly understood, rather than trying to superimpose or *add* it (with respect to the text) during the course of rehearsing or performing, emotion could be treated as integral to the operation of the voice in the first place. Voicing and feeling would no longer be strangers, but work as a team.

The Breathing Organ (2)

Instead of concerning ourselves with breathing for singing we gain more by examining the human breathing organ *per se*. Part of the perceived need to breathe in a special way for singing arises from not recognising that the breathing organ of 'civilised man' has become generically weak.[13] The net result of certain 'civilising processes' is that, even though a deep-down impulse or desire to sing remains (as I believe it does in every one of us), it fails to be wholly or even partially satisfied in the vast majority. Except in a few fortunate individuals, the various 'parts' no longer gel on impulse as they did in infancy. In particular our breathing-out apparatus has become extremely weak, and so therefore has the breathing-in *reflex*.

The perceived need for a larger sound (clearly traceable to the 19th century), by turning peoples' attention to the mechanics of breathing in an unprecedented way, created a problem which does not arise in a naturally functioning voice (more about this in chapter 4). The pursuit of unnatural techniques has proved unsatisfying and damaging ever since.

If we look at how the breathing system is constructed in relation to the throat we see first that the connections are primal, the larynx being a two-way valve regulating the passage of air to and from the lungs. By nature we have basically three breathing modes:

1. Neutral. The throat is relaxed, the breathing slight, automatic and sufficient – as when lying in bed before sleeping, sitting calmly watching TV, and so on. While this breathing takes place automatically, the throat and glottis are neutral (unless we are stressed, or intent upon some absorbing manual task). If we then stand upright, still with this relaxed breathing, the situation does not need to change. Essentially the cycle of our breathing continues being small – there is no reason for it to be otherwise.
2. Inhaling. This is done (a) involuntarily in response to breathing out, and (b) deliberately for increasing pressure in the thorax for the purpose of expelling from either end of the body: for coughing, for example, or defecating. The 'false cords' (instead of the vocal cords) take the pressure before it is released. Needless to say, this mode is well practised.
3. Exhaling – as a deliberate action, as in singing. Joseph Pilates, who advocated natural breathing, recognised the need to fully breathe out if this was to be achieved. Not all Pilates practitioners adhere to this teaching.

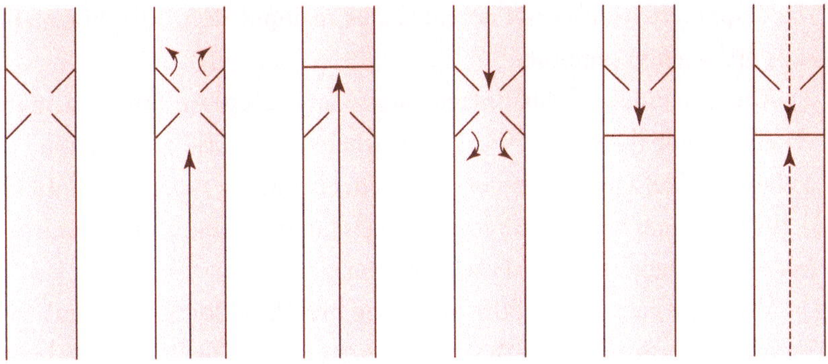

A False cords positioned above vocal cords
B & C False cords close against pressure of breath
D & E Vocal cords close to prevent entrance of foreign bodies or to facilitate strength in upper body
F Outward movement and inward 'tendency': The crucial breathing antagonism in balanced singing

3.8 Diagrammatic representation of the relationship between the passage of breath and the valvular larynx.

Except for the unusually energetic, venturing far into exhalation territory is unfamiliar, and for those not used to it, it should be attempted only by degrees.

A healthy exhalation brings muscles of the flanks and back into play. Normally lazy, these muscles strongly contract only as the exhalation cycle completes, while full engagement of the suspensory muscles (not to be confused with a tightening of the jaw) also happens towards the end of the cycle – as the body's 'desire' to breathe in increases. These muscle systems really count in the best singing.

Exhalation has fundamental benefits for singers. Crucially these lie in the fact that, as in (1) in the above list, inhalation results reflexively from exhalation.

The reflex action provides the outward singing gesture with its counterbalance (thus the term '*inhalare la voce*'). Muscularly speaking the outward action corresponds to the 'closers'. The counterbalance simultaneously stimulates the 'openers'.

Put another way, in the sung tone the vocal folds are closing *against* their continuous 'tendency' to open. Logically, this tendency gathers strength as the sung line proceeds.

Even though this simultaneous out/in antagonism – natural as it is to the singing voice – needs to be stimulated and strengthened in training, the diaphragm itself needs no conscious manipulation. 'Diaphragmatic support' is a non sequitur.

The dynamics of this antagonistic relationship are nowhere more clearly audible than at the vocal folds, where the precise co-ordination of activities is like a microcosm of the broader breathing system. The 'utility' of the breath has become minimal. There is no perceptual pressure, and the folds retain their vibrational elasticity.

With the balancing of the opposing breathing forces, the sensitivity of the diaphragm – as the audible generator of feelings – has been much enhanced, so the emotional charge is as potent as it is subtle.

The sound issuing from the throat of the singer tells us whether or not all is well with the breathing apparatus. Practising inhalation with the express purpose of increasing lung capacity is bad physiology. It can weaken the lungs by distending them. What is needed in singing is not breath or its conscious employment, but, in muscular terms, efficient breathing.

Three notes:

1 **Structural Weakness**

It must be clear by now that the strength of a voice is distributed over its entire musculature. No one 'part' – from pelvic floor to palatal muscles high in the head – is more important than another. All spheres must be equally invigorated. Weak tone may indicate lack of tension at the folds, but that's likely to be a symptom of wider systemic failure. Similarly, tightness in the throat will not be cured by concentrating on the suspensory mechanism alone.

We should be aware that, when there is a struggle to sing, a disproportionate effort is made by the stronger muscles in the system. Typically the abdominal muscles work overtime because of weak or lazy back muscles (m. Latissimus dorsi, for example). Muscles that don't belong to the singing voice often 'help out' where there is weakness. A weak suspensory system will be compensated for by well-practised swallowing muscles (false elevators) and so on.

2 **Vibration**

This is a natural outcome of an energised, balanced and well-tuned singing voice. Cornelius L. Reid defines vibrato as 'a tonal oscillation above and below a mean pitch that imparts vitality, buoyancy and harmonic richness to vocalised sounds'.[14] In addition, the movement of the singing voice is made up of flexible, antagonistic connections between 'parts'. The folds vibrate. The larynx is supported by an *elastic* scaffolding. The diaphragm is highly sensitive to the singer's feelings. Taken all together that's a lot of vibratory activity. Reid quotes Mozart's father, Leopold, on vibrato: 'Nature herself suggested it to man'.[15] All the same, in a well-structured voice vibration is minimal. The wobble, tremolo, bleat or quiver, by contrast, are outcomes of imbalance, flaccidity, force or rigidity.

3 **The Soft Palate or Velum and 'Resonance'**

In singing the soft palate is raised (via the Suspensory Mechanism above) but remains soft and supple. 'Like most elements of the vocal function, the soft palate should never be acted upon directly, but be allowed to form and adjust.'[16] The soft palate seems to act as a sympathetic vibrator, with the effect of reflecting the more or less subtle diaphragmatic movements generated by feelings. Its movements, in responding to a singer's sensitivity to his or her material, subtly affect vocal 'colouring'.

From a singer's point of view at least, resonance and corresponding resonating chambers are largely an illusion brought about by vibratory sensations in various localities such as the chest and head. Any adjustment of pharyngeal space – that, for example, resulting in the easy 'open throat' sensation – is due to the activity of the suspensory mechanism.

While consciously seeking resonance in various physical locations (as in 'placing the voice') can be a useful tool for obtaining a better balance of reciprocal activity between the larynx's intrinsic and extrinsic musculature, it hardly needs saying that the voice is not situated, or to be put, in any one of these places!

Try closing your mouth and humming with and without so-called 'nasal resonance'. With it we hear the vibration of

> the approximated vocal folds. The tone is more or less concentrated. Without it we hear more glottal space – a relatively breathy sound. Although some adjustment takes place in other parts of the vocal tract, the primary and more important difference lies *at the folds themselves.*

For all its complexity there is nothing contrived, nothing to *do,* about the dynamics of the various muscle systems that constitute the singing voice. Through our knowledge and our ears we can detect where it is unhealthy or unbalanced, but ultimately it defines itself by nature, and we recognise it as the singing voice as it gains in health.

CHAPTER 4

Beautiful Singing (Bel Canto)

Introduction

As we have seen, the singing voice has an identifiable structure. A whole voice is one in which its various parts are naturally coordinated and in which its various musical and expressive skills are complementary.

Given individuals' differences in vocal tract and vocal fold dimensions, which influence their natural capacities in terms of compass, dynamic range and distinctive voice quality, the musical skills and expressive properties of a developed singing voice are the same and unmistakable in each and every voice.

There is no choice in the matter. All skills attributable to the singing voice are inherent to it. What's more, they potentialise one another. The only way of having some skills and not others is to contrive some to the exclusion of others. Put another way, a voice is not free until all its skills come together naturally. This means that however much we may desire them, skills and qualities cannot realistically be aims in themselves.

Similarly, beauty is an 'emergent property' of the singing voice, not an aim. Professor Husler used to say of the developing voice, 'Es kommt schon'.[1] The Old Italian School must have appreciated the correlation between healthy (whole) function and an aesthetic ideal. In this chapter I make a brief exploration of connections between a healthy voice and the characteristics of beautiful singing.

Singing Voice and Speaking Voice

I reminded you earlier that our human larynx started life as a two-way respiratory valve (see illustration 3.8). For obvious reasons this system remains vital to human life. It is likely that our intelligence evolved somewhat prior to the 'invention' of speech, but then advanced more rapidly because of it. Be that as it may, there is no doubt that a suitably adaptable instrument was already in place.

All the same, the process of acquiring speech and a specific voiced language is laborious. Infants, whose mainly syllabic vocalisations are otherwise quite spontaneous, wrestle to master the seemingly awkward combination of sheer vocalic sound, which they delight in, with the specific movements of their lips, tongue and jaw required by language. The process gathers pace as the fragments of sounds get strung together, thereby gaining meaning and utility. There is no technique. Infants imitate what they hear, they experiment and repeat until, by degrees, the sounds become well-articulated, intelligible words.

However, in his classic work on the evolution of the larynx, V.E. Negus concludes,

> To think that the larynx and its vocal cords have been evolved primarily for purposes of speech is incorrect. A much simpler organ would have sufficed for the bare vocal needs of man.[2]

The mechanics of voice, involving the three laryngeal cartilages and their relation to the vocal 'lips' and 'bands' are a remarkable arrangement. That the various components re-evolve, so to speak, in each human being – even though, as parts of a wider singing instrument, they are largely neglected – is, to say the least, intriguing. We might ask, 'why a singing voice?'

Voice Orientation

Before we look closer at the heart of the matter – the vocal folds themselves – it may be helpful to orientate ourselves in terms of physical scale. In singing, the larger muscles of posture and breathing, together with the smaller ones that suspend the larynx, have the sole purpose of enabling two very small vocal folds to operate with a high degree of autonomy. On the one hand we have large body-stretching muscles (those, for example, that run the length of the spine – m. sacrospinalis), which I sometimes refer to collectively as 'superstructure', and on the other, tiny muscular folds which, depending on the individual, might be only 15mm or 20mm in length. It may be difficult to imaginatively reconcile these extremes.

Films or photographs of the larynx, or more precisely the vocal folds, useful as they undoubtedly are for the physician, can be deceptive for the singer. What is visible is only a very small area of the total vocal tract. Often enlarged, we get a false impression of size. In slow motion we get a false sense of movement. Vocal tract activity is necessarily disturbed by invasive techniques, and the precise dynamics of a healthy sung tone cannot be made out under these conditions.

Perhaps it is the inability to see the inner workings of the rest of the vocal apparatus that is behind much of its conscious manipulation in the course of vocal training. Interestingly, the Old Italian School said very little about how to breathe.

As far as I know, a comprehensive visual picture of a whole singing voice in motion has not yet been attempted. If such a picture could be made, it would have to demonstrate the simultaneous action of the whole extensive 'superstructure' down to the minute intricacies of the vocal folds via the suspensory muscles. It would have to show this activity distributed in the physiologically correct balance throughout the whole organ. We would then be faced, if we were so minded, with the onerous task of controlling all this apparatus for the purpose of singing. We would need an all-inclusive 'technique'. Such an obvious impossibility makes it imperative to perceive the singing voice in another way than visually.

Fortunately, the singing voice being a design of Nature, we are provided with a natural means of sussing it out. If we are to fine-tune such a vast and all-involving instrument, and not worry about it when actually singing, our orientation has to be aural. Natural singers don't think about how they are singing. The 'neurological understanding' between their auditory and vocal organs has remained intact.

In search of beautiful singing

Towards the end of the 16th century, the Camerata of Florence, a group of cultivated humanists, musicians and scholars decided that '... a far greater and ever-increasing knowledge of the working principles of the vocal organs was of paramount importance for the vocal artistry and craftsmanship they ideally set out to establish.'[3]

This made perfect sense with the then-current development of monody and the search for more dramatic means of expression in vocal music.

Monteverdi's stated aim, for example, was to 'move the whole man'. He believed that music 'must express man's deepest feelings'.[4] Many composers were also respected singers: Jacopo Peri, for instance. In his scholarly history of the tenor voice, John Potter writes of 'Peri's understanding that effective communication had to be grounded in emotional expression and textual rhetoric'.[5]

All the more reason, then, to explore further what is arguably man's most expressive means of communication. They wanted to discover what the fully-fledged singing voice was really made of, where it might take them in their creative endeavours. And of course it would help their teaching. The members of this pioneering group 'sensed, and agreed, that vocal art, to be ideal and perfect, must be provided with a solid and tangible mechanical structure – even as the body is provided with a skeleton'.[6]

Having no comprehensive knowledge about how the voice worked, they could start from scratch. Using their auditory intuition coupled with their artistic sensibilities, they could take their time, experiment and compare notes as they went along.

These artists and creators must have been aware that they were going to study something natural to the human being. In any case, 'Defective or incomplete voices were of little use to our investigators who were more interested in delving into acoustical rather than anatomical problems'.[7]

The difficulty was finding models of completely natural vocalisation. This was a tall order. In those days relatively few people 'took up' singing and most who did were men. It was therefore necessary to seek examples among the peasant and artisan classes who were not generally keen to be 'studied' and for whom singing was not a serious occupation![8]

I see the achievement of those enlightened pioneers as two-fold. Firstly, by painstaking degrees (according to Herbert-Caesari '... it took nearly four generations of investigators...'[9]) they developed a School of Singing: a School in the sense that its various exponents 'taught the very same principles, precepts and procedures where vocal mechanics, or technique was concerned'.[10] By that means they established themselves in all the major Italian cities. Secondly, by the end of the 17th century everything was set fair for what, by all accounts, was to become a Golden Age of Singing. In a nutshell, they achieved pedagogical consensus among teachers and recognisable excellence among singers.

Learning from the Past

Upon what characteristics of vocalisation, judging by the capacities and qualities observed by the teachers, composers and singers prior to and during the Golden Age, can we base this, our second identification and definition of the singing voice?

We have five possible sources:

1 pedagogical treatises
2 what was and is said about the singing
3 recordings
4 the music that was sung
5 that rare creature, the 'natural singer'

Unfortunately, we lack the one element (the sound) needed to illustrate the various terms or processes described in treatises. Exercises themselves, for example, mean nothing in the absence of sound. Exercises would have been executed under supervision, with moment-to-moment adjustments to vocal progress.

Descriptions given by 'observers' are likely to be somewhat subjective. We must therefore look for consistencies in these areas.

When listening to recordings from the first half of the 20th century, we may need to do so with 'new' ears. Otherwise we may be inclined to look back through lenses obscured by the vocal sounds we are used to. These in turn have been influenced by quite different music and performing circumstances.

The music that was sung, from Monteverdi to Rossini, and beyond, shows us not only how music developed but what voices were capable of.

The creative artists of Monteverdi's time, both composers and singers, may have felt frustrated by the vocal constraints of the Cappella period and polyphony, however beautiful it was, or the mere setting of poetry to music. In any case they,

> ... came up with the idea of making language itself, including dialogue, the basis of music. Such music had to be dramatic, for dialogue is by its very nature dramatic: its content is based on argument, persuasion, questioning, negation, conflict.[11]

At first they were 'preoccupied with the exact rendering of the natural accents of the text ... from one emotional point to the next'.[12] The objective of this 'wandering, declamatory music', was to imitate normal everyday

(Italian) speech, pointed up by a sparing harmonic background. Any operatic score of Monteverdi provides excellent examples. As Harnoncourt points out, this must have been shocking for music lovers of the day, who were used to 'highly esoteric and complex polyphonic music'.[13]

I believe nevertheless that it must also have increased the sense of freedom which singers would already have acquired to some extent through their ability to improvise. Singers of the time were already versed in ornamentation and expressive devices such as the appoggiaturas. In his famous treatise *Le Nuove Musiche,* Caccini 'recommends that coloraturas and ornamentation of all types be used only in those places where they reinforce verbal expression'.[14]

The emphasis on clear and expressive text coupled with a declamatory style and vocal agility paved the way for greater emotive vocalisation. As time went on, and *recitativo secco* was varied with *recitativo accompagnato,* and the arioso turned into the full-length aria, the expressive possibilities of the voice expanded along with music which tended always to be innovative. We should remember that many of the composers, in the early stages at least, were singers themselves. It's reasonable to assume that they wrote for what they discerned the natural singing voice to be capable of.

By the 1720s Handel and Bach were writing their masterpieces. The singing voice was coming into its own, and opera seria reached its zenith. Bach's dramatic Passions were peaks of baroque genius. Bach's biographer Albert Schweitzer considered 'the art of bel canto' one of the chief requirements for the interpretation of Bach's music: 'One should not forget that Bach took the Italian art of singing as his model and composed accordingly.'[15]

Another great musicologist says, 'We need to recover the normal technique of Italian *bel canto* as fully as possible in order to give the finest performances of Monteverdi, Carissimi, Purcell, Bach or Handel.'[16] Notice the inclusion of an English composer and a German. He might have added Gluck and Mozart, and even Rameau, as well as Lully, the Italian in Paris. We are not, after all, talking about style or emphasis, but the ability to sing: the capacity of the voice to be expressive as well as skilful in vocalising music of various styles.

By Mozart's time singers' natural vocal range had been thoroughly explored, agility was considered natural to all voices, and long lines were commonplace.

The idea that baroque music, with its orderly structure, should be performed in a mechanical fashion is refuted by Donington, who says, 'There is a way of keeping a steady tempo which is nevertheless not unyielding.'[17] Even the earliest bel canto singing would have had a natural pulse and flexibility in accord with the organic nature of the singing voice. Singers would have sung with the requisite sense of line, and thereby expressed music as distinct from singing notes however smoothly. We only have to try Caccini's famous jewel, 'Amarilli, mia bella' to know what was demanded even at the beginning of the seventeenth century.

The idea that bel canto was simply a vehicle for 'canary fanciers' is ludicrous when we see what, apart from virtuosic embellishment, was required of voices. Which is not to suggest that singers of the day never showed off; who would not be inclined to flaunt such brilliant facility? According to Rodolfo Celletti in *A History of Bel Canto,* there was a period when a taste for the spectacular and acrobatic did get the better of singers and their audiences.

> ... the second half of the eighteenth century, while belonging squarely to the bel canto period, attenuates one of its characteristic features, namely expressive ardour and sensibility, making up for these with a frenzied technical prowess. It was only towards the end of the century and during the first years of the nineteenth century that passion and vigour reappeared ... the art of bel canto was to experience its grand finale with Rossini.[18]

Studying a Rossini or Bellini score shows us that bel canto singing, far from being superficial frippery or merely an attempt to produce a beautiful sound, must have been exemplary in skill and ease over the widest range of musical and emotional expression.

Let us look at some of the bases of beautiful or excellent singing. First and foremost, the highly prized legato, and what technically was behind it.

Legato

An organic sense of line and phrasing is something that a natural singer already possesses. The Old Italian School understood this to be fundamental to good singing. In fact, they would have been much concerned with the implications of a true vocal legato, for the same 'ingredients' that ensure a seamless flow of tone from note to note are responsible for the continuous kaleidoscopic remixing of tone colour, dynamics and emotional weight.

'An inability to sing a true legato indicates the presence of muscular interference within the coordinative process.'[19] Here we are talking about an equilibrium which permits variation, and variation which does not alter the fundamental balance of forces.

Needless to say, to gain this natural, stable, vocal flux took a great deal of hard work over many years. It was not for want of knowledge. But what they were looking and working for (consciously or not) was something that in normal voices is asleep or atrophied – the critical 'edge mechanism'. Furthermore, balance within the vocal organ needed to be sustainable – phrase after phrase, for the duration of a recital or an opera.

> To sing 'for 50 seconds and more' on one breath, and this in large bowed phrases, indulging the while in astonishingly brilliant passages, coloratura and fioritura, means wasting no breath whatever ... The possibility ... is founded solely on that organic perfection which prevents all wastage of breath (not ... on any miraculous procedure that would enable the accumulation of a vast reserve of air).[20]

As I suggested in the previous chapter, in as much as this 'organic perfection' is an aural matter we have no choice but to concentrate on the sound which, if you like, betrays its own source. We can 'read' it. The behaviour of the closing, tensing and stretching mechanisms can be distinctly heard separately and combined. This is what those early investigators had to go by. They would hear, for example, not only that a sound was 'breathy' but also the cause of the leaked or wasted air. They would hear the falsetto and the chest registers and they would learn to blend them via those elusive marginal fibres. They would hear the various movements in the throat. And for every sound that issues from the throat there is, of course, a corresponding movement from the body.

We don't have to do something with the body to make the sound falsetto, or to make a nasal sound, but if we make one of these sounds (or any other), simply by summoning it with our imagination, the body will follow suit. If we make a nasty, crunched-up sound the body will follow suit – with 'suitable' tension. If we adjust the sound (again through appealing to our aural imagination) the body will adjust with it. Adjustments at the throat are likely to be small, and herein lies one of the dangers of trying to initiate things from the body. *Call forth the sound,* and the body, as well as the throat, will reveal itself. *Manipulate the body,* and the larynx will reveal its struggle to comply.

If the body is not sufficiently alive, or the breathing system in its own right is weak, the sounds that can be made with the throat without force will be correspondingly limited. In this case there is no alternative but to wake up and invigorate the body so that it can respond to the throat. This principle of correspondence applies to all four spheres of activity looked at in Chapter 3. All correspondences (or relationships) impact on the throat and can therefore be heard.

In the 16th century the music for each voice would, by the standards of two centuries later, operate generally within a relatively small compass. Singers were encouraged to find the range that was comfortable. As with speaking, venturing beyond the habitual vocal range triggers or necessitates a change of sound. We have come to call this a 'register break'. In reality it is a collapse of the voice from one part or configuration of its mechanism to another. Our Florentine predecessors would have noticed that this split does not occur in the natural voice. They realised that developing a voice was a question of integration. Generally they considered two so-called registers: the chest, which is what they called the voice that was generally employed in singing, and the falsetto (or head), which was what a voice slipped or broke into when it overreached its familiar compass. The aim of 'blending' these mechanisms crops up again and again in the literature. The successful blend was the much-prized *messa di voce.*

Messa di Voce

> Italian, 'to put forth, or bud'; to 'place' (in the sense of everything being *in* place); according to Domenico Corri, a pupil of Porpora, 'to prepare the voice for a crescendo'.[21]

Nowadays, if anyone hears the term *messa di voce* they usually think it is the name given to the exercise of crescendo and diminuendo. Although as an expressive device the < > is much used, and therefore needs to be practised, to leave the matter at that is to miss the point. As with the *voix mixte* of the early 19th century French school, the *messa di voce* denotes,

> 'a blending of all the registers', which, from a physiological point of view, means the constant, uniform co-ordination of all the musculatures required in the formation of the singing voice; and not, therefore, a joining up of one function to another (registers).[22]

What we read of the pedagogy of the time, based as it is on what was discernible by ear rather than any means that today we might call 'more scientific', gives us only theoretical hints about such prized goals as legato and *messa di voce* and how they were reached. But there is no doubt in my mind that those investigators realised that the chief component in the combining of the falsetto and chest registers was the very thing that facilitated the finest gradation from *piano* to *forte* and back again – i.e. the arrangement of muscle bundles and fibres that link the vocal ligament (band) to the vocal folds (lips), which we have called the 'edge mechanism' (see Chapter 3, page 27, for the description by Husler and Rodd-Marling). This crucial combining component would have been discovered when making attempts to crescendo and diminuendo without undue pressure for the former or weakening the tone for the latter. Put another way, the emission of the sung tone and its ability to swell and die away were ultimately a question of integration of the various activities within the larynx – in this case specifically of the vocal lip with the vocal band.

The same can be said for vocal colour and all the other vocal 'skills' that we associate with the singing voice. The edge mechanism facilitates the constant interplay between the stretching and the tensing of the vocal folds. And because it is what ultimately keeps their upper margins firm it ensures that there is no unnecessary expenditure of breath: thus the very long lines achievable and the great carrying power of even the smallest voice. The economy of movement achieved is what ultimately makes it unnecessary to manipulate the voice in any way when singing. It allows it instead to act simultaneously with the singer's imagination, feelings and musicality.

Earlier I quoted Domenico Corri describing *messa di voce* as 'preparing the voice for a crescendo'. This makes perfect sense when you consider that where the singing voice starts is where the tension of the folds begins to combine, at their upper edges, with the stretched and thinned ligament – i.e. minimum tension added to maximum stretching (falsetto). It is from this point of the finest possible mix that the sung tone can grow – as more of the bulk of the folds comes into play.

As I write, the London Olympics are in their fifth day and I have allowed myself time off to watch some of the men's artistic gymnastics final. Who could fail to be inspired? While athletes undergo a tough and meticulous training in order to maximise their performance, the singer's quest for optimal strength and precision is no less demanding. Pupils of the Old Italian School aimed to reach a peak of vocal excellence. Like present-day would-be Olympians they dedicated many years to it, and the results were by all accounts astonishing.

A natural or healthy voice is operationally, and therefore tonally, all-of-a-piece from top to bottom – no 'breaks'. It is not thought out or technically produced, but is part and parcel of the singer's physiological make-up, like seeing, hearing, walking and breathing. It is therefore effortless. The natural singer has by nature the musical skills (even if he or she doesn't yet know how best to use them) after which we lesser mortals strive for many years.

It is fascinating and encouraging to have the intimate 'aural knowledge' of the Old Italian School corroborated by modern 'scientific evidence'. 'The most important concept related to vocal fold structure is that the vocal folds consist of multiple layers, each having different mechanical properties' (Hirano, 1975; Hirano and Kakita, 1985).[23] There are in fact no fewer than five layers, making up the vocal ligament or band, before we get to the main body of the vocal folds or 'vocalis muscles'.

Given such intricacy, it's easy to understand how physical efforts to sing can be misplaced. The small scale of these structures determines how crucial our aural acuity needs to be if we are to work accurately with them or get to 'know' them intimately.

Then, if we look at the music – and we may now do so in greater detail – and see what it asks in terms of finesse at one extreme and grandeur at the other, we can see that such a precision instrument is required both for the exactitude of the one and the containment of the other. And what about everything in between? Should we make a great effort to sing 'big' or inhibit the voice to sing 'small'? If you think in physical terms, the notion is absurd. Does a singer have to demonstrate the big any more

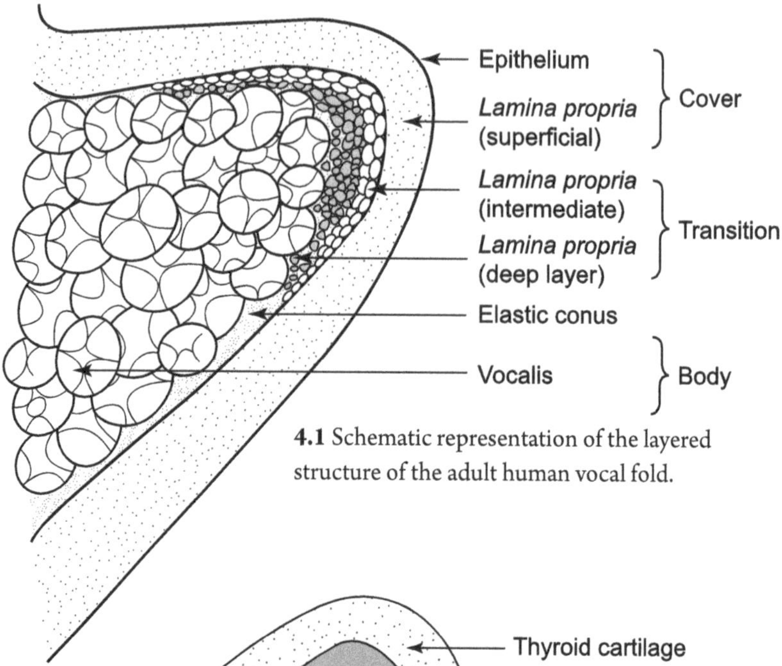

4.1 Schematic representation of the layered structure of the adult human vocal fold.

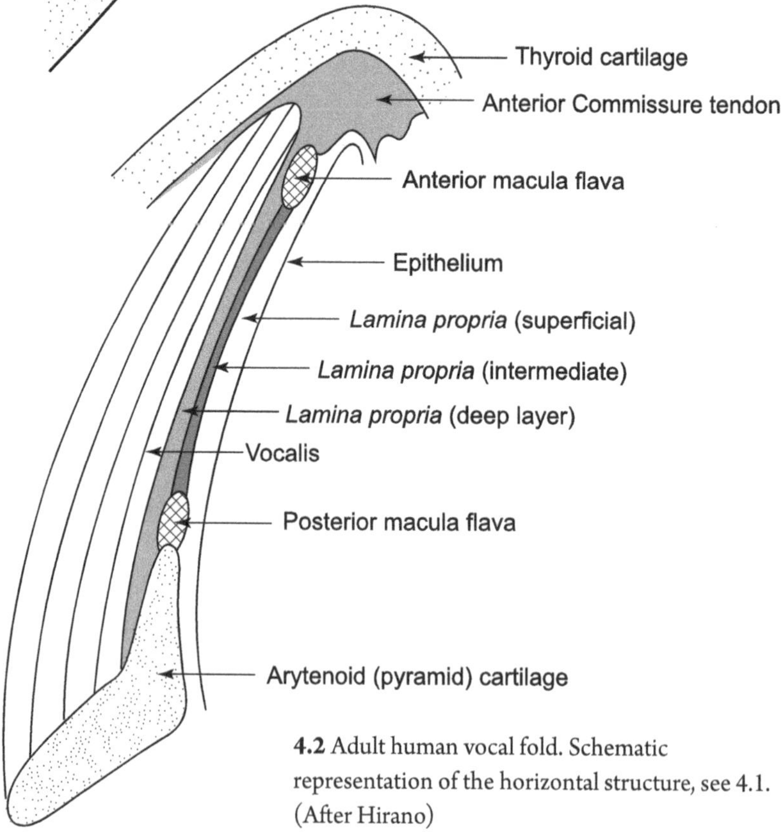

4.2 Adult human vocal fold. Schematic representation of the horizontal structure, see 4.1. (After Hirano)

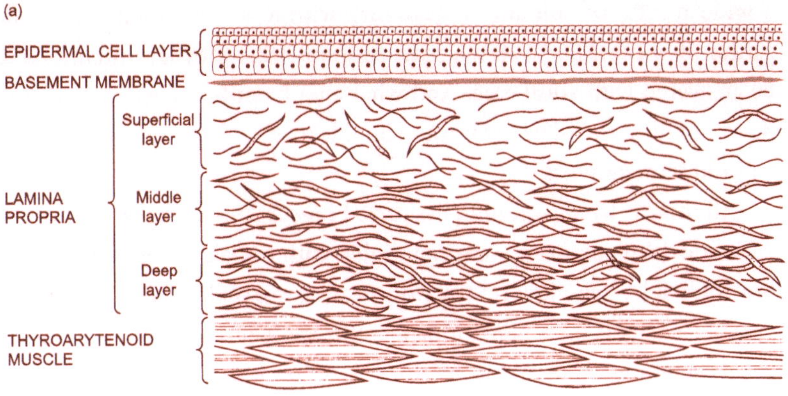

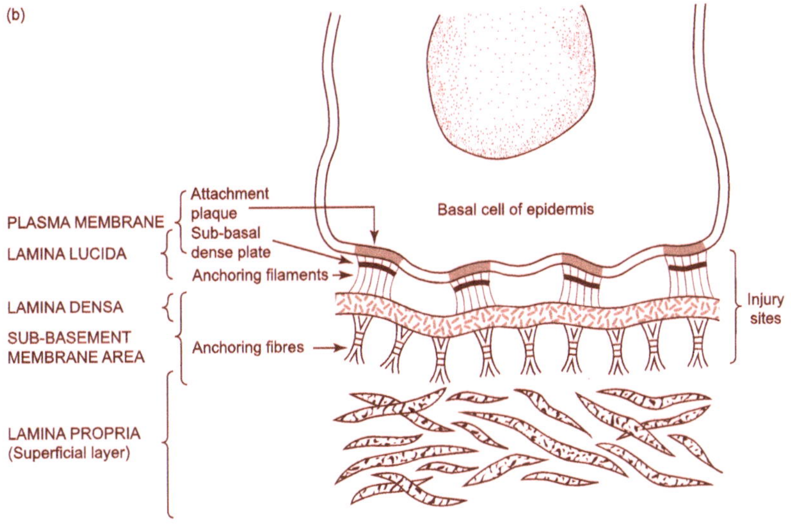

4.3a Basement membrane zone between epidermis and lamina propria. **4.3b** Arrangement of structures visible with the electron microscope from the basement cell to the fibres of the superficial layer of the lamina propria. (After Gray)

than the small? Should the small flow less generously than the big? What a travesty such manipulations make of singing.

Where is the singer who does not desire to have a long, flexible line at their disposal, something seamless and even throughout the range, with the added ability to swell a tone or a phrase without losing focus, or decrease its volume without losing intensity, gradually and easily ebbing and flowing back and forth at will? What singer does not delight in having a wide palette of colours or flexibility within and between the whole gamut of vocal skills? What singer does not wish for their intentions to be answered with vocal ease. And what about words? Whether beautiful poetry or not, who does not want to be able to articulate and declaim them without impediment?

All these – by all accounts the prized possessions of the singers of the 17th and 18th centuries – are achievable with a healthy voice with those tiny folds at its structural centre. And we have not yet looked at the expression of feelings as such. Nor, for that matter, the legibility of the individual's vocal signature. These too, if the singer is to be clear and effective on both counts, are as much the physical province of those remarkable structures as they are a matter of the singer's personality.

CHAPTER 5

Individual Identity

The personal nature of our singing voice – the human heart of it, if you like – may turn out to be its most significant aspect. For many it seems that this inner vocal personality is hard to reach, let alone to embrace and to share. In learning to sing it often seems to be side-tracked or suppressed in favour of something more imitative or 'cosmetic' – perhaps in a genuine attempt at making a 'beautiful' sound, or in order to achieve pre-determined goals as quickly as possible.

Perhaps the attraction of widely accepted norms and techniques is that they are more or less laid down by some 'authority'. One size fits all, and only has to be followed or applied. A contrived way of singing, or imitative singing, can be of some instrumental use, especially when there is a piece to perform in the short term or an exam to pass. It may give the singer the comforting sensation of being 'in control'.

Even so, singers are often to some extent alienated from themselves when singing. Techniques of singing, as distinct from just doing it, are therefore unfulfilling – the authority is borrowed, the control is imposed. To me it has always seemed strange that this type of moulding is so prevalent when it clearly frustrates the efforts of singers to be musical and expressive in any truly personal way.

It is notable that all the best known singers had and have a recognisable individual vocal identity. Even so, few have been able to find the degree of vocal (and by extension personal) integration that I talked about in the last chapter. If we listen to Maria Callas or Elizabeth Schwarzkopf, to take two of the most famous examples, we find that both fell short of the mark, except perhaps right at the beginning of their careers when their voices were full of youthful promise. Both acquired serviceable techniques, which overcame or rearranged their vocal shortcomings rather than eliminating them. Callas says somewhere that she acted (in the dramatic sense) and hoped the voice would follow. Sometimes it did, and no doubt the unpredictability added something to the excitement of her performances. But in spite of her astonishing work in the revival of the so-called bel canto repertoire, her exemplary dedication to her art, and her indisputable dramatic qualities, she cannot be said to have been a true exponent of the bel canto singing we have been exploring. Her voice was simply not free enough.[1] Schwarzkopf was also a great performer, but her progressive need to 'handle' her voice made her singing mannered and predictable.[2]

While sheer force of personality can to some extent override vocal limitations – witness numerous personalities in the 'pop' world, even those with the most constricted voices – if a singer's voice is not free, their true identity in sound cannot come to the fore.

The integration of voice and self is a defining criterion of the true *singing* voice. Examples can be heard from great singers such as John McCormack, Rosa Ponselle, Jussi Björling and more recently Mirella Freni.

Self-realisation

We are used to categorising, pigeon-holing, and departmentalising. Perhaps it gives a sense of organisation, or orientation – we know where things are, and where we are with things. It may seem easier all round if we conform to expectations, to be recognised and marketable as such-and-such a soprano or baritone. But, as Jessye Norman so wisely and wittily put it in an interview, 'Pigeon-holes are only comfortable for pigeons.'[3]

Both the German Fächer system and commercial recordings, instead of encouraging individual vocal quality, have had the unfortunate effect of stereotyping singing voices or (in the sense of taking away their originality or emotive force) sterilizing them.

Such categorisation and standardisation are concerned with external effects, so that while a singer might master a technique or a 'way' of singing, they never truly master their own singing voice. Communication suffers accordingly.

Barriers to vocal freedom and authenticity have normally gone up long before a person decides to become a singer. On the purely personal front, with individual past conditioning and defences in place, a would-be singer has, perhaps literally, moulded his or her body into a particular manageable shape.

> Each of us has found our own unique bodily way of handling our discomforts, be they physical, emotional, or intellectual.[4]

We are so practised at 'managing' ourselves that it's hardly surprising if, when it comes to singing, we look for ways to manage our voice. By the same token, most of us are concerned with our 'image'. An adopted or created self-image can be something to hold on to or hide behind. Through this persona 'we project a limited image of ourselves that we mistakenly equate as our true identity'.[5] Our performances then tend to be imitative and predictable.

Remove these familiar 'aids', this mask, and we put ourselves in the position not only of being responsible for what we 'say' with our voice but of feeling naked or insecure – even (to start with at least) unrecognisable. The fact is, however, that we choose the conventional or the collective mode, or remain blocked, at the cost of our own wholeness.

It can be scary to think of changing ourselves while others continue to follow their familiar formulae. We want to stay in our comfort zone, protective of our current sound signature, by which other people – family, friends, and colleagues – also recognise us.

Doing something different – changing, removing the mask – is by definition going into the unknown. 'Only when this mask begins to drop away can we begin to appreciate its superficial nature'. This is about 'reclaiming that which is intrinsically ours ... It is about returning to our natural state'[6] – and about realizing our true self.

The most conscientious attempts at tapping into a singer's true vocal personality are rarely without difficulties. The process seems by implication to question our way of being, and threatens it. The initial feelings of confusion and vulnerability, even anger, can be hard to come to terms with.

> The tension between being and becoming is a fundamental one in all evolution ... The result of this tension is always pain ... As we reconstruct within we suffer the temporary dislocation of our identity.[7]

The regenerating, restorative process of 'learning to sing' can likewise be disconcerting.

Fortunately, the many and various advantages of gaining such personal freedom can far outweigh the difficulties or pain of the process involved.

In any case, vocal transformation rarely happens in a dramatic fashion. The gradual facilitating of the various facets of expression and performance can support and encourage every step of an individual's opening-up process.

More important is that the pupil wills the process, is prepared to venture into the unknown – and is then appropriately and sensitively guided through it.

Authenticity and Authority

Normally we experience a more-or-less conscious relation between our 'settled' self and the goings-on around us. Searching for a singing voice is searching for a core – the life inside or the relationship of self with self – as experienced and reflected in sound.

As in the Jungian concept of individuation, 'becoming in sound' is an emergent, creative process. It is, like reality itself, a state of flux – an experiential continuum of letting go, exploring, discovering, making choices, changing – becoming. Ultimately we come to the present, a place that cannot be 'captured'. We are with ourselves and with the moment to an unprecedented degree. To be present is to be aware.

> In non-alienated activity, I experience *myself* as the *subject* of my activity. Non-alienated activity is a process of giving birth to something, of producing something and remaining related to what I produce. This also implies that my activity is a manifestation of my powers, that I and my activity are one.[8]

When you and your activity are one, your performance and what you say are grounded in authenticity. This is the power of presence. Power is innate and is manifest in a singer's ability to choose. Freedom of choice means we can question and reject 'received opinions' if we so wish. Loss or deliberate masking of identity, through some kind of superimposed 'way' or 'technical fix' results in loss of power and therefore of choice.

Choice and authenticity support not only the fidelity of our performance but our creativity within it. Both choice and authenticity are provided for by the true heart of the singing voice – the vocal folds. 'The "delicate adjustment" possible through these different muscle-bundles and muscle-fibres "gives the human voice its precision and its personal expression" ... these muscle-bodies have the highest possible capacity for *autonomous* action'.[9]

This 'arrangement' enables us to be fully present to our possibilities. 'The creative person, in the inspirational phase of the creative furor, loses his past and his future and lives only in the moment'.[10]

Recognising a Singer's True Sound Signature

A singer who has already achieved a high degree of natural freedom has a voice as recognisable as their face – it fits. The development process may then be merely a question of subtle enhancement and fine tuning. More often, though, a singer's true quality is difficult to ascertain before a good deal of clearing away of falseness and freeing of tension has been undergone. Detection and nurturing is a question of sorting:

- the genuine from the artificial;
- the natural from the contrived;
- the free from the imposed;
- the individual from the general;
- the down-to-earth from the cultivated.

In this process we are obliged to make the essential distinction between what is commonly recognised as this or that type of voice and what can be appreciated as this unique human being's voice. Needless to say the process is usually one of gradual awareness and differentiation.

The differences are often revealed in subtle changes. The easiest way of expressing recognition or revelation of a voice's identity is to say that it 'rings true' – using the analogy with bells or coins. But even with a great deal of unprejudiced experience on the part of a teacher this is not totally reliable. (Even the great English bell makers of the 17th and 18th centuries who tuned their bells by ear sometimes made mistakes.) As we have seen, the singing voice is a complex and personal instrument. In this regard not only does a person sing with their own unique voice, but the singing voice 'sings' its owner.

The difficulty in searching for a unique voice lies in not knowing at the beginning what it will sound like. What we do know is that this individual's voice is there, and it will sound like singing! And we can only work with what is already audible; the rest we have to discover. This is what, for me at least, makes the quest so exciting. As in archaeology, you know there is a treasure. For all you have been told about what it is, where it is, its history and so forth, you don't know its exact shape or colour, or how deep it goes. Uncovering the whole treasure requires not only a teacher's technical ingenuity, imagination and sensitivity, but also a genuine respect and care for the pupil who is of course the treasure! Neither teacher nor pupil has heard this voice in its entirety. We cannot afford to be prejudiced any more than we can afford to be complacent.

The process is not so vague as I may have implied. We have our anatomical and physiological knowledge, we hear many examples of 'good' and 'bad' singing, against which we can sharpen our critical/analytical faculties, and we have a great variety of 'tools' (see, for example, Husler and Rodd-Marling's excellent chapter on Placing the Voice, with which comes a CD).

We know too that our liberating process must contribute to the singer's ability to make music and to communicate. There are many 'signposts' to such ends along the way. However, we should beware of pursuing a goal-orientated scheme, or putting too much store too soon on emerging musical skills, and thereby missing the real signs and openings to freedom and wholeness.

Since our search for individual identity is not to be found in any technique or preconceived notion of how an individual should sound, it is essential that teacher and pupil work on an equal footing as a team of explorers. This means that both the curiosity and work must be shared and that feedback must be forthcoming from both parties. Such feedback will be about sound, as well as physical and emotional sensations.

In this quest there are many 'aha!' moments for both parties as progress is made and the singer recognises the singing self. 'Aha!' moments are frequently upgraded.

Recognising and working with a person's true sound (as distinct from that of a voice working well, or well enough to satisfy certain performance criteria) demands courage, perseverance, sensitivity and insightfulness on the parts of both teacher and pupil.

A singer's personal identity, true quality or essence, facilitates the critical amalgamation between the expressive advantages of bel canto and a singer's communicative intentions. Communication will be the subject of Chapter 6.

A person's true sound has intrinsic as well as instrumental value, and is, therefore, rewarding both internally, in terms of personal fulfilment, and externally in terms of human communication. These must surely rank high on the list of desirable outcomes from voice training.

Cautionary Notes

1 The voice is a mirror to the integrity of your aims. Any superficial attempt to disguise a lack of integrity is only self-deluding and self-defeating.

2 'Buddhism teaches that it's a mistake to focus on one's identity as an individual, since in reality one is enmeshed with everything in the world'.[11] This must certainly be true if our intention is simply to announce or assert our presence in the world. However, in as much as the ground of our being is the basis of our shared humanity, it is with finding our core that we are best equipped to connect with and participate in the world. We should not confuse focusing on one's identity with egotism. In training, a singer is not only endeavouring to become him- or herself but is regaining something universal. In other words, coupled with personal identity comes the human identity that is a responsibility and a joy to share.

3 The singing voice, being common to all human beings, embodies and promotes the idea of unity in diversity – the universal identity in that of the individual.

4 Self-identity is not something fixed. It is being present to and participant with the flux of life.

5 'Thanks to the media ... the minds of all are concerned with the same set of problems, are cognizant of the same public figures. Thus the furniture of the mind comes to resemble the furniture of everyone else's mind. This may simplify communication, reducing it to an exchange of stereotypes, but it destroys individuality and eats away the sense of personal uniqueness, and hence of worth. For if one is replaceable, if one has nothing unique to offer, one is not an individual'.[12]

6 'Personality can never develop unless the individual chooses his own way, consciously and with moral deliberation. ... The fact that the conventions always flourish in one form or another only proves that the vast majority of mankind do

> not choose their own way, but convention, and consequently develop not themselves but a method and a collective mode of life at the cost of their own wholeness'.[13]

All things considered, and in the ethical as well as the artistic sense, for those of us who work with and for singers, identifying their true vocal character and quality might be said to be the greatest responsibility we have.

CHAPTER 6

Communication

The individuality of a voice lies in its functional integrity. This is where the voice can be said to be universal and where, therefore, empathy begins. It is the condition in which it responds to and reflects the variations in feeling and intellectual understanding of the singer most faithfully.

Having rediscovered their natural singing voice and identity in sound, and through these both the skill and the potency of their instrument, a singer is well equipped for vocal communication in the truest and deepest sense. Their 'message' and its delivery can be totally authentic. There is no need to resort to vocal or emotional effects to get it across. The singer has the power to choose.

This is just the start. The things a singer wishes or needs to communicate according to the music and text – character, image, and human drama for example – are also matters for serious study.

Furthermore, the act of communicating is in itself a skill. Although as human beings we are hard-wired to communicate with others, our ability to do so is often inhibited, neglected or lacking in fluency. Like the skills of the singing voice, those of communicating often need to be liberated and diligently practised in suitable contexts.

How intelligently and effectively a singer communicates depends on skill and commitment combined. There may be intention and no skill – no facility of voice with which to convey music, let alone meaning. Or there might be sufficient vocal skill which, although impressive on a technical level, nevertheless leaves the audience cold or unmoved.

A singer who is committed to the music, the text and the sharing of sentiment and meaning, but has little vocal freedom, will probably try too hard to make up for this lack, and may exacerbate the difficulties. This matter is less important in the 'pop' world where, in the absence of vocal facility, artificial emotion and effects (both visual and vocal) are commonplace.

By 'skilful' singing I do not mean 'clever stuff'. Bel canto singers may have been virtuosi, but this was the result of an unusual degree of vocal freedom which facilitated much else besides rapid scales and flowery embellishments (fioritura). It has been well said that art is by definition virtuosic. In any case, skill in singing means accuracy (of words and music and detail) plus clarity and depth of meaning.

Singers who have the ability to give a good performance in every respect are in a privileged position, with exceptional expressive skills and the ability to communicate human feelings from deep within their own humanity. Because of this, I believe professional performing vocal artists have responsibilities. In order to satisfy the demands of great music, poetry and drama, to which they have access like no others, they must go deeply into themselves.

But it is ultimately towards their audience that they bear greatest responsibility. Only through sharing with other human beings their musical and dramatic material and the feelings that it engenders do they become communicators par excellence.

The singing voice is recognisable in the degree to which it communicates. In addition to the singer's commitment it requires listeners for its completion or fulfilment. The fully-fledged singing performer with a sense of responsibility sings *to* rather than *at* their audience. They do not, like some singers, mesmerise or distract their audience; but they draw the audience into their world, into the intimacy of their thoughts, the clarity of their vision, the intensity of the drama to which they are party – in such a way that the listeners do not remain passive but participate mentally, emotionally and spiritually in the singer's experience and that of the character they are portraying.

I would call a good singer – who can, after all, afford to be generous and vulnerable without fear of embarrassment – an ambassador of the human heart.

Quality communication is where the singing voice and 'good' singing meet. Each is diminished in its effect by the absence or limitations of the other. Bel canto singing at its best was, I believe, the embodiment of both. In beautiful singing the singing voice is capable of conveying not only full-throated emotion but also the finest of expressive details whether in tonal colouration, imagery, dynamics, musical phrasing or inflection, intimate feeling, or whatever else is material to a performance. Of paramount importance of course is the text through which everything else is conceived.

Technically, as we have seen, its articulation should not pose a problem. However, I have always found it impossible to understand why so many singers treat words as though they were of little consequence! Most vocal music springs from them. How can a singer express a single word, let alone a whole phrase, if he is ignorant of its significance. It is words that give birth and life and sense to everything else. The music expresses their meaning or the images or feelings they evoke, melodically, rhythmically and harmonically: enhancing, enriching, emphasising, dramatising them, creating atmosphere and mood around them. By embodying the words as well as the music, the singer personalises or humanises them. This, with the feelings they bear, is how he or she is able to communicate them, make them telling.

It is not what a singer demonstrates but what they convey to their audience and inspire in them that makes them a good singer. It is their instrument, their singing voice, which determines how much they are able to convey and its quality. This is, after all, where the truism, 'you are your voice' really comes into its own.

All too often the musical or dramatic shortcomings of a singer's performance are due to vocal incapacities or weakness. These not only limit the singer's expressive scope but cause them to struggle with or focus unduly on their instrument. Such preoccupation prevents any real communication. Singers (and teachers) often look for 'technical' solutions, not realising that the vocal problems that mar the performance are not isolated technical matters but the result of systemic failure. The free singing voice is fundamental to good performance at any level.

Singing being such a personal matter – from both sides of the lights – audiences can also feel let down or alienated when a performer seems smug or aloof or anonymous. The self-absorbed singer or the nonchalant one insults the audience.

I was once at a lieder recital by a well-known singer who did strange and inappropriate things. While the accompanist was playing on his own the singer studied his fingernails and 'fiddled' inside the piano! There was nothing in the text or drama that warranted such bizarre and irritating behaviour. A baritone with an outstanding voice ruined Mahler's beautiful *Lieder eines fahrenden Gesellen* (for me at least) by singing as though he were saying 'look how well I'm singing this!' It is perhaps surprising how many examples of such performers there are, especially among the higher echelons of the classical singing world.

My belief, and part of the motivation for this book, is that barriers to good performance, whether of a personal or professional nature, can be recognised and overcome early on in a singer's training and education. Singers, both student and professional, should be constantly examining their performance. Above all they should consider to what extent and in what ways their singing voice is enabling or impeding their communication.

CHAPTER 7

False Perspectives and Misperceptions

It is one thing to define the singing voice, quite another to develop it and bring the singer to a level of professional excellence. The work that the thorough training and educating of singers might entail is examined in Part II. This chapter looks at some of the misunderstandings that all too frequently prejudice progress before training begins.

Appearances

It might appear that apart from a perennial shortage of jobs and the capriciousness of funding bodies, all is well with the world of classical singing. There are many excellent choirs and groups, and thousands of artists being employed as soloists in opera houses and concert venues the world over. More than at any previous time people across the world can hear through various media anyone who is considered to be anyone in the singing world, as well as hundreds who are not. However, those whose business it is to promote singers often seem to lack consistent criteria, or even concern, for excellence, and much fondness for the hype-able. As often as not this means the glamorous-looking or pretty-sounding. Exposure does not automatically bestow merit, but the media has ways of elevating mediocrity.

A growing number of singers are hyped for their 'star' qualities, rather than for qualities that add up to great singing. While some stars clearly do have the edge – Anna Netrebko and Elina Garanča are both glamorous and fine singers – there are many who have the glamour and precious little else.

Others have talent but are not particularly glamorous or hype-able. Most of these, I suspect, fight shy of stardom; they just want to get on with the job and enjoy it without fuss. Regrettably, we rarely see or hear them unless we have the good fortune to be working with them.

The net result is that fewer and fewer people can tell the difference between good singing and bad, or what really makes the difference. It is not realistic to put all the blame on the media, whose definition of what is good is based on what is marketable – often it seems they are giving people, at least the general populace, what they want!

Existential Crisis?

In an article which appeared in the *New York Times* of November 13, 2005, based around the American dramatic soprano Jennifer Wilson, the critic Anne Midgette attempts to put her finger on the reason why 'there has been no ... rise in great new talents' commensurate with the acknowledged high standard of vocal training in the USA. She writes,

> One clear measure of the problem is the system's inability to deal effectively with large voices and talents like Ms Wilson's. It seems to favor lighter, flexible voices that can perform a wide range of material accurately, rather than the powerful, thrilling, concert-hall-filling voices on which live opera ultimately relies for its survival.[1]

Certainly good singing is not a matter of taste or mere thrill. Flexibility and power are not optional. Nor is the size of an individual's voice. It is time to get unstuck from the ideas that good singing is a matter of satisfying a fashion, and that different 'sizes' of voice (in the dramatic sense) require substantially different treatment.

Dramatic voices

Staying with larger voices for the moment, symptoms of the current inability to deal with them can be clearly heard if we compare some of the best present-day singers of Wagner, for example, with those of the mid twentieth century. Voices nowadays are relatively 'driven', making them less wieldy and more uneven tonally than their mid-twentieth century counterparts. *Forte* is now made with added weight, and *piano* tends to get 'held back', so that at neither extreme is there an easy, flexible flow of tone. Listen to Jennifer Wilson or Deborah Voigt singing 'Dich Teure Halle' from *Tannhäuser*, and compare Birgit Nilsson or even Montserrat Caballé singing the same piece, and you will get my point. This comparison has nothing to do with greater or lesser talent, calibre or commitment, or even style or interpretation. The differences may, however, have something to do with the misconception that 'a bigger voice needs more support', or with a conflicting body-throat relationship.

In an article called *Voci Verdiani*, written for *Opera* magazine in July 2008, Yehuda Shapiro writes about the casting decisions, which 'grew from the dynamics of the drama', for Antonio Pappano's *Don Carlos* for the Royal Opera House, Covent Garden.[2] He points out that 'over the last 20 years heavy weather has been made of some Verdi operas because voices have been unwieldy and unyielding … Don Carlos makes great demands on the flexibility and sensitivity of singers…'[3] It is refreshing, therefore, to hear what Sondra Radvanovsky, one of today's leading 'Verdi singers', has to say: 'Verdi demands everything – extremely high notes, extremely low notes, loudness, softness, flexibility'. We might add emotional sensitivity and expressiveness, both of which Radnavosky's performances also demonstrate.

In Verdi's day, of course, there was no such creature as the 'Verdi voice'. A hard task master Verdi may have been, but evidently he asked for nothing more nor less than the qualities that he would have found in the best singers of his day. I believe it was the same with Wagner, most of whose music, providing the singer has the voice and stamina for it, is not excessively demanding. The famous critic George Bernard Shaw, born in 1856, said that he thought Wagner 'was the only modern composer to write for the voice with the skill of Handel...'[4] Be that as it may, Wagner's and Verdi's 'modern music', at least with regard to the voice, was not as radical as it later became. The voice was still used in accord with its lyric-dramatic qualities. Even *Sprechgesang* is related to the *recitativo* of old.

I would love to have heard Eileen Farrell sing 'Dich Teure Halle'. I value her recording of 'Sorta è la notte' and 'Ernani! Ernani, involami' from Verdi's *Ernani* as an example of good mid-twentieth-century 'dramatic' operatic singing. 'I just sang … I never had registers … Coloratura? Well, I was a big girl but I could still climb the stairs fast if I had to, or run for the bus. The voice has to be the same.'[5]

Balance

Listen to any of the singers of the first half of the 20th century who sang 'dramatic' roles and were said to show something of the bel canto qualities

– Mattia Battistini (whose singing, incidentally, Wagner admired), Emmy Destinn (who also sang Wagner), Beniamino Gigli, Rosa Ponselle, for instance – and you will hear flexibility and finesse as well as power. Their singing could not possibly be described as heavy or unwieldy.

Great singing, from whatever 'sized' voice, used to be described as 'well placed'. This term is now frowned upon, but only, I suspect, because it is misunderstood. It's the same as 'naturally tuned' (a term applied to the great Irish tenor John McCormack's voice at the age of 21), which simply means that its various component parts are acting as one – in balance, as Nature intended. Nothing is 'out of place'. It is balance that makes power and refinement perfectly compatible. It is only when the voice is *not* well placed that un-physiological 'measures' are felt to be needed.

My belief about the Wagnerian and Verdian voice myth is that, with the loss of bel canto schooling, singers lost the ability to sing dramatically from vocal balance – they lost sight of the truly mixed voice. The mistake that is still made is the assumption that to sing the works of these composers you not only need a large voice (which of itself is fair enough) but you have to use it in a 'beefy' or overcharged manner. No voice, however big, responds kindly to such treatment. The results have been disastrous for the music and most of its exponents alike.

Mixing Objectives

It is sometimes assumed that a voice is built at the same time as the singer learns to use it. But why is this so unthinkingly accepted? Building an instrument and making music are quite distinct skills. No other self-respecting musician would contemplate attempting both at the same time! Lumping both tasks together, before either is ready to benefit from the other in a truly productive way, causes endless frustration on both counts. The voice never gets fully built – I prefer to say 'liberated' – because it has to struggle with objectives for which, as yet, it has insufficient competency, and little music ever gets made because the singer is preoccupied with an as yet unresponsive instrument. Neither task is fully accomplished.

Breathing

This is an area in which singers and teachers unthinkingly erect barriers to progress. Should it really be necessary to teach a singer how to breathe at the higher levels of their training? According to Midgette, reporting that teachers in the USA in 2005 agreed that singers are not being taught the fundamentals, in particular the proper use of breathing, 'Breath support ... has long been regarded as the key to singing....'[6] Well, yes, since about the middle of the nineteenth century I should think, but not before that, when it was understood that a singer's artistry depended on the natural integrity of his or her instrument. In fact, the Old Italian School were at great pains to put the instrument first. Why should it be any different now? 'A properly functioning larynx regulates and trains to a high degree (by means of the ear) the respiratory muscles needed in singing.'[7]

Heavier roles and thicker orchestrations developed and were introduced gradually. The physiology of the singing voice has remained unaltered to this day!

Seeing instead of Hearing

By the beginning of the twentieth century, in spite of the best efforts of pedagogues such as E. Herbert-Caesari to keep faith with a time-honoured tradition, bel canto was becoming a mere memory. Following Manuel Garcia's invention of the laryngoscope in 1854, enquiry into matters technical came increasingly to rely, I believe, upon scientific or pseudo-scientific means of determination.[8] What had hitherto been primarily an aural matter became increasingly a visual one, and what had been heard as a whole began to be 'scientifically' divided up into parts, and physically felt for. Hence the proliferation, throughout the twentieth century, of numerous techniques and proprietary methods, all of which have been based around some favoured aspect of the voice rather than on the whole instrument.

It seems that methods were sought with the specific aim of making voices bigger, disregarding the fact that an individual's voice is the size it was born to be. Trying to make a voice heavier or more robust than it is by nature is counterproductive in so many ways.

Since the mid-twentieth century some notable teachers have endeavoured to rediscover the capacities of the singing voice that were so successfully opened up by the Old Italian School. These pioneers – among them Owen Brown, William Vennard and Frederick Husler – applied an increasing body of anatomical and physiological knowledge to their efforts.

Husler and Rodd-Marling, conscious of where and how things had gone astray, wisely counselled us about using our ears. But in retrospect I think the damage had long been done, especially regarding the entrenchment of 'breath support'.

Nothing could be less scientific, in view of what we now know about the construction of the vocal folds, than to describe the breathing apparatus as 'bellows', or the abdominal muscles as the 'power house of the voice'. But the abdominal muscles are the part of the voice which is most easily felt, most easily seen, and most easily manipulated – all three activities dangerously non-aural.

Midgette states that without breath support, '... it's difficult to hit the proper pitches (particularly the top notes), modulate from soft singing to loud, or even be heard beyond the footlights'.[9] I expect that this is what singers struggling with Verdi and Wagner began to feel a hundred years ago. Having lost aural touch with the optimal functioning of the vocal folds, they had to find another way to achieve their goal. It's time to regain a sense of physiological integrity.

Inspiration

Fortunately for all of us, we are reminded by young singers from around the world that the singing voice is a natural phenomenon. Some of these are heard in prestigious singing competitions. Even if subsequently they lose some of their natural bloom and spontaneity, on these occasions they exemplified the oneness of singer and voice to an uncommon degree, thus restoring our faith in what is possible.[10]

Singing is Easy

To say, as some people do, that singing is easy, may be engaging, a nice thing to say to an enthusiastic amateur, or even what serious students wish to hear. But it can misrepresent the reality. Singing is demanding in a number of significant ways.

A singer must be a good musician and good with languages. He or she must be a good actor and communicator. And even after reaching a natural vocal balance – in itself a great achievement – a singer needs fitness and energy to sustain a good level.

Except in rare cases, reaching the point at which all these things come together is *not* easy. However rewarding it may be, the singing profession is,

I believe, one of the toughest. To imply anything else is irresponsible and may be one of the reasons why young singers often seem to 'go through the motions' rather than buckle down to hard training, and why they rarely fulfil their potential.

Mature Voice?

Youngsters are often exhorted to darken their sound because, it is said, they 'need to sound more mature'. In spite of creating musical and tonal inflexibility and masking emotional truth, a 'plummy' voice, or one affectedly rich or deep in tone, is still widely favoured. In early training it is easy to unbalance a voice in favour of a preferred sound. Artificial or unnatural darkening is one of the most pernicious.

Only recently I was in a position to help two talented young singers, both of whom were suffering this artificial 'maturing'. A 19-year-old in Mexico, where I have always found much promising raw vocal material, had an easy natural baritone. He had no difficulty in mimicking the heavier, more macho sound for which his teacher was asking. But it made him sound old, and he found it difficult to sing music with any ease, let alone be emotionally expressive. Fortunately, he had not been practising this 'artificial' singing for long. Recovering his natural voice, which I must say was beautiful, virile and naturally expressive, was not very difficult. Now he had to be mature enough to find a good teacher.

The other singer was a female singer in Portugal, where one might describe the talent as more sophisticated. This keen and hard-working young singer had practised artificially darkening her voice for some time – perhaps to match the mezzo label that she had been given. Her singing was awkward, monochrome and limited in both range and dynamics. It was beginning to be unsteady. But because she had come to depend on this 'technique', it took some months to get her confidently back on track. First we dismissed the mezzo label, which enabled her to open up, explore and see what would come. This demanded courage because she had to let go of what had become a familiar prop. But as her musical and expressive possibilities began to re-emerge, she became more excited and confident, until eventually her voice began to soar and reveal its true colours.

Both these singers had been led away from their natural voices and acquired limitations in the pursuit of false objectives. Both recognised their true voice and found relief and joy in it. Healthy voices remain youthful!

Low Larynx – High Larynx

In a healthy voice, one in which the suspensory mechanism is doing its job of freeing and stabilising the larynx, a wide spectrum of colours is available. From 'light' to 'dark', this is an individual palette that responds instantly to the singer's imagination and feelings. In a healthy voice, more or less subtle adjustments in laryngeal dynamics take place without resort to conscious technical manoeuvring.

The famed dramatic declamatory style of Gilbert-Louis Duprez apart, the deliberate lowering of the larynx, in order to darken the voice and add weight when singing, actually only gained prominence as a regular practice during the second quarter of 20th century. By this time, I imagine, all practical ties with the ideal bel canto balance had effectively been severed. In any case, the time it took to gain power and emotional depth naturally was probably thought unnecessary when a hefty 'core' of sound could be imposed so quickly, and seemingly safely, by fixing the larynx down. Reid points to another perceived advantage or attraction of the 'low larynx'. It 'persuades the unwary that because something is being "done", much is being accomplished'.[11]

The 'success' of this so-called 'covering' technique or *voix sombre*, if strongly executed, is usually short-lived, depending on the strength of the singer's throat to take the unnatural strain. Flexibility (both inside and outside the larynx) is severely reduced, a *messa di voce* with all its instrumental advantages is impossible, clarity of vowels is spoiled, high notes are forced, and the tone becomes unsteady. The voice is 'inward-directed', *en dedans* rather than open or outgoing. The singer's message is thus held back, garbled or obscured.

Opening = Liberating

It is instructive to note that the German language encourages this kind of 'covering'. Many other languages, such as Portuguese, English and Dutch, favour a high larynx, sometimes almost to the point of swallowing words. But the singing of all normal, non-natural, or untrained voices tends to draw on familiar speech patterns for vocalisation. Typically, the 'false elevators' that lie above the tongue bone (in particular the tongue), fix the larynx upwards.

A 'fixed-up larynx' is no better than an unnaturally lowered one. The difference is that a normal larynx tends to get fixed upwards through force of habit, while lowering the larynx is an intentional practice.

For singing, the immobilising influence of false elevators needs to be relieved. If you compare the relevant illustrations (3.2 and 3.7) in Chapter 3, you may appreciate the importance of the 'depressors' (m. sterno-thyreoideus and m. crico-pharyngeus) in this alleviating process. In fact, it is primarily for lack of strength in these muscles that the false elevators persist.

Husler and Rodd-Marling were probably the first modern pioneers to elucidate the role of the suspensory mechanism and how it works. They were aware of the many fads and abuses proliferating in the field of vocal pedagogy during the first half of the 20th century, and were at pains to explain the fundamental importance of stimulating and strengthening this network of muscles, and to caution that it is *how* the larynx is suspended that counts. The inspanning process has to be in balance – no one part is more important than another. They also pointed out the crucial fact that the sterno-hyoid muscles act by reflex to the stylo-pharyngeus muscles (see illustration 3.2a). That is why in yawning the larynx moves downwards while the palate rises. If the structure and role of the suspensory system (elastic scaffolding) is correctly understood, it will be obvious that in singing the vocal organ is never fixed in any way.

The Tongue and Other Parts – What should we do with them?

'The tongue goes where?' was the title of a talk organised by the British Voice Association.[12] This question is frequently asked, and is typical of singers' technical preoccupations.

Probably the most helpful response is, 'leave it alone'. We might ask a pupil, 'Can you speak?' to which (unless we are talking about a foreign language) they will probably reply, 'Yes'. 'Can you sing?' – the answer may be less sure. Should learning to sing create a problem for speaking? No, hopefully not! Sadly, it's because singers get preoccupied with *what to do* that their voices become (or remain) fixed.

Theoretically the question of the tongue is simple and logical. The tongue is not put in any particular position for the purpose of singing.

Even though it is responsible for shaping vowels it should have nothing to do with the production of the singing sound *per se*. If the tongue is 'trying to help' the production of the sound (to counteract a weakness in the suspensory mechanism) the articulation of words will be impeded. Then we have a problem. The solution is not to be found in the redeployment of the tongue but in getting the voice itself to work without the need of the tongue's participation.

Deliberately putting the tongue in a 'position' is bound to impede the flow of sung tone. It is self-evident that on the one hand we have the singing voice – essentially a flow of tone – and on the other the wherewithal to articulate words, and that these elements complement one another only if they are both free to do so. Tongue-positioning is tantamount to 'tongue-tying'.

Students of singing hear a lot of confusing jargon and contradictory techniques, so it is to be expected that technical questions will arise and be discussed. But a canny teacher will try to disabuse the questioning pupil of the idea that to sing you have to *do* things, *move* things and *put* things. Rather, the pupil should be encouraged to have faith in the naturalness and design of their emerging voice. They should be dissuaded from trying to force the pace of progress, but must wait until their voice can do what it does best by nature. Only then will it satisfactorily serve performing and communicating intentions without struggle.

Recently I watched a television broadcast of a Handel opera – not one with which I am familiar. While it was musically stylish, it took me several minutes to discern that it was sung in English! Handel wrote well for the voice – there is no excuse for 'incoherence'. Singers waste a lot of time on trying to articulate their words when the problem actually lies in the 'mechanics' of the voice itself. Spend sufficient time on liberating the voice and most of the 'what to do' questions become redundant.

Tongue and Acoustics

The perceived desirability of a tongue position for singing has come about not only through the mixing of objectives but through the study and application of acoustics. This is an unfortunate example of how reductionism can cause problems rather than solve them. The only way to satisfactorily 'speak' while singing is for the voice itself to be free and strong first. The tongue can then be free to continuously alter its position in a fluid fashion with respect to the text.

The singing sound is initiated at the folds. It carries well if it is produced naturally and not impeded by any stiffness forward of this source. The mechanism for verbal articulation – lips, teeth and tongue – takes place forward of the larynx, and is successful if (and only if) it is freed by not having to participate in vocal production.

Registers

One of the effects of learning to speak is that our voice is confined, most of the time, to a small range of its capacity. This gives the impression that anything outside this range is somehow not normal – including 'classical' singing. Pop singers use a very short compass of notes around their speaking range, or 'make a virtue' of so-called 'register breaks'. The singing voice is something quite different.

The difficulty seems to lie in coming to terms with the fact that the natural voice is not divided or broken into sections. A whole voice does not have 'registers'. 'Chest' and 'head' (or falsetto), and sometimes 'middle', are terms given to describe sounds which betray vocal disunity. While this is the normal condition, these 'registers' are only natural insofar as they exist as parts of an integrated whole. As singing teachers we must understand how they come together to form that whole. When this work is adequately done, we no longer need to negotiate separate ways of voicing different pitches. The various skills that we associate with the singing voice then apply throughout the singer's range. For more explanation of how the 'registers' combine and support one another please refer to Chapters 3 and 4.

Messa di Voce and Legato – a Reminder

It is the fully integrated voice, with no registers, that gives the singing voice its kaleidoscopic versatility: colours, dynamics, continuity of line (whatever the intervals, rhythms or tempi), constant emotional variation, and the carrying through of meaning, are all blended or synchronised in the mix. We don't have to add these elements. If there is a problem with any of them we have to see where there is structural weakness or lack of synchronisation. Embodied as they are in the sung tone, all singing qualities are continuously interrelating, reinforcing and informing one another, making legato a 'lateral' as well as a 'linear' matter.

Projection

A baby's voice projects – no problem! – even though the vocal ligament has not yet acquired its ability to fully concentrate the sound. That the folds go on developing, even though their singing potential is largely ignored, seems a miracle. But it speaks of a sad state of affairs which begs the question, 'Why don't we all sing?' Why don't we all 'project' or 'get across?'

It is the much neglected and elusive 'edge mechanism' that effectively minimises breath use to a seemingly negligible amount when singing. Given this efficiency, the singing voice projects naturally – like a baby's. Developing this economy of means is the opposite quest from the one driven by the notion that *more* breath, and/or a darker sound, is required in order to 'get across'. The exponents of bel canto understood well that everything that makes the voice the *singing* voice is gained through this finely honed centre.

The best singing, whether we are talking about power or refinement, comes from well-centred voices. A big voice which is heavily produced carries less well than a small voice which has gained its concentrated core. The well-honed voice, whether large or small, projects detail and meaning with clarity, while an un-centred voice loses out on details and transmits a relatively unfocused message.

It can be very exciting to try to get to the centre of a large voice. It is usually tricky, meticulous work, and can be unsettling for the singer. As the voice regains its centre, the singer can have the ungratifying impression that they are singing 'small'. And yet the voice has effectively gained power, and the sound reaches all parts of the auditorium. Its primitive outdoor carrying power is still there! All singers who want their singing to carry well have to come to terms with this phenomenon.

Support – Revisited

It seems that whenever there is lack of continuity or weakness in a singer's tone or line it is put down to 'lack of support'. Most people would be hard put to say what they mean by this. The usual reference is to some aspect of breathing. 'Support the breath', 'Support with the diaphragm',

'Support with the abdomen' are common exhortations. Singers are bidden to support the tone, or the line or the column of air or the larynx. 'How' is never explained in any intelligible way. It cannot be. If the problem is anything to do with lack of integration attempts to manipulate breathing will be to no avail. Whereas if the voice is integrated, 'supporting the voice' is a contradiction in terms.

A fully integrated voice *feels* integrated, not something 'apart'. It does not need holding onto, or holding up, or pushing along. It moves and travels *with* you, not because you make it do so but because it *is* you. Like a river, the voice negotiates 'obstacles' (primarily intervals) with ease, because in the main they don't have to be negotiated. We don't have a keyboard – the notes are differentiated by the very mechanism which forms tone, dynamics and colours. I sometimes find myself saying to a singer 'You can't push the river!' The ability to sustain tone, if that is what is intended by 'support', is first a matter of integration and then of intention – but never of coercion.

Achieving integration is one of the two basic aims in training. It results in ease. Then, a singer also needs to build stamina so that the 'ease' continues. Stamina in muscles means their ability to sustain their activity. This second basic aim must apply to the whole balanced organ, large and small muscles alike.

Control

I recently went to a student recital, an examination, which was remarkable for how the singer's voice responded to her imagination. Musical phrasing, dynamic shading, timbre, emphasis and so forth all seemed to arise spontaneously from her understanding of the text and her desire to convey it meaningfully and with feeling. She trusted her voice, and took risks which mostly paid off. While it was not perfectly consistent, neither was it boringly predictable. It was, all told, a compelling and expressive performance. I later heard that her examiners criticised her for, as they put it, 'lack of control'.

This was, I thought, typical of a certain approach to singing based on the belief that the singing voice can be or needs to be manipulated – the idea of 'taking the reins', or something akin to sitting at the controls of a machine. Either this is based on misunderstanding the nature and physiology of the singing voice, or it arises from a fear or distrust of freedom.

The digital manipulation of recordings has two opposite effects. On the one hand it suggests that performances have to be 'perfect', and this leads to control of the wrong kind. On the other it encourages laziness, because technology can mask imperfections.

One sometimes hears singing, especially among lieder singers and those with a particularly 'cerebral' approach, which is near-perfect in terms of musical and verbal accuracy and consistency of tone, but, dare one say, insipid and predictable.

At the outset of training, many voices are already being controlled by their deficiencies – physical tensions, or the imbalance of strength between the various muscle systems. 'Controlling' the voice amounts at best to smoothing out the inconsistencies or replacing one set of blocking tensions with another perhaps less insidious set. Both can give, at least temporarily, an impression of improved vocal and musical competence. But it is only a matter of time before these new controls no longer serve or satisfy.

I have often found that the original false controls have to be discouraged or inhibited, unhelpful tensions alleviated and weak muscles strengthened, before it can be discovered exactly what Nature has in store. A period of 'losing control' to some extent is therefore usually called for. We eventually discover that not only does the voice 'work', without us having to interfere with it, but that Nature has provided us with a natural control which doesn't have to be thought about or felt for. The neurological realignment of the organs of hearing and voicing comes with the realigning of the physical voice. Signs that this is happening are:

1. The singing and the person feel 'all of a piece';
2. The tone does not need 'persuading' – it begins in a clean spontaneous manner;
3. The vocalisation is consistent;
4. The voice is reliable without deliberate 'support'.

The healthy voice is not the one that we manipulate, control or drive, but the one that responds in a natural and spontaneous manner to our imagination, feelings and musical sensitivity.

Exercises and Practice

To write a book about singing without a single exercise in it may seem odd, but an exercise, to be of benefit, must be timely and serve a functional need. If you are a singing student I cannot tell from here what condition your voice is in.

In prescribing a vocal exercise for a pupil to do on their own, a teacher is assuming that the pupil has some means of knowing when to apply it, and then whether it is doing any good with the long term in mind. Exercising in a routine or mindless way serves no pedagogic purpose. Add to this that would-be singers, until they are quite advanced, are generally deaf to their own voices, and it is more than likely, when there may be days or even weeks between lessons, that assiduous practice will take the pupil down the wrong track, or merely 'fix' things.

Each pupil's needs require different types and different amounts of work at different times. If exercising is to be taken seriously it needs to be apposite and progressive. In exercising the voice for physiological improvements, there is a large element of unpredictability. It is difficult enough for a teacher to pick up as they go what is relevant and take full advantage of it. Pupils cannot do it on their own.

Patterns of notes and rhythms do not of themselves give any indication of the vocal sound that is being looked for. Ooo's and Aaa's vary considerably from language to language. Even giving the instruction to employ Italian vowels will not guarantee the desired vocal progression, even if an exercise is repeated a hundred times. In short, there is no magic in the written exercise. A pupil needs on-the-spot feedback so that their ear and other senses become attuned to a healthy sound as it emerges. Pupils of the Old Italian School were supervised in all their vocal work. A distinction was made between liberating or developing a voice and its application to music.[13] Musical exercises are for music, and only reap physiological benefits by chance, at least until a voice is well developed. From then on there is a wealth of suitable music with which to 'feed' the voice (see Appendix 1).

Teachers of the Old Italian School used their ears for diagnosing and prescribing suitable exercises. In 2013 we are still dealing with sound; whatever we may think we know, neither the singing voice nor its dependence on our hearing have changed. We still need our hearing to recognise the singing voice in all its intricacy. The ear is the great revealer and the knowing synthesizer.

Apart from this primary need (in both teacher and pupil) to recognise aurally what is going on, two things conspire to thwart our best teaching and practising endeavours. Neither was a problem 300 years ago. First, the knowledge upon which we have come to depend is as yet fragmented and incoherent. Second, we are in such a hurry to achieve our vocal goals that we rarely allow ourselves to concentrate on what needs to be our focus of attention – the often tiny steps that lead the way. These matters will be further addressed in Part II. For more about muscle training see *The Human Nature of the Singing Voice*, Chapter 13.

Faster, higher, stronger

Attempts to sing a classical aria on a popular show are, fortunately, still rare – which may go some way to accounting for the lack of discernment by talent show audiences when such an attempt is made. However, voice carers should be concerned that ugly, alienated sounds are so popular and so prevalent; it makes anything less than ugly sound relatively beautiful! Pop singing is often the outcome of vocal disintegration, with all that that implies for health generally. Even so, there has been a worrying move towards approving any way of using the voice that can be explained scientifically.

I am disturbed by the public celebration of vocal feats. They are invariably the result of imbalance. 'Faster, higher, stronger' may be fine as a motto for athletes who are trying to maximise their capacities, but, fun aside, they cannot be aims for serious singers. They are certainly not indicators of health.

We have already seen how some 'classical' singers have tried to make their voices bigger. In recent years some notable singers have pushed their voices too hard, and paid a high price for it. Impressive as such singing might be, it cannot be said to be healthy if it leads to vocal problems.

However, my concern is wider and deeper. 'The British Voice Association is a group of multi-disciplinary professionals who work to promote the field of voice in its broadest sense'.[14] Among its laudable objectives, this internationally respected organisation aims to 'encourage greater awareness of voice disorders and the importance of good vocal health and communication'.[15] It has gone out of its way to embrace all areas of voice use and care – hence its multi-disciplinary character. In its conferences and publications extensive medical and scientific research is followed, discussed and duly disseminated. Throughout the year, and especially on World Voice Day, people in general are advised about taking care of their voices. So far, however, in its long history (I was a founding member back in 1986), while scientific findings and explanations have proliferated, a definition of 'good vocal health' has remained elusive. Conscientious attempts to include all comers from the 'field of voice' may have had the effect of losing any measurable parameters.

A write-up of a Vocalympics day states 'The recordings and video footage were all backed up with scientific explanations as to how it was thought the singer in each case attained their particular note....'[16] Ever since Jo Estill's work on vocal deconstruction, it would appear that a scientific explanation of how a sound is produced is considered the only criterion required for its legitimisation.

Of course, 'mass appeal' in itself is no measure of health or quality; what *does* constitute vocal health and quality is of a completely different order.

Being a Musician

Some people like to joke about singers not being good musicians. Only it's not always a joke. Like attempting to articulate words before the singing voice is secure enough not to be adversely affected by them, trying to be musical before the voice releases its skills can be self-defeating. If unnatural ways and means are devised in order to (prematurely) satisfy musical criteria, the singer has to concentrate on those ways and means. But the result is not freely musical. The singer is distracted – some kind of struggle is going on. The objectives have been impeded by a preoccupation with how to produce them.

The voice is not like any other musical instrument. It should be treated for what (and who) it is. We do not play it. We *are* it. Our musicality and our voice must not just be compatible, they must be *one*. If we don't understand this fact, or choose to ignore it, we will always perceive the problems as external instead of systemic. We will waste time and energy on trying to find specific musical skills through some technical contrivance. This end-gaining frustrates concrete progress. The most that can be hoped for from this path is the ability to reproduce music in a more or less pleasant and mechanical way.

Understandably, conductors and coaches themselves get frustrated when a singer is not free enough to make music. For the singer it is laborious to have to devise new strategies, or skill foci, for each new musical difficulty. Making music can only come from inside. A person's singing voice is what conveys this internal music-making activity. This voice has to be both free and dependable.

If an aspiring singer-musician wants to avoid struggling with conflicting performance interests, they must undergo a purposeful, integrating process of training and learning in which every facet and component makes sense of every other facet and component. This matter begins to be addressed in Part II.

PART II
The Work

CHAPTER 8

Introduction to The Work

When young singers join a programme of work they rarely know enough to assess the true condition of their voice or the quality of their performance. They are not in a position to gauge their own prospects. Some believe that it's merely a matter of time before they find a 'winning formula' that will sweep them to success. The popular attitude that 'anyone can do it – with a bit of luck' is endorsed by the 'success' of indifferent talent and the seemingly indiscriminate dishing out of plaudits.

Aspiring young singers naturally assume that what they need in terms of course content and expertise will be provided. They believe they can reasonably expect to be given the training and education that will fit them for the profession they have chosen. Since they have been taken on by a teacher, or selected by the 'powers that be', for study at the highest level, they can safely assume that they are suitable for the work and, eventually, the profession.

In my experience few would-be singers have the remotest idea about what the profession entails, and a worrying number of them seem none the wiser for their conservatory or college education. Initially they have no way of telling whether the training they are signing up to will be adequate. Too often they discover, too late, that it was not. It may have been incomplete, or insufficiently thorough in terms of depth or detail. Lack of time or facilities often leads to superficial work or end-gaining, and what I call 'outside-in' work, a kind of vocal and musical patchwork which does not hold together for long once serious professional work begins.

Young singers whose voices are in healthy shape at the outset of their studies need time to integrate their many other performance disciplines, attend to details, build stamina, and become professional in habit and demeanour. They may not have had to think much about their voice as such, but they will need thorough advice about how to take care of it in an unnatural environment. They will need to learn how to conduct themselves – even survive – in the most demanding and competitive of professions.

Those for whom sheer vocalisation does not come so easily – and let's face it, these are in the majority – are the ones who really suffer, initially at least, from ineffectual training processes. Even where conscientious steps have been taken to provide what is required, the various curricula are rarely handled in a balanced and complementary way that levels with the individual singer's particular stage and specific vocal needs. Their eventual performance lacks the harmony, strength and creative power derivable from a fully integrated (and integrating) programme.

Any programme of work designed to be of lasting benefit to a singer must be based on or around the following:

a) What the singing voice is and what it is for;
b) The condition of this voice;
c) The recognition that a singing education must include all subjects that are likely to have a bearing on success as a performer;
d) An understanding of how these subjects affect one another and behave together;
e) The singer him- or herself.

In other words it must be foundational, individual and with a view to the long term. It must be a process that always, and in all respects, feeds the individual singer's growth. It must be experiential and revelatory rather than premeditated and explanatory; the former honouring uniqueness and leading to freedom, the latter doing neither.

It must be systemic rather than an accumulation of knowledge-modules or a rag-bag of separate skills. It must, above all, be personal – about who the singer is, and is becoming. This will make the student comfortable with themselves and their material, and will help them to become the most compelling performer and communicator that they can be.

I am assuming, throughout this book, that the reader is interested in the highest possible standards of vocal and musical performance.

In composing the following curriculum (with suggestions regarding frequency) I am going to take the four criteria that I used to define and identify the singing voice (Chapters 3, 4, 5 and 6) as general guidelines. If all disciplines or facets of the work are to make sense of each other while at the same time serving to capitalise on the natural capacities of the singing voice, they must accord with these defining and identifying criteria. Here they are again:

1) Physical Structure (instrumental freedom);
2) Beautiful Singing (musical skills and awareness);
3) Individual Identity (personal growth);
4) Communication (performance).

The subjects, which I will call departments, discussed in the following chapters might serve a new singing school or the singing faculty of an already established musical institution.

CHAPTER 9

The Voice

Readying the singing voice for a serious training course

I have said a lot about the singing voice, and it should by now be obvious that I consider a healthy (whole) singing instrument the *sine qua non* of a singer's genuine progress.

How great a priority the voice *per se* is made will depend on the individual's vocal condition at any given stage of the course.

In a lecture given at the Royal Academy of Music, London, in July 2010, Janice Chapman made a bold attempt to address the matter of 'Priorities in Developing the Young Adult Classical Singer at Music College'.[1] A well-thought-out if brief critique of the current situation, it offers a lot of good advice. Chapman concentrates on the first year of study, which she says 'we should consider ... as a voice and technique building period'. Although I take issue with the meaning of 'technique', the idea is clear and this emphasis makes sense.

But most entrants to this level are nowhere near ready to take advantage of what's on offer. For most, one year to get their voice sorted out is not enough. Considering the nature of the vocal instrument and the amount of practical work that a student needs to do to reach a professional level, either they should enter better prepared, or the course ahead needs to be extended. In any case, young singers have very different individual needs and develop at different rates.

Just as with any other physical development in which muscles are gaining coordination, flexibility and strength through specialised exercising, the development of a voice is a 'building' process. Considering the make-up of the singing voice, with its very large and very small muscle systems, and considering how muscles are best trained, voice training must be done in fairly short bursts: anywhere between 10 and 30 minutes at a stretch. Then, to make 'hard training' fully beneficial physiologically, a student should leave the voice alone for a suitable length of time after each session – not rush off to a rehearsal!

Assuming the training *is* hard training, one session a day might serve as a minimum amount. Importantly, teachers must be there to supervise this specialised, progressive work.

A careful distinction should be made between exercises for the development of the instrument and those with a specific musical objective. Musical skills are released with the voice; singing as such does not necessarily release those skills.

Any music that is employed while the voice is gaining its freedom and strength should manifestly contribute to this end. A short phrase, carefully chosen and sung on suitable vowels, can serve the purpose. It's not necessary to sing a whole aria to enjoy oneself with music!

Tests for progress can be made against structural integrity, musical qualities, a pupil's self-revelation in sound, and the ability to say something with the voice. Work done meticulously and thoroughly lays the foundation upon which the whole of the singer's career depends. Taking time to get this right can save a great deal of heartbreak or frustration later on.

Too many graduates leave college in a poor vocal state. Many students have told me their voices were 'easier' (usually meaning they could do more with them) before they went to college. This is shocking and inexcusable!

What it takes to be a voice teacher

Helping singers to find their voices is an exacting privilege. It requires not only intimate knowledge of the workings of the instrument and ways of enlivening it in young bodies, but considerable maturity and wisdom. Teaching singing, as well as being specialised, is a highly personal matter. Having a degree does not of itself qualify one to teach singing any more than it equips one to sing. One cannot learn to be a voice teacher by reading a book, studying a method or following instructions.

Nor is a career as a professional performer any guarantee that you can help a singer to develop their own individual voice. Many great singers are hard put to explain how they sing, and end up trying to get pupils to do what they imagine they do. Their instructions are often quite unfounded physiologically. There is a delightful YouTube clip in which Luciano Pavarotti states that all tenors have a break at f or f#, and then proceeds to sing a scale without one.[2]

Many pianists set themselves up as singing teachers when their only relevant experience is some musical coaching or playing for singing lessons. That's like a nurse becoming a surgeon without the appropriate studies or experience – ouch!

Teachers need many personal qualities specific to the job of teaching *per se*. Then they need specialised knowledge regarding the singing voice. Above all, they need to develop a suitably analytical ear.

In a modern musical institution there is no place for charlatans to hide. However, we should beware of placing our faith totally in either 'received' or newly- available 'knowledge'. As yet it is fraught with inconsistencies (some of which I pointed out in Chapter 7). No fixed 'method' can possibly cater for the innumerable differences and varying needs between singers.

In our conscientious attempts at getting up to date we should not sever our roots with the past. The Old Italian School knew a thing or two even if we have only hearsay evidence. The singing voice has not changed any more than the rest of the body. We are dealing with one and the same God-given instrument. Their concern was to make the very most of it. Ours should be the same.

Considering the nature of voice training, it stands to reason that a singer needs constant, caring and progressive attention. It is not good enough to clock up the requisite number of hours.

CHAPTER 10

Music (Singing)

Obvious musical talent, along with obvious vocal talent, needs to be at the top of the list of requirements for anyone seeking musical and performing education with an eye to becoming a professional. An aspiring professional singer's musicianship needs to be up there with that of other instrumentalists when entering college. A good measure might be Grade 7 or 8 of the Associated Board of the Royal Schools of Music in some instrument, not necessarily singing.[1]

My choir school background was a fortunate start for a life in music. There was no better musical education for a child. I was surprised when I first went to music college at how poor the general level of musicianship was among first-year singing students. To have to study in such a basic way at this level does not bode well for an individual's future, and may even be a waste of time unless the student possesses an exceptional instrument with a better than average feeling for singing.

Poor musicianship poses a serious problem for a singer. Musical difficulties cause them to hesitate and feel their way. The singing voice does not take well to hesitation. The singer tends to hold on to their instrument, losing rhythmical vitality and, because of the need to move the voice deliberately from note to note, spoiling any sense of legato or continuity. Having a lot of catching up to do adds urgency to the deliberations.

On the other hand, a student with the musical background but an insufficiently free voice is likely to make the most of what they have, but unlikely to advance very far vocally. A serviceable technique becomes the most attractive option because it helps to achieve musical goals while keeping the voice together. It may help pass an exam, but what it means to be truly expressive is missing.

Challenging a voice with things for which as yet it has little facility can arrest its freeing process and be intolerably frustrating for the inner musician. A would-be singer is well advised to study music in some other way than singing. Many great singers from the past studied the piano. Studying music to degree level while taking well-paced singing lessons alongside, and entering college when more mature and better equipped musically, has sometimes proved a good option. Every case is of course different. Entrance requirements will be discussed more fully later on.

Being able to play a keyboard is always useful to a singer. The voice is 'saved' while preparing text and music. The basic work having been done, it can then respond spontaneously. With a keyboard one can familiarise oneself with the all-important harmonic progressions and changes of mood which help a singer to be expressive.

Unless the singing voice is free, the singing itself never gets beyond 'application' – of instrument to music. To make music we must go beyond rudiments and intellectual exercise. We can only do this with the voice if it is free of inhibiting tasks. In good singing, voicing (which is not an intellectual exercise) and music become one, and thereby transcend one another.

There's an existential difference between singers and other musicians in the way of making music. With our natural, inbuilt instrument (ourselves) so finely tuned to our musicality (a natural predisposition if we can realise it), our music making is like making conversation. All other musicians, however at one with their instruments, must 'converse' as though by proxy. This is probably why so many of them wish to emulate singing. On some level they 'know' the power of this inimitable 'oneness'.

While we can rationalise the making of music by analysis of its various components, we can only experience what is greater than the sum of its parts intuitively. Meaning is not a linear matter, as the written music and text seem to suggest, but the experience of continuous wholeness.

We can apply these guidelines:

1) How elastic (structurally together) as distinct from rigid (consciously manipulated) is the voice at this point?
2) How 'musical' is it in itself? Line (flowing melody), timbre (changing colours), dynamic variations and 'feeling' – all inherent qualities of the singing voice when singing – coalesce

as the voice gains its integrity. These natural musical attributes are summoned by the singer's understanding and imagination, not 'engineered' as and when deemed appropriate.

3) To what extent is the singer emerging (coming into their own) or still 'demonstrating' a selected or preferred sound? To what extent are they still being self-conscious.
4) Is something genuine being conveyed in the vocal gesture? How clear is it? How telling?

Rhythm

> There is rhythm in nature before poetry, painting, architecture and music exist. Were it not so, rhythm as an essential property of form would be merely superimposed upon material, not an operation through which material effects its own culmination in experience.[2]

All life has rhythm, and nowhere is that more palpable than in our bodies. Getting in touch with our inner rhythm can help us to be more self-aware. Just as through the voice we actually embody melody, timbre, dynamics and emotion – since these are its natural constituents – so we must look for the inner experience that is rhythm, the pulse that vitalises our life.

A blocked or struggling voice can make it difficult to tap into this natural musical resource. The rhythm of the singer's music can be awkward or mechanical. The Italian School, moving on from relatively rigid rhythms and unvarying dynamics, would have explored both emotion and rhythm as expressive means. The natural voice facilitates the expressive developments of emotion and rhythmic vitality. Conversely, these enliven the voice, enabling it to expand and take flight – an exciting physiological discovery!

While a blocked voice can disrupt a person's natural rhythmic sense from being fully embodied, sometimes rhythmicality is impeded by a perceived need to 'work out' the rhythm.

Whatever the reason, a lack of rhythmic sense is worryingly common among singers. Understandably, this irritates conductors and other musicians. A singer more than any other musician needs to be able to embody rhythm, to feel the pulse without counting or measuring it.

Music springs from rhythm – the rhythm of the dance. True musical rhythm is elastic and can be subtly varied. This is why encouraging singers to dance their music can have such a releasing effect.

In a school aiming for excellence, I would create a Rhythm Department. In one form or another this would be a compulsory activity and serious fun. It would consist of all or some of the following:

Dancing (compulsory throughout the course)

> The language of action was originally indistinguishable from 'dancing' – both the 'dance of gestures' which expresses thoughts, and the 'dance of the feet' which communicates the various conditions of the soul.[3]

Dancing, as an essential part of the curriculum, would cover different rhythms, tempi and styles. It would be done solo, with partners and in groups. It would be formal or free, ancient or modern. The dances would come from many different cultures.

Bodies want to move, and given the chance they know how to. So it's mainly a question of finding the right triggers. The particularly shy, inexperienced or awkward could begin with one-to-one or small group sessions if it seemed appropriate.

I believe that a sense of rhythm is a corollary of true physical fitness; we observed this in the London Olympians. Yet I have observed that people can have a good sense of rhythm without being particularly fit. I once saw a great production of *Show Boat* in which a number of the cast were overweight – but could they dance!

Dancing skills are often required of singers. In addition to discovering and enjoying their natural rhythmic vitality, dancing would serve a desirable professional competence. Furthermore, it could make a considerable contribution to the social side of the school.

Drumming

> By rousing a muscle's rhythmic sense, deep-seated energies within it are released ... Life without rhythmic content is never very vital.[4]

Another way to stimulate an energetic sense of rhythm is to work with drums. This, too, could take different forms and be great fun. Depending on individual needs I would make this compulsory for the first year. There would be scope for improvisation and the cultivation of alertness through interaction and subtle or sudden pattern changes. 'Body Music (or Body Percussion)' might act as a viable alternative!

Eurhythmics

> Rhythm and movement engage our inner creative resources and connect the body, mind and emotions.[5]

Eurhythmics classes can benefit would-be singers at any stage of their development. Singers need to develop their kinaesthetic sense or physical awareness in terms of position, weight and moving in space. This sense is not something superimposed or got hold of. It is sensations brought to awareness by way of monitoring our physical being.

Ironically, it's often a lack of physical sensation that leads people to look for palpable sensations in singing, when what is required is the aural awareness that enables them to get on with the job of singing, without undue physical interference.

Having said this, singers are often out of touch with their bodies when conscious physical movement is required. Schnebly-Black and Moore make the observation that although 'Humans are naturally flexible in the torso ... our surrounding environments are such efficient spatial arrangements that we seldom need to bend in our mid-sections'. As for the use of our limbs, they observe that 'Ergonomic engineers strive to prevent large movements'.[6]

Eurhythmics recognises the partnership between the kinaesthetic and vestibular nerve receptors. I believe this body-ear, and by extension body-voice, partnership of neural checks and balances is of fundamental importance to the singer-actor. The proper alignment of body, voice and ear forms a holistic basis from which the specific skills (acting, voicing and music) can flourish in harmony.

CHAPTER 11

Physical Expression (Acting)

The great advantage of the language of action ... was its instantaneousness.[1]

The singing voice with its particular expressive qualities, and the body with its particular expressive qualities, are perfectly compatible. I'm not talking in either case about physical feats, but the freedom of each to be itself, so that in singing they can come together naturally as one. Where there is conflict – that is to say when either of these two is not free to express itself in its own right – then the other will suffer.

We often see this and hear it in performance – not only in the obvious place, the operatic stage, but also on the recital platform, where voice and body often betray their disagreement. It is a conflict of being. And so, far from being instantaneous, the language of action becomes obscure or indistinct. Sometimes the demands of an unsympathetic stage director will cause a counterproductive breach between the singer's body and his or her voice. What is compatible and productive needs to be understood by both parties.

Singers come in for a lot of flak because they can't act. Of course they must be able to act. But it is precisely this compatible enabling that so rarely gets done in training. The unfettered voice and the unfettered body are able to be instantaneously expressive – each complementing the other. Sounds and actions should not need 'explaining'. A stage director needs a singer to be bodily free and available so that actions don't have to be contrived or qualified in some way. A powerful, truly moving performance is not one that is in any way 'demonstrative' or 'explanatory'.

But even a performance that is a perfect example of movement or 'acting' will not necessarily be believable. The truly moving performance is one that is lived. Or, as Lorna Marshall puts it in her book about performance and expression, 'owned', in contrast with work which is flawlessly functional, but in which 'you don't have the sense that there is anyone at home inside'.

> Every single move they [performers] make should reflect some kind of vibrant inner reality ... we should all try to 'own' everything we do. We acknowledge a connection between what we choose to do and who we are as individuals. It is 'me' that performs. Not egotistically, or self-indulgently, but genuinely and openly. I use myself, my experience, my inner landscape, my imagination, and enjoy permitting these to engage with the work. I adapt and shape what I do according to the demands of the situation, but I own every action, every shift and nuance. I recognize my right to be fully present in everything I choose to explore.[2]

This may seem advanced, but as Marshall wisely counsels, 'it is good to engage this sense of connectedness right from the start, even in the most basic exercises'.[3]

So long as a singer is preoccupied with vocal technique, the body cannot be entirely free to act. To my mind the Physical Expression department and the Voice department of a school need to be monitored alongside each other. This is perfectly logical when we remember that the singer's body is their voice and vice versa.

Given that this is understood, I don't believe there needs to be acting tuition especially for singers, as though they were a different type of person, not at least in the 'classical' world where Nature and Truth (and Beauty, for that matter) rule. That said, David F. Oswald's *Acting for Singers,* from which I quote later, is full of wisdom and practical advice about believable performing. No doubt singers can learn a lot from actors and vice versa.

As for the 'outside-in' approach – the 'do this, do that, come here, go there' school, often still adopted by unimaginative or dictatorial directors – it's anathema to my mind. Like other actors, singers need to be able to draw on their inner resources.

It is when the inner contacts are made, embraced and nourished that both the singing and the acting come alive and can serve their various purposes without coercion or conflict of interests. This self-connectedness in turn connects with the audience and connects them with themselves. The rest is show.

Stanislavski said:

> I tried to develop in my pupils not the outward rhythm of movement and action, but the inner rhythm of that unseen energy which calls out movement and action ... to develop in my pupils the sensation of ... the entire inner pulse of life.[4]

Stage Craft

This used to mean, and is still applied to, 'the art of writing or staging plays'. It does not normally mean 'the art of acting', even though aspects of acting and stage craft combine and affect one another. I use stage craft in the sense of the now common definition, 'Skill in the Techniques and Devices of the Theatre'. This means, among other things, how to make the most of stage lighting, microphones, TV monitors and cameras, and how to handle sets, props and such like. All singers need to be competent and feel comfortable on stage.

Stage craft must therefore include walking on and off the stage, with or without high heels, sitting on a chair and getting up from it, with or without tails. It must include how to handle various styles of dress and headgear. Opera singers will need to know how to feel comfortable and safe on a raked stage. All singers need to know how to bow (solo, with a partner, or in a group) and to gracefully acknowledge applause and receive flowers and kisses, and how to thank or 'include' fellow performers confidently and, again, gracefully.

Stage craft should include how not to be clumsy with a score or a music stand, or notes or a drink of water. It should include how to negotiate pot plants or other musicians' music stands en route to the performing area.

These things may all look easy enough on paper, or even in your imagination. You might think nothing of them in the comfort and safety of your home. But walk out onto a vast stage (or even a small one), or up the aisle of a church in front of a large (hopefully) and expectant audience, and everything changes.

What you do matters! Every twitch and gesture is visible. It's no good being self-conscious on stage, but there is every reason to be self-aware, comfortable and confident. Your body is, after all, the interface between your audience and your self. Free or blocked, how you are on the inside will show on the outside.

How you move matters! Not only for you as a performer. Done in an awkward, botched or careless fashion, movements on stage can be embarrassing for an audience. They can irritate, or they can look tasteless to anyone with a modicum of aesthetic sense. Incompetence is not to be pitied – it spells 'don't care'.

How you behave towards your audience and with your colleagues matters! I'm not advocating stiffness or starchiness. On the contrary, your audience is more likely to feel comfortable if you are. And there must be room for humour, especially if something goes wrong. But those who have come specially to see and hear you will appreciate the care you take in presenting yourself and your material. It shows that you care about what you are doing and about them. There is a 'craft' to professional conduct on stage. It is a visible and telling facet of the performer's art. Students should start learning to be at home on stage (with or without accoutrements) from Day One.

Presentation

Presentation is bound up with stage craft and communication. It has a lot to do with attitude. It's worth considering the relationship between what an audience sees and what they hear. I would say that, by and large, whether performers and listeners are locked into a totally intellectual performance, or whether there is something more of life to it, the visual aspect tends to be the more influential. This is because its influence works two ways: presentation is not for the audience alone – it affects how an artist performs.

I recently heard a concert of 'early music' which sounded as unphysical and joyless as it looked. I found myself wishing that the musicians had dressed in colours instead of all black – it wasn't even a mass or a requiem! – their performance might have gathered some vibrancy. By contrast, I vividly recall shifting to the edge of my seat in anticipation as a female singer strode onto a concert platform, full of confidence and *joie de vivre.* It was indeed a confident show – of stunning artifice! Anything less than a show would not have sufficed for this singer. The audience seemed duly impressed. While artists are not normally out to deceive, they do well to consider appearances – what is appropriate, compatible and honest.

Although it may sound vulgar, artists need to 'sell' themselves, not just to obtain jobs in the first place, but every time they perform. This is not a question of deception or artifice, but of honesty. It's a quality that arises from an attitude of respect and sincerity, which needs to be cultivated from the outset of professional training. Put simply, an artist's work, and their performance, is affected by their attitude towards it. In as much as they are one and the same, selling ourselves implies also 'selling our product'. Whether for our audience, our performing materials or ourselves, respect is key.

Auditioning

Similarly, an audition which is executed with due respect and sincerity is much more likely to be successful than a 'demonstration' of vocal or theatrical prowess. Members of panels don't want to be 'told', they prefer to decide for themselves what they think you have that is interesting to them. Being aloof or apologetic is not professional. Nor is being ingratiating. The panel are professionals and they want to feel they can work with you.

Auditioning is partly a question of being prepared and partly a question of organisation. Although the circumstances are not 'normal', an audition is nonetheless a performance. All the qualities of a public performance (including stage craft and presentation) pertain. Allow plenty of time to get to the audition venue. You may have a chance to warm up. At least you will have time to get warm from the cold outside, and gather yourself. In any case, 'late' is decidedly unprofessional. Better half an hour early than five minutes late.

The panel hasn't time to waste. As a performer you must be able to walk in confidently and say 'good morning' – or 'good afternoon' if you're lucky – with a smile. Shaking hands might or might not be appropriate. If it is, do it confidently – with eye contact and a smile.

First impressions count. You need to look good the moment you walk through the door. Being over-dressed is as bad as looking sloppy. Smart-casual is a good rule of thumb. And they want to see your eyes – get that hair out of the way! Find out beforehand if the audition is likely to entail some improvisation or other work, and dress accordingly.

The panel doesn't want to know you have a sore throat – why are you there if you are not going to sing your best? They want to know what you are capable of. Only ever sing your best. The same applies if you make a demonstration CD or video – only your best, with the best equipment possible.

If it's your choice, you must know exactly which piece you will begin with – no hesitation, no fuss. The panel may or may not wish to know why you have chosen it, or what else you have brought along, so wait until they ask. You should offer them a copy of your music.

Unless the audition is for something specific, you should sing a variety of thoroughly well prepared pieces, always from memory, which show the virtues of your singing as a whole – accuracy, ease, expressiveness and so on. Don't choose something with which you have to struggle in any way.

It's unprofessional to sing with the music – it's a barrier. Except in an oratorio context, don't do it. Be prepared to tell the panel clearly what your song or aria is about, if they ask, and why you've chosen it.

If you take your own accompanist, with whom you can thoroughly rehearse, so much the better. If not, try to get a chance to run through pieces, or at least the parts where ensemble is tricky, with the official accompanist. It might even be that he or she can receive copies to look at in advance. It's up to you to be so well prepared that you can manage to give a good performance even if the accompanist can't. Occasionally the official accompanist is bad! At the very least give the accompanist a clear indication of your tempi before you begin – no discussion!

Compose yourself and take a moment (but not five minutes) to get into mood or character. Panels usually understand this need.

Remember, juries want you to do well. Why should it be otherwise? They know you are unique, and they are generally interested and happy to hear something new. But you cannot second-guess what they are looking for, or what they will like. Besides, they may have already decided whom they want. And however well you perform, your face might not fit. Hundreds of singers audition for a few jobs. You can expect to be rejected nine times out of ten. Logically that means that you will have to do ten auditions or more to get one job. Sing your best, and with a bit of luck they will make a note for the future.

There are lots of things to consider here. Are you ready to audition? My experience is that singers are often unprepared. It is not good enough to have 'the right idea', to do suitable 'visualisations' – although these can certainly help – let alone 'go through the motions'.

The fact is, auditioning is a crucial aspect of most professional singers' lives. It needs practice – lots of it. While the voice needs constant attention, performance practice (Chapter 13) will be a good start. From the end of year 2 or the beginning of year 3, regular auditioning practice, even with one simple song, should take place in front of the other students – who, let's face it, are in the same boat – and discussed and evaluated by everyone in a constructive, non-judgemental manner.

From about the third year, say once a term for those who are ready, there should be a more formal audition – with all students present. This would be 'staged' in front of an employer, conductor, stage director or casting director, who would be asked to give his or her professional and candid feedback. Students could thereby get a taste of reality, and gauge their progress accordingly.

Part of the audition preparation could be the scrutiny of CVs and promotional materials – videos, photographs and the like – so that by the end of the course all performers would be competent in this important area. CVs (if necessary fake ones, just for practice) would be appraised for clarity as well as content. Future employers don't want an autobiography. They may want to see what you have done in the past, but are more likely to be interested in what you are doing now, what you can do which is relevant to their needs. Any visual or audio material must be similarly clear and apropos.

Visual Impact and Feel Good Factor

For some time while I was teaching in London, my pupils were fortunate enough to be able to call on the services of a beautician. Some people have good dress sense, knowing instinctively what suits them in colour and style. But many haven't a clue. As already discussed, how we look and present ourselves as performers can mar or enhance our performance.

I was surprised how good everyone could look with suitable but minimal adjustments to their wardrobe, in terms of cut or colour, plus a little make-up, applied by someone who knew what effect it would have.

Sometimes a change of hairstyle was in order, and there was the question of jewellery – but all only to make the most of what each had by nature.

Singers should learn how to apply their own make-up in order to make the most of lighting – or lack of it – and distance. Note that it is always beneficial for eyes to be fully visible. They are, after all, where expression begins.

Students, both male and female, should have workshops for making the most of their looks. It can be fun to experiment, in and out of school and on each other. Experiments could be made as a 'catwalk act' (see Chapter 13) and discoveries tried on occasions like auditions and concerts, when it really matters.

When considering clothes, singers should take into account the nature of their concert. How formal is it? Does it entail much movement? Is it a trouser role? What are the other soloists wearing – short or long? What colours? – so you don't clash. What is the décor of the performing space? Are you liable to catch cold in a draughty cathedral or out in the open? What about shoes? What you wear must be fitting in all senses.

CHAPTER 12

Language (Text)

Apart from the voice, there is nothing that lets down a singer's performance more than a lack of interest in words. In fact they are so important and so under-considered that I think any school that trains future professional singers should run a Department of Literature.

It's all very well being 'emotionally expressive' with a beautiful melody – and of course the singing voice thrives on melody – but when there are words it makes no sense to ignore them. Even the expression in a melismatic passage or a cadenza is based on the text. Words are there for a purpose! There are plots and stories and verbal exchanges between characters, which all need articulation and coherence. Poetry and imagery are part and parcel of any art song.

We don't even have to look at a song or aria to know that its *raison d'être* is going to be its meaning. Rhythms (which logically come first in any vocal composition), tempi, melody, harmony and marks of expression are all inspired, conjured and directed by the words. They are the basis of what transpires – they tell the story and transmit characters' thoughts. We have words to recite and meanings to convey. The only way a singer can convey meaning, or be a believable character in a drama, is by understanding the words and making them their own. The words – their meaning, and what they conjure up – is where expression, in terms of colour, weight and emotion, begins. They give the voice its reason for singing.

More than Words

There is more to songs and operas than what the words say directly. Otherwise we might just recite the text. That is not to decry what actors do.[1] It's just that singing, at least with the singing voice, is of a different order. The great lieder singer Dietrich Fischer-Dieskau wrote, 'Music and poetry have a common domain, from which they draw inspiration and in which they operate: the landscape of the soul'.[2]

Our singing voice, through its deep structures and mysterious communicative properties, uses poetry to tap into our lyric nature and plumb the depths of our being. The words direct us intellectually to this place, but it's the music and the singing combined, each acting as the medium of the other, that carries us there. Great singing is great because it transports us to this level of origin.

Clearly such mysteries are impossible to describe. One is tempted to talk about music and feelings and leave it at that. The singing voice is primarily the voice of emotions. That is why in classical singing we can 'say' things with it which cannot be said with words alone.

Similarly music can express things that it is uniquely qualified to express. The appeal in both cases, and even in the absence of words, is uncannily universal, both being able to undermine or cut across cultural norms to express something which is fundamental to being human. The vocal and musical messages don't need explaining in a person's native tongue, or in any tongue for that matter.

The Human Narrative

You might say that for this reason the words are not so important after all, and in certain respects that is right. Sometimes even composers seem not to care for words as such. But the 'narrative' too is human. However much it can be comprehended on those deeper planes, singing is still a bearer of the human story. The text leads the way, and provides the intellectual layer of our performance. It is as though the human voice then provides an all-important sub-text without which the performance cannot be fully comprehended or genuinely shared.

People often choose to relate almost exclusively to one or another of the various aspects of singing. In some circles it's the intellectual aspect that is considered pre-eminent, for others it's the physicality. Others indulge emotionally. For some it's the aesthetics that attract. In each case they are missing out on things by which singing in the classical sense is defined. They are missing the singing voice's unique capacity to express all facets of human expression combined. This is the power and the mystery given to classical vocal music as distinct from any other type. Furthermore, an emphasis on one aspect to the neglect of others jeopardises the voice's artistic integrity, and by extension that of the singer.

Intelligent singing must look to the physical *and* emotional for its full human expression. The physical must be balanced with the emotional *and* guided by intelligence if it is to be anything more than a primitive thrill. The emotional must be contained by the physical and tempered by the intelligence. The aesthetic must draw on resources provided by the other spheres, and so on.

Translating all this into our education and training programmes, the four guidelines will help teachers and singers to gauge the balance between the physical, aesthetic, emotional and spiritual manifestations of the singer's development.

A Literary Department

A Literary department should be a beehive of practical study. Directly or indirectly relating to each student's repertoire and performing needs, this department would require the advice and supervision of a tutor, and should be incorporated into the regular schedule, say at least 2 or 3 hours per week, depending on need, for the duration of the course. It would include:

1. Reciting and reading aloud. For a start this would satisfy the occasional need of the singer to speak on stage. It would contribute much to a singer's familiarisation with any text. It would also aid reading for those who find it difficult.[3] The main aims would be to make reciting or reading intelligible and interesting.
2. Saying recitative or reciting a specific song text – either with other characters involved or, where they are not, having at least one other person to whom to express the words. This again would serve to gain deeper meaning or greater understanding before singing. Others present could question the speaker about characters and situations in order to 'get the picture'. This could also be a productive *aide-mémoire*.
3. Preparing summaries of songs and arias, duets or scenas (with colleagues), and the background to works currently being prepared. This would encourage the practice of preparation

skills and provide examples of 'information for audiences' that could be used later at school or other concerts. One aim could be to answer the question 'Would I want to hear this piece?' Again, fellow students could ask pertinent questions.

4 A class for the appreciation of word-setting. Obvious foci of study might be the works of Monteverdi, Purcell, Schubert, Puccini and Britten, among many others. Look at Britten's *War Requiem,* for example. Say the words from 'So A-bram rose…' (just after Figure 69) with the exact rhythms and accents of this great word setter. The objective would be to study how music and words work together – how music can affect meaning and how words can inspire and shape music. A simple example: in the following illustration, why did Caccini write the first rhythm for 'Amarilli, mia bella', and not the second version? What's the difference in feeling?

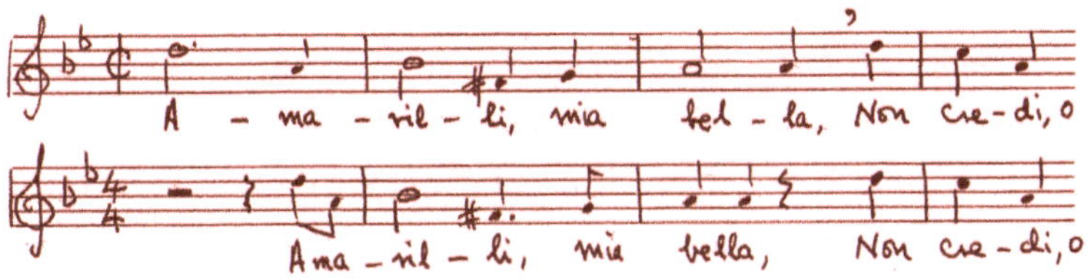

5 Appreciation of poetry. Students could find poetry they would particularly like to share with others, from their repertoire or elsewhere. Poetry was once the province of the bards. As far as we know its aim was to appeal to the ear with the speaking voice. That would be the aim here.

6 The Foreign Languages department (see below) could be linked to this one. Students could explain (in their native tongue), or translate, their pieces before reciting the words in the original. Saying a foreign text in your own language usually aids comprehension, and the ability to express it in the original.

7 Use of speaking voice. An important by-product of this department's work would be the monitoring of students' spoken voices. The aim would be vocal health and intelligibility at all times, plus the enhancement of meaning through

> appropriate emotional involvement. Taking an interest in a text can lift or lower a voice to a healthy pitch. Similarly, animating the speaking voice can spark interest in what you are saying. Interest and animation should join forces in singing.

In general a Literature department would aim to elevate words to their rightful level and thereby make a major contribution to students' preparation skills and the depths and efficacy of their performances.

Foreign Languages

Singers need to sing in a variety of languages, predominantly Italian, German and French, with Russian, Latin, Czech and Spanish not far behind. There is of course a great deal of worthwhile repertoire in English. In my experience, however, outside the English-speaking world music with English texts is not sufficiently appreciated to make the language compulsory. A more important reason to speak English is for general global communication.

It seems reasonable to expect an entrant to a major school of music to be already conversant with at least one of the main languages other than their native one. It would save a great deal of time if Italian became a universal entrance requirement. In any case, Italian and German should be tackled from the start and be studied for the whole course. A year here or there for any language usually proves far from adequate.

Languages do not always come easily to singers – even those with a good musical ear. They should be presented and learnt in the most attractive, open and practical ways available. Being stuck away in a laboratory is ridiculously unsuitable for singers; 90% of the work should be practical, with as many opportunities to actually speak and converse as possible.

To reinforce a systematic 'direct method', students could help each other devising scenarios, holding French or German days or foreign-language-only evenings. Props – French berets, strings of garlic – can do wonders for students' accents and inflections, which are often the main difficulties. *Haute cuisine* could be washed down with a decent French table wine. Such occasions might help to lighten serious pursuits and enhance the social cohesion of the school.

Translations of a great deal of the singer's repertoire are now available. Lois Philips's classic *Lieder Line by Line* is still available.[4] This can save a lot of time, but singers should beware that translations vary in quality. A 'singing translation' might not be entirely accurate, or may be out of sync with the music and therefore out of line with the composer's expressive intentions.

Language exams in the conventional sense are unnecessary. A student's ability to use a language effectively in singing can be assessed periodically by well-qualified vocal coaches; there is no one better placed for the job. There should within reason be coaches available for all languages being sung.

Repertoire

At suitable moments a singer's emerging skills need encouraging and reinforcing with suitable music – something that continues to feed (rather than hold up) the freeing and growing process of the singer's voice. In other words, a suitable challenge, not simply something that he or she 'ought to be able to sing'.

It is sometimes difficult to gauge what musical material will be most beneficial at a particular moment. Since no two singers develop in exactly the same way or at the same pace, it is unrealistic to prescribe 'set repertoire for different stages'. While it is advisable for singers eventually to learn the standard concert repertoire for their voice, and might indeed profit from studying the relevant scores at any time, this may not be the moment to attempt something so vocally demanding. In a general way, singers do need realistic challenges from the start. But just as a fully-fledged singer will hold back from moving to heavier repertoire prematurely, a young singer should not be presented with musical challenges for which as yet their instrument is ill-equipped.

Tackling unsuitable repertoire in the early stages always has a deleterious effect. If nothing else, it is demoralising not to be able to sing something which is expected of you. Determining progress and gauging merit will be looked at in Part IV.

At this stage we should be following our guidelines as closely as possible:

- How is the structural balance? Do all facets agree or interconnect to some degree? What seems to be out of balance or insufficiently supportive?

- What is emerging vocally which of itself can be called musical?
- To what extent is a student's vocalisation a reflection of his or her self?
- What comes across positively and tellingly in terms of communication?

The questions can be put in various ways. Answers are rarely straightforward or conclusive, but they give us some idea of the direction or emphasis presently required of the training. To be continuously productive the choice of musical material should be based on where the individual is vocally. The great thing about this situation is that the field of choice of material is wide open.

We are not yet thinking in terms of the singer's musical or artistic merit, let alone excellence (see Chapter 23). We need vehicles for the growing process, music that will stimulate the singing voice generally and in specific areas of the gradually integrating structure. The voice loves to sing, so the act of singing itself can bring out the best in a voice once the balance warrants it.

If the work is being undertaken in the studio, and the teacher knows how to diagnose their pupil's responses, they cannot go wrong with the material they choose. All the same, it makes sense to have a broad range of possibilities. Remember, we are somewhere between technical work and beginning to sing. Appendix 1 is a little library of possible sources. There are of course many more.

Things to remember

Until they are adequately trained, muscles have a job to sustain their work. All muscles, large and small, that comprise the vocal organ need to match in strength. They need to be able to keep going in concert, continuously able to pull their weight in their respective tasks. So long as the voice is out of balance its stronger muscles (like some abdominals) will tend to dominate, thus preventing the development of the weaker ones. Non-singing voice muscles (like the false elevators) will tend to compensate for weakness. Sung on too early, this unbalanced configuration is unlikely ever to be righted. Training must first be for the balance which gives the freedom to sing, then for stamina and sustaining power throughout the organ.

It follows that, physiologically, faster, shorter bursts of work are better to begin with than long sustained phrases at a slow pace. Music can, if necessary, be taken faster than intended by the composer. Similarly, dynamics, ritenuti, pauses and other marks of expression can be employed judiciously at this stage.

As the voice regains its natural balance, its ability to sustain activity will accelerate. So will the ability to do more detailed work. The voice wants to sing, but, like the singer, it needs to be sufficiently unrestrained by demands before it can benefit from doing so in significant developmental terms.

It can be very disheartening to not sing – even if the physiological reasons are understood. I always say to pupils in this difficult situation, 'sing when you feel like it – just don't do it insistently or seriously!' To help singers through this crucial training period, conditions must be supportive. Students must work with their voice teachers as often as possible – at least daily, in carefully measured doses. There must be a real sense of buzz and continuity in The Work generally. There will be many other classes and activities for students to enjoy and feel they are making progress with in the wider programme. In general the work of the faculty must in any case be approached in the right spirit – playfully, experimentally and light-heartedly. The over-seriousness and over-reverence that one sometimes encounters in the classical field is as inappropriate as careless frivolity. It tends to slow progress, which is more easily made through playfulness and joy.

Regarding pitch: almost any song or aria can have something about it that constitutes good developmental material or a useful tool, but the original key can be prohibitive, some songs being a little too high for the present, while others, like the popular songs of Shakespeare's day or the Broadway songs, (see Appendix 1) are almost bound to be too low.

In the early stages we cannot afford to be purist in the matter of a piece's pitch. While it is true that many songs will have been written in keys that best suit their mood or flavour, others will have been written for a particular voice type or even a particular singer. It is of course better to comply with a composer's wishes, but singing students are feeling their way and need the chance to flutter their wings. While it is a mistake to sing everything in the middle range of the voice, in early training the pitch should suit the singer's capacity, not the singer struggle to 'fit' the pitch.

Our concern so far has been primarily physiological. It is a lack of physiological integrity and awareness that leads people to try prematurely to gain musical skills – high notes, sustained tone, agility, *piano* etc. – and to do so by practising them as isolated objectives. The singer's natural tessitura (comfortable mean pitch) reveals itself only with the restoration of balance. Only then has the voice a reliable guide to its true working range.

From Training to Singing

The period of at least two years up to this point will be the most crucial of the singer's development. It is a question of getting the priorities right in terms of work emphasis and balance, and of laying a solid foundation, so that the higher levels of competence can be built securely and stand for a long time. This is where things so often go awry with young trainee singers.

The lack of a solid vocal foundation is why their progress is so often frustrated and why they find themselves having to re-train later on. Even though they were accepted for a high level of musical education and training, their future depends on their state of preparedness at the end of the course. *Foundations are everything if the course is to be truly productive for the long term.*

If all has gone well in the first years of vocal training, there is usually still a good deal of specialised vocal work to be done by way of refinement and strengthening before a student can become a fledgling professional artist.

The voice must still come first. But as ease of voicing increases and skills emerge, so does confidence and expectation. The enjoyment of being able to sing and make music deepens when there is no struggling with the instrument. A virtuous circle is in place.

Serious repertoire

As a singer's repertoire becomes more a question of serious concern – learning whole songs and arias – various criteria for good or timely choices come into play. A voice will be coming into its own, at least sufficiently to show, in a more clear and consistent way, what it is made of in terms of weight, agility and expressive powers. The level and quality of the training up to this point reveals itself in what the singer can begin to do, not only musically but also artistically and in terms of communication.

The character of a piece can be very important at this stage. The singer must be inspired to make the most of what they have gained, and to bring their own identity to it in such a way that they begin to communicate with personal authority.

Preparing repertoire

I frequently ask my pupils to think about and research their own repertoire, to imagine what might suit them and look for pieces they might like. I then vet the choice for vocal suitability. In this way they gain greater self-knowledge and motivation.

A singer can begin to create imaginative recital programmes (an enjoyable art in itself). The repertoire at this stage will be guided partly with an eye to the future. *Thorough preparation of text and music must be done before singing,* so as to permit maximum vocal freedom.[5]

Some students may still not be able to fully commit to much repertoire. This matter has to be carefully handled. A singer can only go as far with a song as his or her present freedoms allow. Teacher, pupil and coach between them can ensure that aims and challenges are realistic. Repertoire based on character might usefully be recommended by the tutor of Physical Expression at this stage. Confidence is gained by singing well, not struggling!

Musical Coaching

The musical coach is a key member of any musical establishment. A crucial link between voice training and performing, their work is not to be confused with that of a répétiteur, whose job is to teach singers their notes. A good coach helps a singer to transform raw materials – instrument, text and music (already sufficiently learnt) – into something harmonious and telling.

A coach should be a competent pianist and more than competent musician, with wide or specialised knowledge of singers' repertoire and its various styles, a good command of the relevant languages, and the crucial ability to sense what a singer is able or not able to do. They will be able to draw out the best of the singer, and avoid making unreasonable vocal and musical demands. A bad coach will blindly (or rather, deafly) insist on the composer's indications, thinking perhaps that the singer's job is to find a 'technical way' to satisfy them whatever their present ability.

Singers should beware of coaches (or, worse, pianists) who set themselves up as voice experts. Some technical knowledge of the voice or the ability to play the piano does not qualify one to be a singing teacher, any more than knowledge of repertoire or keyboard skills necessarily make a singing teacher a good coach. Teaching singing (in the technical sense) is highly specialised – it should be left to specialists.

The singer has a voice teacher with whom developmental work is under way. In London I was in the fortunate position of being able to send pupils to various trusted coaches. I could consider which one was best for which pupils or which repertoire. Liaising or working alongside a coach can be an enjoyable and productive experience.

In musical institutions there are good coaches on hand, and necessary exchanges of information or on-going discussions about pupils' progress are possible. In working together, teachers and coaches can make valuable contributions to a singer's awareness and understanding of the possibilities of a voice-music synthesis. An experienced coach will have a fund of repertoire suggestions.

A coach will want to feel confident that the challenges they propose are realistic for the singer. They might ask the teacher what aspects of the singer's developing voice can be reinforced through their repertoire, or where from a vocal point of view their weaknesses lie. A singer's *overall* progress is usually evident in their singing, so the coach is uniquely placed to monitor the 'growing process' in general, and can give the singing teacher valuable contextual feedback.

A singer's voice needs a diet of music to support and encourage its various emerging expressive skills and to enable the singer to become fully aware of them. This is why it is not helpful to a student's vocal and artistic sensibilities to specialise. So, you want to be a singer of that lovely baroque music? Get your singing voice fully up and running. Facilitate its many natural skills, and then you will either become a better baroque interpreter than you would have been, or you will be in a position to change your mind. Become a fully aware artist and performer in command of a free instrument, and whatever you choose will benefit.

There are other practical matters that coaches and singing teachers can fully discuss, like a pupil's preparation competency, or what length of coaching session is likely to be most beneficial at any point. If the pupil is included in such discussions, so much the better for the understanding of all concerned.

A coach needs to bear in mind that all voices start off relatively lightweight or lyrical, and may or may not proceed to become more dramatic. We are born with a certain constitution and capacity. A voice that seems to have 'dramatic' characteristics, for example, needs time to grow into them. That means time to gain its best balance and time to gather all-round strength, while retaining its natural flexibility and quality. We can no more prescribe predicted roles for an ill-prepared singer than we can give a child a bar of weights that are as yet too heavy, just because he or she is built like a potential champion weight-lifter. Similarly a lightweight voice needs time to gather its depth and fullness, not be changed in character or encouraged to sing 'big' or 'mature' for the sake of it.

Coaches, like singing teachers, are often too eager to 'label' a voice. While a category-label can seem to make the repertoire question easier, it is in reality unnatural – an expedient or strait-jacket. The *Fächer* system (which didn't exist in bel canto times) makes people dealing with singers lazy, and its premature application can damn a singer's career. There's nothing more disturbing than witnessing an enthusiastic singer struggling and straining to sing, as though the more effort they put into it the better they will perform.

The German language tends to encourage vocal 'covering'. Just as it is vocally logical to find the singing voice before introducing words, it is logical to start with Italian and proceed to German.

I have often had the impression that coaching was a waste of time, money and expertise, simply because students were not prepared for it. It is not only the instrument that must be ready but the material. How to be well prepared in all respects should be practised from day one of college.

When I first came to Portugal, most singers I encountered considered that being ready to perform was simply a matter of knowing words and music. And it must be said that they pulled out a few unexpected stops on the night! However, at the Stúdio we were concerned *to make the most* of their talents.[6] Once they got the hang of coming to rehearsals prepared to move beyond accurate reproduction of the words and music, they began appreciating the qualitative differences in both their music making and their communicating.

The best coaches I have come across always made the words the basis of their work. I shall always remember how much Philip Langridge got from the Stúdio students simply by appealing to their imaginations and feelings through the comprehension of their texts. Without interfering vocally he got the best of their singing from them. Of course a singer has to be *able* to respond both physically and mentally.

Whenever we employed a coach, for the performance of different styles each month, the singer was accompanied by a house accompanist. We took advantage of this to instil a better attitude of partnership between singer and pianist. We are lucky in Britain to have, since the great Gerald Moore, a tradition of accompanying. This rapport, so critical in music-making, cannot be taken for granted. While musicianship counts for a lot, it is only the basis for the ensemble work required of great music-making. The 'sensitivity to the other and the other's music' is a commonly undervalued side of the singer's art. It must be nurtured.

Practising

It is easy for an enthusiastic student to emphasise the wrong things in practising. Often they will give too much attention to stretches of a piece which are easier and seemingly more rewarding, and too little to the difficult bits. Singers quite often do a kind of 'generalised practice', repeating a song, attempting to make overall improvements. This is a waste of time.

Students rarely know how to benefit from their practice. It is often thought that the more you do the better you will get. But the more of what? And what does better mean? Einstein said, 'There is nothing that is a more certain sign of insanity than to do the same thing over and over and expect the results to be different'.[7] Constant practice without a constructive purpose can have the opposite outcome from that intended.

Of course, the singer's desire is normally two-fold – to sing better and to be able to reproduce something reliably. The problem with mindless repetition is that either the attention that informs or observes the process (and by extension the progress) is absent, or it serves only to fix something in place mechanically. Neither provides for positive movement towards improvement. Neither aids our memory except very narrowly or incompletely.

If the *aim* is envisaged, but the *how* is nowhere to be seen, or if we have an instruction but don't know what it's for, our practice is doomed before it begins. To do things purposefully we need to have a clear idea of our aim and, crucially, adaptable ways of finding and taking viable steps towards it. No end-gaining, only steps as they are revealed or suggest themselves. Singers need to be able to read the signs that the voice gives them of its progress, not simply be aware of their inability to do something.

Once again, we can say that singers are a special case among musicians. Until their voice, their instrument, reaches a sufficient degree of freedom and responsiveness, they tend understandably to look for the closest approximation to their musical goals. This is unlikely to be the right route for long term vocal development. Others will be preoccupied with their voice's shortcomings and badger it until it seems to do what's required – if reluctantly.

Once again we are faced with the mixed objectives dilemma. If a voice is not ready we cannot make it so at the same time as endeavouring to create a better or more reliable performance. Freeing a voice is a training matter. Making music is creating a performance out of that freedom.

There is no obvious solution to this conflict of interests, except to understand its nature. Then two things will be realised:

1. Nothing of real value is gained by trying to make a voice do something it is not ready to do.
2. Whatever point of instrumental development the voice has reached, what counts in attempts to improve a performance is what inspires the voice to sing – not what you do to make it sing.

Instead of technique the singer will then always look for the following stimuli:

- what is expressive in this piece;
- wherein lies the music;
- what is beautiful about it.

Any practising will be done with these elements in mind.

As already explained it is in the nature of the singing voice to respond spontaneously. Therefore, conditions must be created in which that is possible. Preparation, of which text and rhythm are key, facilitates such a response.

The singer's aim must be to be more musical and expressive without jeopardising the very thing – the instrument – that makes those aims feasible. The movement patterns which are the basis of being able to reproduce the material can then be established by means of *purposeful repetition* without fear of fixing or mechanising. 'Successive repetitions follow the cycle of stimulus, perception, storage and retrieval, thereby creating a nearly automatic path of recall that is successful even in times of stress'.[8]

This is why singers who are aiming at a high level would be well advised to delay practising on their own until their degree of vocal freedom and their musicianship match. Only then can a singing voice build on itself in a significant way as it sings. It is then that we are honouring its inherent genius.

Curiosity

Singers are understandably often curious about the workings of their voice. Yet curiosity can sometimes, at first, create problems. Strictly speaking muscles and cartilages should not be the stuff that singers concern themselves with. On the contrary, they must be able to trust their teacher to deal with this side of the work appropriately, and wait to receive the relevant explanations (if they still want to know) after the event. Information given too early feeds the singer's desire or perceived need to control the voice. It focuses attention on aspects of the instrument which are better left to a natural process of release. This is the teacher's province. The student's job is to respond and gain awareness. Both have what they need. Their jobs are difficult enough without confusing their roles.

Experimentation

I have found that singers can hasten this process by experimenting on their own with the myriad sounds that their voice is capable of making. This is not practice, and there should be no forcing or insistence. But the singer's curiosity with regard to their voice can be satisfied in a spirit of exploration which can then be carried productively into supervised training sessions.

There are many ways to contribute to good habits of work and personal development. With regular supervised training, a student should always feel that he or she is progressing in observable ways.

CHAPTER 13

Performance

To be able to give a good performance, a synthesis of skills, knowledge and intentions must be achievable. The constituent parts of a performance will only come together in an authentic, believable manner if they each come naturally or easily to the performer. A student's performance is the culmination of the work they have done on these constituent parts; by degrees, through acquiring and relating many strands of knowledge and skill, they have been empowered to make the most of their personal creative faculties.

A Performance department should provide the facilities and framework in which students can give of their best. I can remember occasions when conditions for a student performance were not conducive to doing good work. A colleague said something like, 'It will be good for them – they will have to face difficult conditions later on'. Well, the second bit was correct. The first bit was simply bad psychology. Before poor conditions can be 'good for them', students have to have not only a level of competence but the confidence that comes from doing something well. Only at an advanced level, when the singer is sufficiently confident and strong, might obstacles to good work be deliberately placed in their way, if and when it is judged that this would be truly helpful!

Progressive performing

There is no guarantee that when the student is ready in other ways, they will find it easy to be on stage in front of an audience. Performing is a skill in its own right.

In considering Physical Expression, we have already looked at facets of singers' work that make powerful contributions both to the foundations and to the art of their performance. They will gain confidence through being able to move with ease and be physically expressive. They will learn through stage craft how to conduct themselves in an unfamiliarly large space, with or without the presence of other performers. They will know how good they can look!

Not everyone is a born performer, but the fact that a singer is not particularly extrovert does not bode ill for his or her future on the stage. Even so, the prospect of what may seem like 'showing off' may not sit comfortably on a genuinely modest person.

It is in the very nature of being a creative artist that you bring something fresh or new to your work. Individuality must be given space in which to find itself and grow confident.

Performing from Day One

In as much as it means getting up in front of people and showing them what you can do, or sharing with them something special that you have, performing is another facet of the singer's art which needs to be practised from the start. This is a matter of exposure and rapport, so it really doesn't matter what one performs by way of an exercise or experiment. On the contrary, a young person may not be ready to sing, but a special 'act', perhaps involving a different skill, can help to foster self-confidence as an individual within a group – no competition, every reason for admiration! For example, someone might welcome the chance to play an instrument. Another will be good at telling or reading stories, or reciting a poem. A third might like to share a pet subject. Yet another might be good at juggling or performing magic or 'party' tricks. Another can make people laugh. And so on.

The performance over, it could be discussed or appraised from various angles, in a friendly, appreciative atmosphere. Fellow students could be 'instructed' in front of the class in how to do something they had never done before. Regular performing – perhaps as often as once a week for the first year and a half, will contribute further to the social cohesion and enjoyment of the school. The individual act does not need to be more than a few minutes long to begin with. From time to time friends and family could be brought in to vary the audience and test the performer's rapport.

Quasi- informal occasions make it easier for students to experiment and 'make mistakes' without feeling bad about it. It is a suitable situation in which to observe the self in action and to explore different ways of communicating. Performers could experiment with conditions such as lighting, handling props, wearing costumes, etc. In short, they would have permission to play!

Each performer would be encouraged to introduce their 'act', and to gauge the quality of their own presentation. Alternatively, students could take it in turns to compère the show.

When it comes to singing

As the young singer develops overlapping and complementary skills, and their general competence increases, confidence grows and performances become more sophisticated. These facets feed off each other. Nevertheless, singers can fight shy of attempting something special or detailed, preferring perhaps to play safe with something more 'general' or 'normal' in character.

A genuinely refined performance entails tapping the centre of oneself and employing the 'centred instrument'. Part of the difficulty here for the growing singer is the consequential unambiguous directness for which they must assume full responsibility. In one way or another, we have been working towards this – directness and responsibility – from the first day of study. Excellence may still be some way off; it will be discussed in Part IV.

CHAPTER 14

Supporting Cast

If Voice, Music and Physical Expression are three protagonists who, while somewhat estranged to begin with, are finally united in triumphant joy, Language, Foreign Languages and Performance are secondary roles without whose involvement the drama could not unfold in any intelligible way. The following can be seen as an important supporting cast.

Improvisation

Improvisation as a skill of embellishment was expected of baroque performers, flourished to excess among the castrati of the 18th century, and was still going strong, especially among keyboard players, during the first half of the 19th century. Beethoven is said to have moved his audience to tears with his improvisations. In short, the skill was considered of the highest importance among 'classical' musicians until the last half of the 19th century. It was regenerated in the 1960s. Interestingly, Stockhausen preferred the term 'intuitive music'.

'Dalcroze believed improvisation to be the pinnacle of musicianship'.[1] It plays a leading role in his eurythmics work which aims at harmonising the body's sensory system through improvised movement to music.

A singer's voice is so often slave to the mind. In our physical expression work and dancing, we can change this incapacitating relationship. Dalcroze made the observation that, 'When internal communication flowed effortlessly between body, mind, and spirit without interference, the level of performance, insight, and creativity soared'.[2]

While a physical improvisation may be based on some specific musical task, it can help a singer to push the mind out of the way and let the musical impulse take over. There is no time to deliberate. Anything is possible, and we become adept at trusting our intuition in responding to situations. The stage director and teacher David F. Oswald says,

> Improvisations provide the ideal playground in which to exercise feelings appropriate to specific situations and to let those feelings motivate actions. Improvisations allow you to arouse your feelings as a character, practice spontaneity, and practice sharing your feelings in public. Singing improvisations allow you to combine all these benefits with the singing process.[3]

We learn to live in the moment of perception, and our imagination becomes lively. 'The essence of improvisation is the intimate two-way connection between imagination and execution.'[4]

Essential benefits can accrue to a singer through vocal improvisation, the main ones being:

a) What has just been said of the relationship between imagination and execution. The singer must eventually achieve freedom to trust the voice to respond to the imagination. This removes the perceived need to make the voice be expressive.
b) Voice lessons often require the pupil to make unconsidered spontaneous vocal gestures, using only the aural imagination. This can help to naturally stimulate those parts of the voice that might otherwise remain blocked by mental control, habit or timidity. The process of voice development can move on when a pupil is willing to 'let their hair down' and explore, using only their perceptual intelligence.
c) Eventually, in more contemporary music, a singer may be called upon to improvise in performance, or use their voice to make sounds that are not fully vocal and may be fragmented. Learning to improvise in the context of training can serve to 'legitimise' this kind of temporary voice use.
d) As they develop, a musician needs to be able to respond and react in a creative and perhaps quite subtle way with fellow music-makers and actors. Improvisational skills can sharpen the ability to respond and react appropriately.

With practice, and because it obliges us to 'let go' of the usual mind-over-body control, improvising helps us to gain a feeling of inner connectedness between the senses. This becomes a reliable 'flow' which translates into a sense of authenticity. Our mind finds our body, heart and spirit 'open for business' on an equal footing.

Through improvisation we can open up to the seemingly infinite possibilities of our individuality, because they are not dictated (and thereby limited) by external sources, but instead arise inevitably from our own personhood.

As George Hadjinikos puts it, 'The roots of music stem from our inner being'.[5] It is there, not in the rudiments, that the 'musical and expressive information' resides. 'Expressing oneself in music is a form of communication that is individual, intimate, and when done well, capable of touching the emotions of others'.[6]

A Note for Teachers

> A good teacher ... must develop the ability to improvise, no matter what the subject. A teacher who takes cues from student responses can make on-the-spot revisions that catch what the students have expressed and guide it through an improvised route to the target of the lesson.[7]

Improvisation as a creative tool can benefit all facets of a singer's practical work and should therefore be practised, in one form or another, every day or two, at least during the first two years of any training course. While it can be fun to do out-of-class improvisations, if the work is to do with the use of the voice it should be monitored by a voice teacher.

Clowning

Clowning can mean many things apart from circus stunts. Taken seriously, clowning is an art with many applications, including community building, theatre and teaching. Having experienced clowning myself I know for a start what a tonic it can be. Simply for health I would recommend it to anyone as a general life-enhancing therapy. But that's just the first of its benefits. There are other more specific reasons why I believe clowning is good for singers.

An obvious benefit is that, insofar as its humour is based on self-deprecation, clowning can help one not to take oneself too seriously. To be productive or positively effective in life we need a balance of seriousness with light-heartedness. Put another way, we need to be buoyant as well as grounded in order to move freely. Balance again! So it's good for the creative spirit and can get a work session or a whole day off to a good start.

Self-acceptance

Clowning is an excellent way of uncovering physical sensations and tactility with minimal emotional pain. 'By accepting the sensations of the body, we begin literally to love ourselves. Only from such a base of self-acceptance … can we effectively extend our feelings of love outward.'[8] This is, of course, the basis of effective relating and communicating.

Embarrassment

Many times we fear being creative, or communicating something personal, because it means going out on a limb. It makes us vulnerable. Being 'different' exposes us to possible embarrassment or ridicule. But consider,

> The parts that embarrass you the most are usually the most interesting poetically, are usually the most naked of all … the goofiest, the strangest … and at the same time, most representative, most universal …[9]

Clowning workshops provide safe tools for exploring these personal-universal traits. As a physical performance discipline it helps in dealing with tricky subject matter.

Failing

Most people fear failure. Some are so hard on themselves that they fail before they start – a kind of paralysis. 'The word "fail" … ceases to apply if we know that whether we try something new or practice something old, we are merely gaining information.'[10] Clowning helps us to loosen up and venture forth from our comfort zone on our information-gathering mission. 'Theatre director Joan Littlewood said, "If we don't get lost, we'll never find a new route".'[11]

Our early conditioning puts a stop to the natural, healthy, active curiosity which we call play. In clowning, as in improvising, there is no 'right', so … no 'critic'. We are given *carte blanche* to explore, create and discover things that we had forgotten or didn't know were in us. Just like young children who, through play, discover themselves, the world around them and their relation to it. The shame is not in making mistakes, which is how we learn, but in not allowing our adult selves to go on playing!

> Art proper is characterized by discovery of something new in yourself as a human being, either by creation of the art object or by the enjoyment of it.[12]
>
> Humour is one of the very few ways we have of changing perception. In humour we switch, suddenly, from looking at things in one way to looking at them in another.[13]

A weekly dose of clowning, say first thing on Monday morning – or 20–30 minutes from time to time – could considerably change students' approach to their work, helping them to let go of the habitual restraints of an overly serious or over-defended life, and open up to new and exciting performance prospects.

Filipino Tinkling Dance

Try this for rhythm, exercise and fun in failing!

Alexander Technique

F. Matthias Alexander was one of the first people to appreciate the indivisibility of the body and the mind. He understood that the inefficiency of movement that resulted in strain or wasted energy was attributable to the loss of psycho-physical coordination. This loss (which varies in degree from person to person) results in bad habits acquired over time.

As I have pointed out with regard to the singing voice, the downside of so-called civilization is the strain it puts on our ability to be completely and efficiently ourselves, and consequently on our sense of being.

Alexander saw that over-effort (sensed as the subjective feeling of wasted movement) was often the result of end-gaining – in which, on having a desired goal, we attempt to grab it or struggle to achieve it. Such wrong-headed actions cause further blocks or strain. And since unhealthy tension reduces our field of awareness, we are not usually conscious of our lack of coordination or equilibrium.

One common example of defective equilibrium in singing is the matter of countering gravity. This frequently results in efforts to push upwards (see note on anti-gravity, page 8).[14]

Alexander's approach to using the body effectively breaks the vicious circle of effort and tension by considering *the means whereby* a goal or action might be achieved. Taking care of the means amounts to correct psycho-physiological use of the self, which results in healthy management of the body and economy of effort.

I think the Alexander Technique should be incorporated into the work of learning to sing. In fact I have never come across a singer who could not benefit from this optimising approach to physical action. My own first-hand experience of the Alexander Technique over the years has proved most beneficial to my teaching, both for myself and my pupils.

The quest for psycho-physical coordination is by definition an individual matter, and the outcomes are correspondingly individual. Realising the full potential of our individual conscious selves is what Alexander described as 'man's supreme inheritance'.[15]

Meditation

For a singing student, success depends to a large extent on well-being and preparedness. Clowning can lift inhibitions and raise spirits, and the Alexander Technique can prepare bodies for optimal efficiency. Meditation can help to put one in a healthy state of mind of receptivity and creativity. Practised on a regular basis, it can eliminate stress and increase inner happiness. In raising the quality of one's awareness, it can clarify thinking and help to turn intentions into results.

In spite of its growing popularity, people often think of meditation as something esoteric or necessarily religious, but this is to limit its appeal. Meditation can be simple and practised by people of any background or ability. Practised in a group at the beginning of each day, it can make a significant contribution to the atmosphere, communal relations and productivity of any school at any level. This technique for raising consciousness has been proved to be effective in education generally. Deepak Chopra puts it in a nutshell: 'Consciousness is the potential for all creation'.[16]

Listening and Hearing

Since hearing is fundamental to both singing and making music it stands to reason that 'listening resources' can have a defining influence on singing work at any stage.

I am not talking about musical perception and skills as such. Gained in aural training, *these* need to be of a high standard before a student enters the higher education level. A good musical ear and a good instrument are the basic tools for developing into a professional musician. Given these, even if a student is behind musically they can catch up.

Hearing what is Good

My concern is with perception in the critical sense – the ability to discern what is 'good'. Good in the sense of healthy, when dealing with the voice, and good in the artistic-aesthetic sense (see Chapter 23 on Excellence). I believe the Old Italian School understood and appreciated the correlation between health and beauty. This understanding is of particular significance nowadays, when young singers' ears are assailed by a plethora of ugly – and from our point of view unhealthy – vocal sounds, and an unprecedented level of noise. *Forte* seems to be the dynamic of choice, and music of all types suffers technological reinforcement. We are not only in danger of premature deafness, but of our ears becoming musically and aesthetically brutalised.

Clarity

The blur of noise pollution makes it more difficult to differentiate sounds. To gain clarity of perception we need to get back to the blank canvas of silence. So any singing school should have areas of silence. These could also be spaces for meditation – to help quiet the mind.

Also, all singing teaching rooms should be completely insulated from external disturbance, and acoustically on the dry side, so that all sounds are heard for what they are – clear and unenhanced. More about 'purposeful spaces' and acoustics in Part III.

Examples and Models

The communications revolution has brought about the unprecedented promotion of any one who can 'sing' in any way. Not only has this brought into the limelight many singers who 20 or 30 years ago might have had a job to get heard at all, but it has extinguished the lights on many of the great singers from the past. Many of these singers are well worth the effort it takes modern ears to get used to studying them. The old recordings are instructive because you hear voices with little or no acoustical enhancement. Try Amelita Galli-Curci or John McCormack for starters.

It is easier to acquire a sense of taste if we have plenty of examples to compare. But, just as we appreciate the pros and cons of our own present circumstances in life by adopting an historical perspective, so can we best determine the pros and cons of present day vocal practice by studying its antecedents.

Sound-proofed cubicles equipped with state-of-the-art listening technology should be available for (a) repertoire research and (b) listening to 'classical' singers from the beginnings of recorded sound to the present day. This latter exercise should be followed up by group sessions designed to compare singers' voices and their various interpretations and performances. In particular students should learn to detect what is good through virtue of the fact that it arises from a free, healthy instrument.

Analysis

Other group sessions should be arranged in which aspects and attributes of the singing voice could be examined live, with pupils for illustration. The content of this workshop would be based on our four definitions, so students would learn to listen for:

1. Health in each other's voices;
2. Musical skills and qualities related to or arising naturally from the structure, as distinct from something contrived;
3. How well the individual and their voice seem to correspond;
4. Characteristics of communication – how clear, direct, telling and so on.

It becomes more and more obvious as time goes on that these facets are not separate entities but all in their distinct ways indicators of the same articulate whole.

Open Coaching

From time to time, and where appropriate, coaching sessions by in-house coaches and guests should be open to all students, in order to familiarise them aurally with the process of music-making.

Outings

As well as in-house concerts on different scales, students of singing should be encouraged to witness the singing of professional soloists, and live music making in general. These outings could be written up as though for a review and/or discussed in class. It is important that students are able to measure the qualities and characteristics of their own performance against those already in the profession rather than against their peers. Much can be learned about music making and artistry also from other instrumentalists, both soloists and members of small ensembles. Students should develop a critical ear, regardless of their taste.

Aesthetics

Singers can benefit enormously from other art forms, both performing and visual. In addition to classical music performances of all kinds, they need to be encouraged and enabled to go to, for example, the ballet and to art galleries. A creative artist needs consistent nourishing of interest and imagination. Such outings can inspire in the singer a sense of wonder, and the desire to broaden learning and comprehension.

It's a lot easier to employ colour, form, line, proportion and movement meaningfully and effectively if they are not merely concepts but concrete qualities that have been studied and appreciated. It is easier to create shape and line if we have learned to value structure, easier to be an integral part of a musical creation if we have learned to appreciate texture.

Beauty

The appreciation of beauty is more than the striking of the senses by what is seen. It is more than the appreciation of an object by a subject. This duality shuts out quality. Beauty is born of the harmonious ordering of parts involved in the beautiful object or performance. It is how these parts relate that makes them significant. This is something we feel. We are no longer merely an admiring observer, we are involved. Beauty in singing arises from its wholeness – which comes about from the harmonious relating of its parts. As those great Italian teachers and composers realised, in the singing voice Art and Nature concur. This is how people the world over know when singing is 'the real thing'.

Aesthetic sense

Where the cultivation of an aesthetic sense really counts, and where beautiful singing comes into its own, is in the employment of the singing voice in making music. Even when a voice is working well its successful employment in musical and artistic terms is by no means secured. This is why for example the graceful line needs to be felt, the structured phrase embodied, and why the exquisite needs to be marvelled at and studied closely.

It is by means of this incorporation that a singer can develop a craftsman-like feel for a work of art. There are strong connections between the hands and the voice, so there is every reason to encourage students to draw, paint or model. A room could be set aside for this purpose.

Quality of work comes through the artist's care for what they are creating, the 'harmony' that they are bringing about.

Communication

The more its 'parts' come into harmony with one another, the more the singer's singing draws in the listener. This is another reason why the holistic paradigm, applied to the singing voice, implies participation. By participating in beauty we are reconnecting to ourselves. Our mind can no longer see our body as 'it'. I am the body that I rediscovered in the physical expression classes, in improvisations and clowning. I am the sound that I unlocked. This I can give, not to 'it' the audience, but to you, participants in the beauty I have found.

The Work Curriculum

In Appendices 2a and 2b I offer samples of a curriculum, and hours to be allotted per subject per week for each year. Based on what I consider necessary constituents of The Work, as described above, these are only to show what might be practicable. In the training and educating of singers, given their personal nature, a curriculum must take into account each individual's strengths and weaknesses. While I consider that most of the subjects are needed by all singers, regardless of their knowledge and experience at the time of school entrance, the proportion of time allotted for individuals' work, such as voice training and Alexander Technique, will vary from singer to singer. Likewise, the point at which a student is considered sufficiently prepared to begin serious work with a musical coach must vary.

The Work constitutes a variable and progressive course for would-be professional soloists. Given physically fit, vocally and musically talented students, together with the 'conditions', to be described in Part III, I would estimate that a minimum of five years' intensive training is needed, divided roughly as follows:

Years 1 and 2 Basic voice and body work of 'freeing' and 'building'. A student would attend individual lessons and take part in classes for between 5 and 7 hours per day (Monday to Friday). Emphasis and apportioning of disciplines would depend on individual need.

Year 3 A transition year, in which the beginnings of 'serious' music making and performance would gain in precedence. Particular care would be taken to monitor the performance of individuals' voices so as to prevent the slightest structural regression. The hours would be much the same as for years 1 and 2.

Year 4 An intensification of the singing/performing priorities, with increasing attention to detail, both artistic and professional.

Year 5 By year 5 I would hope that true excellence would be attainable, and a student would take at least one sure step into the professional world.

A final word – fitness

It is axiomatic that a student embarking upon such an exacting training and education as that of a singer needs to be, in general terms at least, physically and mentally fit for the work to be undertaken (compare the requirements of ballet and athletics training).

PART III
Conditions

CHAPTER 15

Instrumental Differences

If the quality of work depends on conducive conditions, these must be based on the nature of the work and what it is trying to achieve. From the four interdependent definitions – structure (body), beautiful singing (music-making), identity (self), and communication (other) – outlined in Part I, we saw that the business of finding an individual's voice is deeply personal.

Part II underlined the fact that singers' training and education differs in three major ways from that of instrumentalists.

1. The singer has to find their voice, or re-find it, before it can be 'played'.
2. The singer has to be able to articulate words and work with them.
3. The singer has to be an actor so that, as Aristotle put it, they can mediate between the message to be communicated and its recipients.

Each of these factors, if not thoroughly addressed, poses a potential threat to the integrity of the singer's eventual performance. They are normally in conflict. The training and education must combine them in such a way that they can be creative in concert.

We have seen that, as things presently stand, the voices of most singers on the threshold of advanced training are only partially intact. They cannot serve either the music or the expression of text adequately or artistically. The differences listed above, and what they imply for practice, must be fully understood if significant improvements are to be made in the field of voice training and singers' education generally.

'The Work', and the five years I have given it in Part II, would constitute a significant step in the quest to improve the lot of singing students, but it nevertheless represents a compromise. Three or four years would probably prove sufficient if students' voices were in perfect shape at the outset. Otherwise they need at least one year, in most cases two, of intensive vocal training and 'physical education'.

As things stand, too, the practical musicianship and aural competence of many entrants leaves a lot to be desired. It is difficult then to see why it has been considered desirable to turn all courses into degree courses. No amount of knowledge can take the place of practical experience. To make way for this experience I would stiffen entry requirements. The necessary theory and history is not difficult to come by on the internet and learn by oneself prior to going to college. It could then be realised, reinforced and expanded upon during the course of the all-important practical work as outlined in Part II.

The singer's instrument being inextricably bound up with their emotions, it's a wonder that it was ever imagined that singers could manage to gain a sufficiently high standard to become good professional artists after only three or four years of study, in which objectives are invariably mixed and various disciplines make little practical sense of one another. Most would-be singers *don't* manage.

Fifty years ago, when I was contemplating my own path towards the singing profession, there was a 'Performers' Course' at this level. The intended emphasis, at least in theory, was obvious. The problem as I recall was that so much of this course was optional, and so much that a singer needs in order to become even a competent performer was missing. So, for example, unless you were in the opera class (which I was not) there was very little in the 'physical expression' department. Performance practice and auditioning as regular disciplines were non-existent. Language classes were thin on the ground, and I had to learn German privately.

By the time I embarked on this top-level but insubstantial Performer's Course, I was a better musician than the average intake, and was doing two second-study instruments. I loved words and what I thought was acting, but had only 'O'-level French, little Italian and no German. Although I had been singing 'seriously' since the age of 9, and at 17 was given to understand that, but for my poor academic showing, I would have been accepted for a choral scholarship at Cambridge, my singing instrument was (I saw later) in poor shape. The whole experience of trying to sing the music I loved in the way I wanted to sing it proved therefore very frustrating. Add to this that I was a reserved, emotionally inhibited Englishman, and it is a wonder that I lasted the course! The Royal Academy seemed to me a pretty daunting place; doubtless it exacerbated my reserve.

I'm not saying this experience was common, but I do think it reflects the typical limitations and practical inadequacy of high-level courses for singers, and a lack of disciplinary coherence that still prevails in many institutions.

Fortunately, much has changed for the better since my student days. Musical institutions are no longer so stuffy or inhibiting. They tend to be more welcoming and down to earth. Young people generally are less inhibited, take things more in their stride, and appear to have more fun. In many of today's schools the teaching is better informed, and teachers and pupils enjoy more equal relationships. Curricula, by and large, are more comprehensive.

It bears repeating, however, that the singing voice is unique among instruments. The singer and instrument are one and the same thing. Therefore, when it comes to developing, releasing or bringing out a voice, we are developing the singer. The implications of this are huge. What affects the singer directly affects the instrument of music making and communicating.

With this difference alone, we should not expect singers to become professionals in three or four years at college, as other instrumentalists do. Instrumentalists, before embarking on their advanced professional studies, have been playing a 'whole' instrument for years. They have learned their musicianship with it, never jeopardising its wholeness. Singers generally have not yet found their whole instrument, let alone learned to 'play' it, much less to 'be' it. And the dangers of trying to 'play' it too soon are all too evident.

It is clear that a singer's course must by its very nature be fundamentally different from that of an instrumentalist. It needs to be essentially practical. My contention is that advanced courses for singers need to be improved on three fronts – the three Cs if you like:

1 Content;
2 Conditions;
3 Coherence (between disciplines).

We have looked at content. But even if the necessary curriculum is in place, conflicts of interest and wastage of time will only be avoided if the conditions provide for disciplinary coherence. The holistic paradigm comes to our aid. Coherence can come about:

a) if the work is based on an understanding of the nature of the singing instrument;
b) if it is understood how the various disciplines or competencies affect one another;
c) if the complementary nature of these various subjects is faithfully and intelligently attributed.

CHAPTER 16

Environment and Attitude

Environment

Environment affects behaviour. I believe that most students of singing are selected for advanced training because of their perceived potential. We say they 'have talent'. Talent, if there is such a thing, lies in the genes. But 'genes are not destiny', they reflect only potential.[1] For the potential to be realised, it needs suitable conditions, conducive surroundings, enabling structures, appropriate nutrients.

Purposeful Spaces

I have often wondered how it is that architects and designers can create a building that does not adequately serve its designated purpose – theatres and concert halls with poor or uneven acoustics, hospitals that are more likely to depress than revive, music schools without practice rooms, and so on.

Décor

Spaces influence the quality of our work or our approach to it because they affect our mental states and moods. A colourful décor can enliven our spirit and stimulate our interest, whereas a gloomy or insipid one is more likely to dampen or dull it. I was once asked to teach for a week in a black box theatre, a large, all-black space (apart from the comforting exit signs) which is ideally suited to experimental theatre. It did not feel ideal for the experimental teaching of singing! Although I knew I could escape at the end of the week I feared for my sanity in the meantime, so I got a pupil to bring in a dozen or so large balloons of different colours. Magic! The brightly coloured orbs transformed the oppressive space into something humorous and joyful. Not only did we all survive, we enjoyed many productive, if somewhat surrealistic, sessions!

Calm

Singers and teachers also need quiet, calming spaces. We are enveloped in sound for long stretches, during which aural concentration is often at a high intensity, and stress is not unknown. We need relief from this, and an environment in which to prepare for fresh listening. In a culture of slick communications and easily accessible, rapidly changing images, there is an increasing need for tranquil spaces where, iPods off, we can collect our thoughts and renew our powers of concentration and reflection. Whether for meditation or recuperation, such spaces might have more muted colours, and some green plants.

Light

More important than colour is light. Quality of light affects our health. Natural light is best by a long way. The healthy school, therefore, might be built around a large courtyard so that the maximum number of studios can benefit from natural light. A surprising number of existing studios do not have this basic necessity. It is unfortunate that fluorescent lighting, which is often chosen now for its economy, can have negative effects on our health by upsetting our body's regulator mechanism (circadian rhythms). Among its negative effects, this can cause stress, fatigue, eyestrain, immune system suppression, and reduced productivity.

Air

It hardly needs mentioning to voice-carers that the quality of the air we breathe is also of vital importance. If we cannot open a studio window there must be an efficient air conditioning system (regularly cleaned), and heating that is properly regulated – not just 'hot' or 'cold' relative to outdoors.

When it comes to comfort in the working environment, there needs to be a balance. If we become over-relaxed or snug we are likely to lose focus. If the environment is too Spartan we are likely to be distracted by our discomfort.

Spaciousness

The size of a working space, suitable for teaching and performing, needs to be not too confining. A small cubicle might be fine for an instrumentalist, although I rather doubt it. Even given natural light and a suitable acoustic (a matter that we will be looking at shortly) being cooped up is contrary to the nature and spirit of singing. For all its intimacy, singing is something expansive and giving. A generous spirit is unlikely to be fostered in a confined space!

On the other hand, when it comes to performing, a too large space can be intimidating. Otherwise, by giving the impression that it must be filled, it can encourage a singer to be effusive or demonstrative in a quite uncharacteristic way. Until they have come to terms with their voices, singers often strain to 'get across'. Stanislavski, who was very keen to create the right conditions for nurturing his actors, put it like this:

> I had dreamed that the actor who grew up in the Studio would make his first timid artistic steps in a small room which was built so as not to violate the inner creative life of the beginning artist.

He had a small amphitheatre built to seat between 100 and 150 spectators, so that the young actors could 'begin to live their rôles, naturally developing and strengthening ... their voices, gestures' and so on.[2]

Conviviality

A convivial space is essential for the meeting of budding young artists who have a shared aim and enthusiasm for their work. It needs to be a place for humour and camaraderie: a place for a drink and a joke as well as for serious discussion if wanted. This space needs to be separate from the canteen and always open. It needs to be welcoming and comfortable and, except on special occasions, without music! It must be large enough to accommodate all the students without a crush. This space, I feel, should be at the heart of the school – the communal hub.

Acoustics

I am treating this subject separately to emphasise its importance, especially to those of us, teachers and singers, who value our hearing so highly. In reality, sound should be part of the health equation of any artificially created space. In our context the design of the 'convivial' space, for example, could turn a number of innocuous conversations into an offensive hubbub, like that experienced in crowded pubs, in which you can neither hear the person next to you nor be heard by them without shouting. A more user-friendly design might be like one of those open restaurants in which, in spite of the large spaces, the many tables seem to be in their own sound capsules, undisturbed and undisturbing.

When it comes to teaching and practising spaces, there are many important issues to consider. Singers should resist the temptation, or perceived necessity, to adjust to the acoustic of a space, however dry or bright. For many this is a hard lesson, but the reasons behind it are logical and its implications are far-reaching. Understanding them can make all the difference to a singer's progress and the quality of their performance.

As we have seen, the singing voice has an identifiable structure which is behind those qualities we attribute to healthy singing: a range of notes, evenly produced, a range of dynamics which varies without the forcing or weakening of tone, a range of tonal colours which arise imaginatively and naturally from structural integrity, emotional freedom in sound, without destabilisation, unforced carrying power, agility – all perfectly natural to this voice.

As a result of structural balance these properties are dynamically supporting and complementary. There is lateral fluidity between them as well as linear fluency because of them. In other words the singer doesn't have to create flexibility or colour or emotion, or help the voice go up or down, or make it loud or soft. These natural musical and expressive 'possibilities' are, if you like, in a continuous state of relational flux. Undue effort made in achieving any one of them, let's say a crescendo, results in temporary dislocation or suspension of other properties which should be 'simultaneously possible'. It is the conscious effort to produce desired qualities, often the aim or outcome of techniques, which disrupts the natural organic integrity of the singing voice.

The primary issue with regard to acoustics seems to be whether the voice is carrying or 'getting across'. Indeed, 'projection' is often a technical aim. Unfortunately, measures to combat or compensate for 'difficult' or unfamiliar acoustics invariably unsettle vocal equilibrium, so that what might be experienced as a gain in one department is a loss in another.

Ironically, the sense of improvement that the singer feels is usually not experienced as such by the audience. So, while from a purely musical point of view it might be beneficial (in a reverberant space) to make adjustments (like slowing the tempo of a piece) so that not all details are lost, it makes no vocal sense to adjust voice-production with each different acoustic with which one is confronted.

Having said all that, a high degree of freedom, strength and awareness needs to be achieved before a singer has the confidence to sing with integrity *regardless* of the acoustic. This is part of what a singer's training and education is about. It is the responsibility of the school to provide suitable teaching spaces that materially assist both teachers and singers in their exacting task.

The Importance of a Working Acoustic

> Sounds from a source do not only come directly to the ear, but come also secondarily resulting from reflections off the walls, whereby the total impression of the sound is deformed by the acoustical characteristics of the room.[3]

I have taught in several prestigious institutions where the teaching studios had 'bathroom' acoustics. In each case the barrage of sound, while often impressive, precluded the detection of the small vocal clues that lead the way in training. In one case I opted to teach my students in the relative dryness of my front room at home, and soon realised what a strain the 'bathroom' listening had been!

Whatever is intended outside the studio, we teachers should remember that our job is to train the singer's voice for what it is. We should remember that it has a specific structure, the detail and wholeness of which can be perceived accurately by the ear. In a bright acoustic it can be difficult, especially in more obviously athletic work, to distinguish between 'helpful energy' and 'impeding effort'. If the sound is always being distorted in some way, the work cannot be adequately detailed.

Fritz Winckel, writing in Germany at the end of the 1950s, says that perhaps the new halls being built with 'good definition' suited the music of the time, just as 'good definition' favours polyphonic composition. But then, referring to the blending and fullness of sounds, he states that 'it is not suitable for the sound requirements of the Romantic period'.

Debatable as this is, singers who depend on external conditions for effect are unlikely ever to find the balanced centre of their voice, which affords so many simultaneous skills including projection and clarity. These skills, both musical and expressive, are needed whatever the acoustic or style of music. Given that every vocal nuance made by the singer's larynx is very much magnified externally, the less 'interference' with the true sound of the voice there is in the teaching space, the easier the inner vocal-aural connections can be re-established within the singer. In other words we need the definition if we are to do well by our students.

While some instrumentalists might be troubled by the inexactness that a dry acoustic exposes, and therefore prefer a brighter space to play in, vocal work – involving such a tiny centre of activity as that of the human vocal folds, upon which so much in terms of accuracy and skill depends – needs complete attention to exactness.

Winckel takes the matter a step further:

> Just as a violin body is so constructed that as far as possible a relatively equal sound volume is emitted in all positions, so it is desirable for a music room to have a similar equality in its frequency response, that is, for all audible tones to be heard with approximately equal volume.[4]

Some typical results of being influenced by acoustics

a) A pupil learns to sing in, say, a front room, according to its acoustic. This is more or less comfortable, if not very impressive. Minimal effort is required – everything is heard. Then, a larger space seems to require greater effort. Maybe the singer is told they cannot be heard, and feels obliged to make a greater effort in order to amplify the sound, or to 'project' the voice or words. The voice has not been rigorously brought out. It has not gained strength at its core. It has not learned to be itself, only to accommodate the smaller, dryer space.

b) A singer learns to sing in a reverberant space, singing according to its acoustic. Since loudness and projection seem to be taken care of, laziness in terms of structural detail is encouraged. The acoustic alters the singer's sound in such a way that no weaknesses are discernible. Little by way of fineness or detail can be achieved, because the amplitude obscures or distorts the fine activity at the vocal folds. Weak structures sound robust, so the exactness of the way the sound is produced seems to be of little consequence. Any attempt at structural detail is swamped in an impressive, seductive wash of sound.

Then, in a dryer space this unrefined voice, which has been so used to 'outside help', is suddenly experienced as less impressive. It lacks clarity and flexibility. Once again it seems to call for greater effort. Fineness or exactness at the core of a voice is the equivalent of the details of craftsmanship that go into constructing a fine violin. We are not talking of decoration here but of those things that make for efficiency and quality.

c) A singer auditions or rehearses in a reverberant space, and the sound, to the undiscerning, is great! Weaknesses which will later tell in a theatre or dryer space are not noticed or else ignored – perhaps with the expectation that a suitable adjustment will be made. The singer is signed up, the music rehearsals are done, only to discover later, in the performing space, that there is indeed an adjustment to be made. This once again leads to vocal struggle or strain in an attempt to accommodate the ungrateful acoustic.

Attitude

Details

I believe the seriousness of a project or undertaking is reflected in its detail. Whether it's lighting, décor, safe staircases, truly nutritious food, well-tuned pianos, available drinking water, or chairs that support good posture (which most do not), taking care of such things demonstrates care for the students and teachers and respect for the work they are doing.

Professionalism

What is the attitude of a good teacher if not based on empathy, caring and responsibility? When teachers' work is not supported or properly provided for, or when they are continually having to fight for suitable working conditions, or their surroundings are simply uninspiring, teachers cannot do their best. They are discouraged by being obliged to work in conditions which are not conducive to good work – the thing they care about. Their empathy, care and responsibility is being challenged by matters which should not be their concern.

What message does gloominess or out-of-tune pianos convey? What does neglect or indifference do for enthusiasm? The pupils suffer because their teachers cannot take good enough care of them and because the inadequacy of the working conditions suggests that respecting the work, taking due care of it and doing it well – i.e. being professional – doesn't really matter. The message to the student is that they can get by without bothering about quality or the details upon which it depends. This message may prove all the more invidious for being received unconsciously.

If the material conditions have been taken care of, those who stand to benefit from them – teaching staff and students alike – will see that their needs as professionals are understood and respected. The organisation cares about what they do and how well they do it.

Such an attitude is palpable. It can be shared and savoured by all the professionals concerned: cooks and cleaners, professors and porters, librarians and piano technicians, principal and administrators. All can feel, without it being stated, that they are part of an important joint venture in which their role is valued.

Pupils, however keen they are to sing well, don't necessarily know what matters, what being professional entails, what it looks like, what it feels like. They need examples. From day one they need to witness it broadly and in details, to absorb and share and delight in the 'school for beautiful singing' ethos. The cultivation of a professional attitude at institutional level should be so prized that its influence spreads to the profession at large, where almost invariably singers are treated as second-class citizens.

CHAPTER 17

Ethos

Schools need to be vibrant places that are conducive to the enjoyment of hard work and creativity; somewhere you really want to be. Given healthy, supportive and inspiring conditions one can expect teachers and students to feel positive about their situation. But of course a school is more than bricks and mortar, however well designed. Its pupils, teachers, administrators and others who work there together comprise a community. It is these people and what they are doing that will generate the spirit of the place and an appropriate communal atmosphere.

A large school in which hundreds of students are pursuing a wide variety of forms of knowledge is somewhat like a city with many businesses and lifestyles. It is so big that a 'sense of community' is possible only in small neighbourhoods or ghettos. A small school is more like a village in which the locals share and are bound by common concerns, which are easily made known, discussed and dealt with to the benefit of all. The place belongs to them collectively, and they feel they belong to it. At best, they take a pride in their surroundings and care of each other. The communal spirit of such a place can generally be felt.

A specialist school or department, such as a school of singing, suggests something else again, since almost all its inhabitants are similarly engaged in creative work. The ethos to which this gives rise is not only one of community, of sharing (facilities and knowledge) and participation (classes, ensembles and so on), but also one of sharing a very specific and specialised purpose. In Part II we saw that various 'subjects', such as dancing, offered opportunities to nurture a feeling of community. We will look at the idea of co-operation in Part IV. Meanwhile, I want to examine what I believe should be at the heart of a school devoted to singing, and, considering its shared purpose and the nature of the work, the basis of a sustaining and sustainable ethos.

A School of Singing

'School' can imply an approach and an attitude towards the cause it espouses; thus the Old Italian School and the Husler School, both of which advocate a basis for work that arises from their understanding of the singing voice. While the thinking behind the work of these 'schools' is rooted in principles, these do not signify the grounds for a specific technique. A 'school's' way of thinking involves questions such as 'What is the essence of our work?' and 'What (therefore) is the substance of our involvement?' Answers to such questions can be found in my criteria for defining the singing voice (explored in Part I), which are not only yardsticks with which to measure individuals' progress, but pointers to the very nature of the work:

1 The structure of the singing voice, its anatomy and physiology, entails physical training.
2 Beautiful singing, implying artistry in practical and aesthetic terms, demands the cultivation of taste and an artistic sensibility.
3 Individual identity requires self-examination and commitment to growth.
4 Communication involves self-awareness, appreciation of performing material and respect for the listener.

These definitions are indicators of health. They bear the personal stamp of the individual singer. They are all recognisable facets of what could be described as 'a process of becoming in sound'. It follows that, while the work is similar in kind (physical, mental, emotional or spiritual), it varies in particulars, emphasis and proportioning from individual to individual. Crucially, the various properties of each definition are audible. They are also recognisable through their relational nature. Hearing *that* and *how* they are relational obviates other forms of validation.

Care as a Characteristic of the Present

Taking care of the individual's 'becoming', through these audible relationships, leads us to the ethos of the school.

The quality of teachers' care depends not just on their willingness but on their depth of understanding, their standards and how much they 'care' for singing. As for the students, even if initially they understand little of what a high standard really is, it must be assumed that they are willing to do whatever it takes to fulfil their ambition. The student's input is as crucial as the teacher's – the work can only be successful if teacher and pupil work as a team.

Let us suppose, then, that we have organisational competence, teacher expertise and student talent, all three bodies committed heart and soul to the cause. For all these 'givens', the real challenge is the unknown. This would not be an issue if learning to sing were an academic subject such as geography, chemistry or mathematics. But there are no maps or formulae as such. Conditions for learning to sing and an appropriate ethos are as important to the growth of the singer as soil, weather conditions and the gardener's care are for growing flowers!

In life, generally the future grows out of the present. For all our informed guesswork or forecasting we cannot engage with the future, even less with specific future outcomes. We can create what we suppose to be a suitable environment, and intend to follow a curriculum, but progress can only be built on what we perceive and do in the present, on the experience of now. We can only deal with the singer's vocal and musical talents, for example, as they present themselves in this moment, the singer's fears and failings as they are. This fact will be the same tomorrow and the next day. The best we can do is begin a process with what we know, the 'material' we have in our hands, and be alert to the signs and symptoms of progress.

Put another way, as singing teachers, if we are honest and don't work with a sausage machine mentality, we have no option but to 'feel our way'. However expert, teachers only have their previous experience with quite different students plus the perceived potential of the new student to go by. They must of course be trusted to be able to see 'the angel in the marble' and carve until they 'set him free'.[1] (The fact that the new student may have been chosen by others is a matter for serious consideration. Selection will be looked at in Part IV.)

Students, too, face the unknown. The work of releasing and developing a voice requires the student's participation in terms of personal application and therefore of fitness of body, a positive frame of mind and emotional access. Even given such readiness, they usually need to learn not only what voice training and learning to sing really entail, but how to become the main motivating force behind the process. This may be asking a lot when education has traditionally been a kind of spoon-feeding or even force-feeding – aided and abetted by the belief that the teacher has the answers.

In our context, except that we can have intimations of the treasure within, the analogy with Michelangelo's sculpting is of course inappropriate. Far from being a passive block of marble to be chipped away at, a pupil is an active flesh-and-blood body and mind with reactive emotions and spirit. Nevertheless, in so far as these human characteristics can find themselves in conflict, they are all potential stumbling blocks. The 'angel' may never be set free.

The pupil's mind might be strong but the body weak. Or the body might be strong but the emotions on the defensive. They may be low in self-esteem, or hiding behind a mask of false security. They may block progress with impatience or an inflated ego. They may feel the need to exercise mental control over everything they do. The state of body, mind, emotions and spirit can vary from moment to moment.

Human beings, singers not excepted, are complex creatures, and the path to freedom is rarely straightforward. There is no ABC, only a melting pot of positives and negatives, of foibles and propensities, out of which it can seem impossible to clear a way forward.

The various departments outlined in Part II provide references or frameworks for focus. So instead of mixing objectives and thereby causing unnecessary confusion, frustration and stress, they can each be worked and enjoyed until they are competences in their own right, and so able to complement one another without contrivance or strain. At a stroke many potential conflicts are removed, concentration is facilitated and care is well placed. Well-focused work attracts the attentiveness and patience that care implies. Time devoted to a specific discipline is far more productive than time spent on several that hamper each other's progress.

It is, after all, logical that if two disciplines are to complement one another they must be evenly matched in freedom and competence. Otherwise the attempt to progress is like two race horses, one that's recovering from an injury and the other on racing form, trying to train side by side.

Typically in our work as singing teachers, a pupil's development is badly held up by weakness in one or two aspects of their work. It could be posture, general fitness, inability to act, something emotional, musicianship and so on. In the private teaching sphere it can be difficult if not impossible to find or pay for a remedy. When a private pupil needs to hold back on some disciplines while putting most of their energy into something that is seriously holding up progress, they can feel demoralised or exaggeratedly inadequate. They may have no understanding or sympathy from any other quarter. (After all, they are supposed to be having singing lessons!)

Take the case already mentioned, in which a would-be singer needs to work on their voice, the instrument of singing. This is so common that it can be said to be the normal situation. It is also commonly not done, or not in a sufficiently concentrated or rigorous manner. But this person's whole future as a singer depends on that instrument. If delaying the actual singing were a commonly recognised practice, or if the pupil understood their own vocal shortcomings and the need for training time, perhaps they would experience little difficulty or frustration while doing only technical work and singing vowels for two or three years until the voice was a truly serviceable instrument. But since the dissolution of bel canto practice, and with the modern have-it-now mentality, progressive training practices have been superseded by illogical, temporary problem-fixing.

A singing school designed for the purpose has the conditions and ethos to do necessary work thoroughly, and therefore make a matching-through-separation approach viable. When there is a shared understanding (by teachers and pupils alike) of the nature of the work, and a general acknowledgement that all potential singers are in the same boat, whatever is required to be done can be worked at care-fully, progressively and in proportion to individuals' needs without them feeling inadequate, deprived or excluded.

Some of the classes, such as clowning and presentation, tackle blocks or reservations more or less head on. In others there will be a gradual dissipation of fear or uneasiness. An ethos born of genuine care and co-operation will make it easier to pursue a process that is always foundational. It matters that weaknesses are not somehow covered up or 'preserved for the future'. We cannot in all conscience cut corners, skim over difficulties or simply deal with symptoms of malfunction.

Everything that comprises a singer's singing voice is there. Our task therefore is searching for that wholeness and encouraging it to reveal itself. Looking for the good in another is symptomatic of love.

Towards a Process

An inspiring working environment designed for efficiency and enjoyment, a spirit of community and mutual support, and an attitude of care, all add up to conditions that nurture. A person might be blessed with vocal and musical genes, but without the nurturing, their talents are more likely to languish than to flourish.

A number of books exploring this issue have come out in recent years. It seems that however obvious a young person's aptitude it comes with no guarantee of future success. People who have studied this matter seem to agree about the 10,000 hours (of practice and experience) that are required – in any field – in order to realise potential and achieve success. Furthermore, it's not just the time put in but the purposefulness and quality of the practice that counts. Crucially, in addition to expert tuition and advice, the person concerned must have motivational support and encouragement.

One reason why, realistically, a course should last a minimum of five years is that few singers have previously undergone continuous, purposeful, quality voice work – their circumstances simply do not support it. Even if a voice is exceptionally mature at the age of, say, 15, long practice every day – common enough among budding instrumentalists – is simply not physically possible for a singer. The training of the smaller muscles in particular needs careful pacing. Developing a voice needs specialised supervision. Often young singers do not consider singing 'seriously' until their adult voice begins to show itself. Other skills for becoming a professional performer also need time and pacing.

Eight hours of study per day, for 40 five-day weeks per year, adds up to around 4800 hours in three years. However you recalculate to make this more realistic or manageable, it is unlikely that 10,000 hours could be achieved in six years. There would still be compromise – on time-scales as much as on content – the hope being that conditions and the way the school is run and the students taken care of would ensure a high standard for all suitably qualified entrants.

Whatever the nature of their talent, a person's potential for growth is a basic human tendency. We encounter this first in young children, whose unconscious play is deadly serious! When it comes to art, 'the *playful* attitude becomes interest in the transformation of material to serve the purpose of a developing experience.'[2] Conditions, while they don't in themselves create change or growth, must be 'enabling'. It is how we apply ourselves, given the conditions, that counts.

The industrial revolution, with its flagrant abuse of nature and unconscionable determination to control the living world, has made human beings arrogant. The idea of 'fixing' a voice is, I believe, partly a consequence of that mindset. A student passively seeking a 'technical fix' is not enabled to grow. That narrow, end-gaining purpose prevents the gaining of wisdom, of knowing oneself as a whole. This in turn bars the realisation of talent.

Growing implies extending boundaries. In our context this means exploring the whole. Only the student can take the appropriate steps. The drive to explore and actualise the self are two aspects of the same thing. As adults we may find exploring (playing) and actualising (becoming) risky. But the risk is reduced if the aspiring singer identifies (mentally) with their objective.

> Inspiration and aspiration are intimately linked. Each leads to the development of the other. If we are inspired, we will develop higher aspirations. If we cultivate high aspirations we are likely to open ourselves to inspiration when it occurs.[3]

An enabling situation is an accepting one, offering the student freedom and encouragement to move out of their comfort zone. Since the process of learning to sing can at first seem somewhat nebulous, trust needs to be built. Both teacher and pupil need to be open and straightforward, and adopt unconditional positive attention to what they are each themselves doing.

An environment that allows students to grow also has to be individually validating, to encourage students' independence. As students push the boundaries of experience, they gain confidence through realising what of themselves they can bring to the work – it is new and unique, and therefore empowering. As competence grows, so does self-esteem.

Important to our enabling conditions is the fact that each student is unique. Each is equally important. By implication, competition has no place in students' development. It is rather the opposite. A spirit of caring is more likely to foster co-operation. I hope the reader can begin to see from various angles the meaning and value of 'participation' as implied by the holistic paradigm. To embark on a process of growth is to participate in its progress.

CHAPTER 18

Process

'Joy is man's transition from lesser to greater perfection' writes Spinoza. For 'perfection' we should read wholeness and integrity... Joy brings power, rationality, virtue, freedom, activeness, the ability to be self-causing or self-directed and to make ourselves intelligible to others. Joy confers power; power enables effectiveness.[1]

With conducive conditions and a positive attitude we, teachers and pupils alike, can already achieve much. Being supported and validated, students can trust themselves to take steps towards the future, and gain confidence in doing so. They are encouraged by the belief that their talent is not only appreciated but being given due care and attention. But what are the steps we must take?

Product-orientated work

There are those for whom the idea of 'process' – in the sense of evolvement – is puzzling or disturbing. They are usually the ones who think there is a specific way to shape a person's voice for the purpose of singing. This has become a commercial aim. The way is predetermined, as is the expected result. 'This is what we want, and this is how you do it', they say. Such product-orientated approaches may be the result of a lack of insight, insufficient confidence to think outside the (conventional or linear-directed) box, laziness or sheer greed.

Product-orientated approaches are attractive to the student because the desired product – which, in our 'click on' culture, should be attainable at once or very soon – is attractive. While it may be unspoken, the ulterior motive for many young people is fame. And five minutes of fame is better than none. The sooner this is achievable, for the least amount of work, the better. The more naïve believe that all you need is sufficient information and the opportunity. Others search for a formula. This formula (vocal method or technique) is often, at least subconsciously, attributed with magic – 'How it works we don't exactly know, but it worked for so-and-so'. Implicit in such techniques is that if it doesn't work for you, it is somehow your fault!

The mystery surrounding such methods makes their opposite – the well planned, scientifically explained, one-size-fits-all versions – all the more attractive. A little knowledge is all that's required to pass these methods on.

Techniques and methods usually have some kind of anatomical tag, or bear the name of their inventor. Since they are imposed from the outside, or learned by mindless rote, little or no participation is required. The subject-object duality is perpetuated, and the alienation (from self and other) is officially endorsed. Instead of self-reliance and the freedom and authority to be truly creative, the pupil becomes (or remains) dependent on technique and praise.

I listened recently to a broadcast lieder recital. After the first few phrases I knew exactly how each subsequent phrase would be sung (or should I say negotiated). This singer's technique was dependable to the point of monotony. His demonstration of perfection would have been praiseworthy, but for the fact that it was void of character or feeling.

Another approach to training is one in which the singer manoeuvres their voice into a position that feels right – because it fits their defective coordination, as Alexander would have put it. Other singers find themselves replacing one unsatisfying technique with another.

Many would-be singers 'fail' because they can neither fit a prescribed mould nor accommodate their vocal shortcomings. Their struggle to achieve perceived goals only serves to reinforce their difficulties. We do well to remember that undue effort produces tension, which in turn reduces our field of awareness.

In our technological age, short-term 'technological' solutions – artificial ones – have become a habit of mind. As we are experiencing with regard to the environment, we apply them to nature at our peril. We apply them to the (natural) singing voice, except to get out of a temporary difficulty, at the peril of our music-making.

Vocal techniques are often based on false premises. For example, that the voice is a musical instrument that has to be played, or must be consciously manipulated to satisfy various performance criteria. This is only true when the singing voice is *not* free, or when the singer is obliged to sing unsingable music, music that is not based on the singing voice as such.

Another false premise is that to sing – in a classical way – we have to 'add' something to the normal voice. In this view 'normal' is taken to mean natural. By definition, therefore, the singing voice is deemed to be unnatural, and it would seem appropriate to employ unnatural methods.

Other techniques are based on a narrow (and therefore limiting) definition of 'singing voice', or an underestimation of its inherent capacities.

Whatever the case, fixed perceptions make it impossible to be constructive. This is why ultimately techniques are unsatisfactory and unsatisfying. With the 'instruction-giving-and-obeying' mindset, and its over-reliance on looking and feeling, in which everything tends to be overdone,

> We miss the essence of an experience as a constant discovery, a consciousness of being, a journey with a view of peaks and far horizons rather than a necessary trudge along a dusty pathway.[2]

The joy is missing!

Healthy evolvement

The holistic paradigm raises our level of consciousness by making a quantum jump away from constraining thoughts and habits into a broader field of vision and possible action. Once our hearts and minds are free of prejudices we are free to pick up or search for solutions that are entirely apropos. The holistic perspective means that the process is fed from all sides, is informed by all that is going on. 'Information', mainly audible, is thrown up in unpredictable ways from moment to moment – if only, instead of being distracted by some irrelevant agenda, we can stay present and catch it as it flies.

So much information comes at us that we need to be selective as we go. I will come to the idea of 'prioritising' the work shortly. Meanwhile, selectiveness requires mindfulness and the skill to use information constructively and intelligently. Sometimes the information is confusing. That which tells us how best to proceed is sometimes difficult to detect. Since we are not trying to pin something down but to release it (so that we can develop it), the more a student 'lets go' in response to cues, the more freely the process can flow. Action is managed or ordered in reference to the consequences of risk-taking.

'Solutions' amount to an on-going detecting, releasing and affirming of a singer's vocal and performing potential. This process gradually optimises the co-ordinating possibilities between a complex set of variables: voice, person, music, text and so on. It does this not by prescribed steps or the accumulation of ideas, skills or subjects but by the continuous making sense, interweaving and intensification of relationships, whether of a structural nature within the singer's body or between the disciplines that constitute the singer's art.

Growing implies change

I have mentioned the need for mindfulness (the *sine qua non* of the process), I have recommended that the curriculum includes meditation and that the conditions provide for quiet times. Absence of clutter and distraction, increased awareness and the confidence that comes from braving and accepting the new, help to nourish the perception of quality and the acquiring of taste. A quiet mind helps us to go with change. Change is characteristic of process, which means that process itself is subject to change! Once more we see that inflexible systems cannot work.

Resistance to healthy change is often physical or visceral:

> The contractions that are maintained in all action as a personal manner of doing, irrespective of the act, always express an emotional attitude. The attitude found most frequently is that of insecurity or the masquerade of ignoring it. Physiologically stiffening the body, lowering the head, sinking the chest, contracting and flattening the abdomen – when performed not in the course of a purposeful action, but as acts in themselves – are protective acts ...[3]

Feldenkreis attributes all incorrect action to 'premature or too violent demands made on the person'.[4] It is easy to see how hurried work or disproportionate emphasis might prove counterproductive.

Taking care of the 'how' – flexibly

Progress is a matter of constant evaluation, clarification and revision, the aim always being to take care of the 'how', and monitoring its effectiveness. Alexander said, 'If you will pay attention to the means, the end will take care of itself'.[5] While unpredictability can be difficult to go with, a well-conducted process is constantly rewarded by revelation. It reveals achievement and effectiveness without either being fabricated. The natural voice is there. Uncovering it shows us that it is efficient.

An unpredictable process of voice training and singers' education demands flexibility – within each discipline and between them, within the organisation, between staff, and between teachers and pupils. If the nature of the work is properly understood, aiming to achieve pre-determined goals in a pre-determined time span makes no sense.

Rigid time frames encourage the cutting of corners, formulaic approaches and the skipping of seemingly small but crucial issues. In particular they allow no individual adjustments with regard to pace and rhythm. It is more than likely that students will need different amounts of attention for different disciplines. This is totally unmeasurable until the entrance audition or until the course begins. Thereafter, change of pace or emphasis must be constantly re-accommodated. It stands to reason that if a process of such personal consequence is to be one of genuine growth, it needs thoroughness for each individual. Hastening or skimping training or education (the foundations) has been a major reason for the crumbling of careers, even before they began.

Time is, however, of the essence. Rather than quickening the pace, this means making the most of the moment. I remember when teaching in musical institutions that whenever an examination loomed on the horizon real progress more or less ceased – sometimes for a term or more – while students fixed and fretted and fiddled over their material. This was a lesson in itself, because it pointed up two irreconcilable goals that students constantly have to deal with. On the one hand they must build for the long term, which entails releasing and strengthening their various skills so that they are sufficiently secure and flexible to serve the creative challenges of an unknown future. On the other hand they are encouraged to 'fix' the future (exams epitomise this) and, because they are as yet ill-equipped, they spend precious time cobbling their as yet unevenly-matched disciplines. Measures of progress will be tackled in Part IV.

Patience

We are so used to being in control mentally that we think that we can put something right just by having the right idea. We don't realise that we have gone down the wrong track for, perhaps, many years, so the fault is a habit that has to be undone. Bad habits can be so ingrained that we don't even know we have them. Then when we are turned in the right direction it can seem wrong. Often we must correct our course many times before we 'set' it. Staying with the process requires patience as well as trust, perseverance as well as courage and imagination, so that we keep constantly interested and engaged.

A word of warning: To rush ahead as soon as something good is experienced – greater ease, easier access to higher notes, or the ability to sing louder without pushing, for example – is unwise. Ease comes through balance, which is achieved by (sometimes very small) degrees. Those muscles that finally come into their own and are therefore able to trigger the balance are often the most fragile or vulnerable. They need to build their staying power. The latest muscle development is also the first to weaken or unravel.

Prioritising

Our four definitions act as references for the growing process. Growing is not an end in itself, it is a means towards fulfilment, towards 'becoming' (as manifest in the voice), and by extension the releasing of the capacity to make music beautifully and to communicate deeply and directly.

We should not fall into the trap of making the definitions ends in themselves. The process, for example, sounds our individual identity, and this identity is heard in our singing. This is why it's a helpful 'definition', something through which we can ascertain the genuineness of our singing voice. But identity in this context does not mean dependence on objects, feelings, sayings, attractions, etc. – on externalities or their acquisition. Such dependent identity does not make for impartiality. Rather it is our realised self – our independence – that enables us to be impartial. Finding our selves in the process of learning to sing reduces the need of approval and gives us confidence to be master of our own performance.[6]

Because singing (as such) is too often treated as an end in itself, to be gained as an objective, work on the instrument of singing rarely comes fully to fruition. The irony of this might be lost on those who think that singing has to be artificially produced. The fact remains that, even if the act of singing inspires the voice, it is primarily the instrument that facilitates the music making, not the other way round.

The structure of the instrument reveals the individuality of a person's singing voice, and it is the individual instrument with all its skills, personality and intimacy, that makes for authentic, authoritative performances and for communication on both a personal and universal scale. The abilities to manifest musicality, authenticity or communicativeness are all indicators of a healthy singing voice.

We should bear in mind that the singing voice per se is not music and words, even though it facilitates both. The intellect is relatively modern. As we have already seen, at an early age its need for expression takes possession of what is inherently our singing instrument. This fact should help us to maintain a healthy balance between intellect and voice.

Notation is also a modern invention. An all-too-common misconception among singers is that what is seen on the page – notes, expression marks and so forth – is music, and that what has to be done is to apply our mind to its accurate reproduction. George Hadjinikos dispels this notion:

> The roots of music differ radically from the established rudiments of music education ... The rudiments are abstract notions that were conceived in order to find a way of writing music, while the roots of music stem from our inner being and correspond accordingly to the laws of nature.[7]

This is why a course for those wanting to perform needs to be practical, why rhythm needs to be embodied, why eurhythmics, for example, can be so helpful. We are blessed with a natural physical-emotional instrument that, as it unfolds, opens us up to our innate musicality, and makes it possible for us to tap the roots of music that lie deep within.

But such a wonderful gift is to no avail if it is locked or hidden away. In my experience the intellectual approach and the blocked (vocal) channel are mutually reinforcing. The intellect tries to control or manipulate the unresponsive instrument. The instrument can only respond by self-distorting, and so the mind perceives the need to stay at the controls.

There are two basic opposite approaches to voice training, and numbers of variations in between:

1) Based on the idea that the voice needs to be produced or made to work, your focus is mainly on the expected product. You attempt to deal with symptoms of inefficiency. You do what you think will effect quickest results. Your energy is insufficient or inappropriate to the process.

   Disadvantages (mainly to do with performance and personal fulfilment): training can be boring and repetitive. Predictable, 'mechanical' results. Unexciting singing. Superficial/false expressivity. Serious limitations in range, flexibility, emotional expressiveness. Absence of spontaneous creativity. Each new musical problem necessitates a new 'technical strategy'. Never deeply satisfies (expressively, musically, artistically) because never wholly at one with the voice. Weaknesses begin to tell after a relatively short time.

   At best the resulting singing is accurate, pleasant (or impressive) and dependable, and takes less time to obtain because it must or you fail. Consolidates with suitable experience. Sometimes this approach produces results that seem to be improvements in terms of product.

2) Based on physiology, and with an eye both to its instrumental and personal nature, and with suitable energy applied to a process of regeneration, you encourage the voice to reveal its innate capacities. Rather than deal with symptoms or try to get round difficulties, you look for what is good and follow this to the voice's roots.

   Disadvantages (mainly to do with training process): can seem (at first) to be 'emotionally threatening'. Is mainly practical, requiring well-focused application. Needs fitness, commitment and perseverance. Demands specialised conditions for specialised work. Needs to be understood for what it is – not end-gaining, but a process of release and growth.

   At best the voice unfolds and matures naturally. Aligning itself to the singer's personality and musicality, it gathers depth, quality and nuances. It thereby engenders exciting, imaginative music-making which is expressive on all levels. It's enjoyable for all involved. Well nurtured and kept in trim it should serve for many years, improving with experience.

Two Distinct Activities

Voice training is not yet singing, and singing is not an activity in which to be technical. Your voice is your voice at whatever stage of development. Technical work and singing are differently motivated. Technical work consists of training muscles – a bit like going to a voice gym. It's a game that requires not thinking or analysing but a great deal of aural concentration and non-judgemental observation. You can expect to sweat, or at least feel that you've worked out. Although from a certain stage of freedom singing suitable material helps the voice to develop, it is only in the studio that the voice *per se* can be improved in any radically significant way.

Trying to be 'technical' while singing spoils the singer's performance; the focus is in the wrong place. The things that motivate a vocal performance are the qualities that inspire the voice (you) to sing – the transmission of words and feelings, the painting of images, the embodiment of characters, and the joy of it. If your voice is not serving these ends without struggle, you are not ready to sing professionally –at least not at a high level.

If there's any technique to the 'act' of singing it is in the recognition and fostering of complements. The things that complement each other are broadly encapsulated in our definitions. Attention to these must be apportioned according to present benefit rather than future advantage. So, for example, a singer might ask, 'Am I being musical?' 'Am I being faithful to the text and making sense of it?' 'Am I singing with authority?' 'To whom am I singing?'

The various attributes that together we call singing can only achieve full integration in the context of a performance. Otherwise a crucial element, the audience (the Other) for whose benefit we are singing, is missing. Meanwhile, if we overly favour communication, we might start 'demonstrating' instead of transmitting. If we are trying to be musical instead of letting the music flow we are likely to treat the voice as a type of musical instrument that it's not: 'bowing' it and 'fingering' it. If the words are our preoccupation, we are likely to stiffen the articulatory mechanism.

We should not be putting the voice together while singing a song, any more than a violinist should be constructing their violin while playing a sonata.

> He is getting to the stage when things are happening. He was at the stage before when things were beginning to happen, and he was enjoying feeling them. Now he has got past that and he thinks that nothing is happening.[8]

As disconcerting as it can sometimes be, this is the feeling of coming home to yourself. You can do anything because you don't have to *do* anything. Spinoza insisted,

> ...that an important aspect of our joy (and a condition for being able to be joyful) is 'repose in ourselves', a satisfactory knowledge of our own activity, our process of living, our creativity and our achievements.[9]

CHAPTER 19

Systems and Organ-isation

Voice

We have seen that the singing voice is comprised of opposed muscle forces. These are not separate or sequential events, but simultaneous movements 'organised', so to speak, within a dynamic whole. To recap, we have:

a) A breathing system – exhalation, counteracted by an inhalation 'tendency' (*inhalare la voce*) which increases in dynamic force as the sung phrase proceeds;
b) A flexible system of suspension for the larynx: upwards and backwards – forwards and downwards (the latter a reflex of the former), upwards and forwards – backwards and downwards, all simultaneously operational;
c) Vocal folds that simultaneously stretch and thin, and tense and thicken (shortening by their own contraction), open and close (a delicate but secure process of adduction);
d) A framework of postural muscles against which the specific breathing muscles effectively brace.

These subsystems act with and through each other in a continuous elastic, give-and-take way that allows for infinite variations of emphasis and bias within the system as a whole. The various subsystems have an all-pervasive influence, each impinging on the rest and affecting its performance. The organic nature of the singing voice, while allowing for temporary bias, does not 'recognise' one sphere of activity as being more important than another.

This shared organ-isation throughout the singing voice structure can only come into its own if each sphere is balanced within itself. The stretchers and tensors, for example, must be equally capable and active in their give-and-take relationship.

Then, as we've seen, the specific balance and efficacy of events within each operational sphere depend upon that sphere's balanced relationship with the other spheres. This is important for how we go about releasing the voice, constantly cross-checking between spheres. Diagnostically we can view the conditions of the whole in the functional integrity of its parts and vice versa. This balance is also instrumental in the voice's ability to support itself, and for the outcome in terms of performance fluidity, or perhaps we should say lucidity.

Recognising the singing voice as 'organ-ised' should ensure that our unlocking and developing approach is in accord with its organic nature. The fact that there is no 'it' prevents us labouring to impose our will on it. Put another way, we cannot make ourselves 'be'. Either we are, or we are in the process of becoming. Perpetuating the false dualism of 'me' and 'it' blocks or muddies our quest for self-integration and the ability to relate.

At the heart of our 'being in sound' are the marvellous intricate vocal folds – those two remarkably short lengths of tissue which vibrate at hundreds of vibrations per second. These folds vibrate best when they are equilibrated. But we should not think of equilibrium as a 'settled state'. The vocal folds are far from settled in their activity, or the voice would not be so variable in timbre and dynamics while simultaneously voicing different pitches or moving between them. Nevertheless, it is the order (or integrity) at this pivotal vocal point that is critical in facilitating an infinite variety of muscular events. These 'vocal configurations' are in continuous flux – active on the vertical as well as the horizontal plane.

Singers and teachers alike need to come to terms with the fact that the subtlest variations at this vocal heart are hugely 'amplified' on the outside. While this means that the teacher's hearing has to be sufficiently acute and perceptive in order to gain a true sense of scale, the lesson for the singer is often that he or she should be more observant (simply) but 'try' less hard.

Conscious physical efforts by singers to effect such lightning-speed variations are always manifestly out of all proportion to what's required, so minute are the movements involved. Like a tightrope gymnast or figure skater, a singer has to heighten their sense of balance. However, in the singer's case it is an aural sensitivity to balance that must be cultivated. Once this neurological matter has been achieved – through the physical-physiological regenerating process – intuition and imagination can take over. The singer no longer needs to remain in the vocal driving seat.

Given the scale of this well-balanced precision instrument, the natural or well-trained singer 'lives on the finest edge' of vocal possibilities: the finest line between opposites, between louder and softer, darker tone and lighter, between something more delicate and something more robust, and so on. Similarly, this critical vocal edge acts as a kind of watershed between the emotional extremes of laughing and crying. As this delicate balance comes into being, so does it feel increasingly natural and inspiring to live on this 'edge of possibilities'.

So fine and sensitive is this structural peak that it takes no thought for the voice to veer one way or the other. Its systemic design means that its response to imagination and feelings is both biddable and immediate. The characteristic self-regulation of the system enables the voice to adapt with contextual appropriateness, without being thrown out of gear. Just as the lungs are automatically replenished at the end of a sung phrase, so is the equilibrium that gives the voice its potential for variation constantly re-established.

And just as the singing voice has its mean pitch or tessitura, so does it have a wide spectrum of expressive possibilities throughout its natural range. It is the *messa di voce,* the re-united structure, the ultimate opposition if you like, that makes such variety possible. The two extremes of falsetto (finest stretching) and chest register (thickest 'bunching') act as two polarities in tension. Like yin and yang, neither one is primary. The ranging between them (unlike *passaggi* to be negotiated) is merely a matter of proportion. Singing is the progression of this dance.

Music

> 'Tis true; there's magic in the web of it.
>
> William Shakespeare[1]

When we talk of the singing voice being a precision instrument it is sometimes assumed that we're talking about its accuracy and efficiency, as in singing in tune, or with agility, or 'phrasing' well, and executing such things with a degree of ease. All of this is true. It is also true that, consciously selected, such aims can be (and often are) anything but organic in response. Similarly, when it comes to interpretation, conscious efforts are often made to 'bring out the meaning', as though it is something to be pre-planned or superimposed. What we miss from this selective approach is, I suggest, the 'wisdom of the whole'.

I said at the beginning of this book that I think people generally underestimate what the singing voice is capable of. But I didn't mean 'what can be done with it'. I mean they underestimate on the one hand its inherent skills and on the other its intrinsic ability to respond.

Two singers typify what I am talking about. Christian Gerhaher's album *Romantische Arien* (Sony Classical) demonstrates exemplary declamatory singing. Here, the words rule, but Gehaher's voice responds without undue effort. The singing of Patricia Petibon on *Rosso*, a CD of Italian baroque arias (Deutsche Grammophon), is another example of vocal response – 'acting out', as she puts it, 'what the music says'. Her extraordinary flights of fancy seem quite spontaneous – as I'm sure they would have been in Handel's time. There are many fine singers on the threshold of excellence whose performance would benefit from such risk-taking if only they could get away from the perceived need for 'digital perfection', or always making a beautiful sound.

More imagination let into a lot of the classical repertoire would be like replacing stale air with fresh, and would, I believe, enhance its appeal in the world of music at large. Whether or not the result is to your taste is beside my point. Both Gehaher in his declamations and Petibon in her vocal peregrinations are able to play, risk and be vocally faithful to what they imagine. They sound as if they are enjoying themselves into the bargain!

Some singers do achieve fine things with a less-than-free instrument, while others, with relatively unlocked voices, do nothing special. Most people will agree that to be a singer you need to have a sufficiently pliant or compliant instrument. But the voice must have something to respond to. So, to be a good singer you need intelligence and a thoroughly good musical education.

In explaining how young singers can adequately prepare for their career in all its aspects, I have insisted that it is the singer's instrument, defined by its integrating properties, that must take pride of place. It serves the singer's purposes best, not because it can be manipulated or comply with instructions but because of its natural skills and responsiveness. Once this multi-talented organ is set free, the singer doesn't have to *demonstrate* musicality or even feelings; they will emerge naturally. The free singing voice responds to the singer's natural musicality, to their feelings and imagination, in a remarkable – almost 'magical' – synthesis. No deliberate orchestration of parts, only comprehension of material plus intention. The 'parts', such as they exist at all, enable the mix that is desirable in each fleeting moment of expression. They are, after all, in constant communication with one another. The singing, with all its subtle variations, becomes intuitive. It is the brain's synchronistic properties that enable the person to move as a whole. In the best singing, 'greater than the sum of its parts' suggests 'a subtle dynamic order that transcends the collective influences of … other parts of the organism.'[2]

> The parts and their sum can be discerned through rational analysis, but the *greater* can be apprehended only through intuition. It is experiential rather than conceptual, a realization and a feeling, an intimate identification with the wholeness, not an inference or a fact to be imparted verbally.[3]

Equally remarkable is the intuitive creativity of fine singing. Giving birth to our creativity, we give birth to ourselves – and vice versa: a virtuous spiral. Singing, as well as being an act of personal expression, is by definition a creative act. Indeed, when singers find this to be so, it is not necessarily because they set out to be creative, but because in the 'inspiration' of the moment the voice seems to have a creative mind of its own.

This has nothing to do with the nonsensical 'waywardness' of some singing, but is a kind of illumination that adds authenticity to the elements of a well-prepared work. The healthy voice 'maintains continuous sensitivity to unpredictable demands' from elsewhere in the system. The 'demands' come from the singer's dealings with music, emotions, words, imagination, the desire to communicate and so forth. Myriad multiple possibilities or potential 'recipes of expression' coexist within the system. They are resolved appropriately by context.[4]

Perhaps because it is not possible to comprehend the complexity of this creative system, people prefer to simplify it. 'How can we handle the complexity of it?' is a question we might ask of life itself. But over-simplification underestimates the singing voice. It encourages people to take control of what they *can* comprehend, often to the exclusion or devaluation of what they cannot. The other elements of performance – text, movement, presentation, communication and so on – suffer because they too are conceived in manageable compartments.

Of course, no explanations can take the place of experience, but a higher estimation of the singing voice's genius can help us to forestall inadequate, unhelpful or counter-productive approaches to its release and to its interaction with the other elements of the singer's art. The holistic perspective enables us to create simplicity by indicating what to work on and what to leave alone.

Between Disciplines

We are nearly ready to look at the 'third front' on which I consider advanced courses need to be radically improved if they are to foster true artistry (the others were Content and Conditions). I hope that by now, with a suitable Ethos in place, a Process in motion, and gathering 'systemic awareness', the need for *Cohesion* between the various disciplines will not only be obvious but also an exciting prospect!

Over the years I have talked with a number of colleagues about the education of young singers, and declining standards of both teaching and performing. It is reassuring to know that I am not the only one unhappy with the status quo!

How to change things for the better? It is not easy to express radical ideas succinctly on paper. But the practicalities of any significant change can seem overwhelming – especially to the individual. It is discouraging to find that even organisations with the wherewithal and power to implement life-improving measures either fail to do so or are oblivious of the need.

We are all familiar with governments' seeming inability to get things done, sustainably. We suffer because solutions are sometimes incompatible. Decisions are made without due interdepartmental consultation. Sometimes, because they have not been properly thought through, they give rise to new problems, or even to the opposite of what was intended, causing inconvenience and bad feelings. Philip Ball, in *Critical Mass*, cites as a classic example, 'The increased congestion that can follow from the building of new roads'.[5]

Peter Senge, the Director of the Center for Organizational Learning at MIT Sloan School of Management, says, 'problems never come in isolation, whether in business, society, or individual lives'. He points out that:

> ...we tend to assume that cause and effect are closely related in space and time. Usually... they are not... the problems and solutions are seldom in the obvious places, and creative ideas come to the intuitive person who can face up to the insecurity of looking beyond the obvious.[6]

And, I would add, beyond the comfortable.

'Obvious' and 'comfortable' often mean considering problems from our own point of view, and so our 'solutions' tend to reflect this bias. The results may be fine in our everyday personal decision-making, especially if we don't look too closely at the wider consequences of our actions. Looking at complex questions which are not on our doorstep, we sometimes bury our heads in the sand rather than accept responsibility, even if this may contribute to problems further along the line.

We can only know where we really stand in the greater scheme of things by considering other points of view and including them in our estimation. For organisations, the need to grasp the 'bigger picture' is axiomatic. Products and services cannot be effective unless all elements are considered. Organisations can fail for various reasons: poor communications between departments, a lack of foresight, linear thinking, etc. Even if an organisation has taken on board the desirability of close liaison between departments, how can this be achieved with maximum flexibility and efficiency, and with minimum disruption?

In our particular area, we are faced with the practical coming together of subjects which hitherto have been treated in more or less isolated units, without enough thought as to how they might best relate or complement one another. Instead of leading to a distillation or cohesion of studies or instruction, it usually amounts to an arbitrary picking of cherries.

Sometimes the relationships between skills are unclear for the opposite reason: subjects have been lumped together so that how they relate is unclear. Instead of an organic entity in which clearly distinguishable skills can range and interrelate with mutual respect and freedom, there is a selection of ill-matched 'means-to-ends' that may be confused or in conflict.

Given a shared holistic view and thereby an understanding of how the various disciplines work together and influence one another, and given a

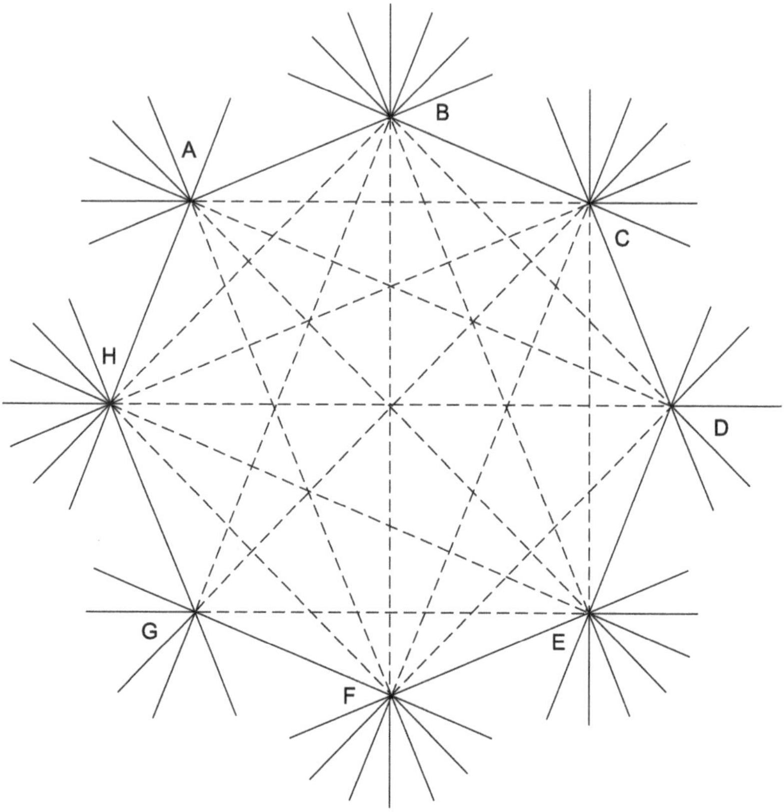

19.1 It is not always easy to discern interrelational connections or detect crucial links.

shared enthusiasm for 'the cause' (all of which could reasonably be considered essential criteria for employing staff in the first place), interdisciplinary co-operation is likely to require awareness of mutual influence and more time outside teaching hours.

Even if teachers agree in principle to continual re-evaluation of students' progress, adjustments to their programmes, and working in close proximity to colleagues, they may find the practicalities bothersome.

A good step towards dealing with problems would be to set aside one day each month for detailed reappraisal of each student's work. This would necessitate the meeting of all teachers together with the students individually.

Since the process is one of looking for and fostering the 'good', decisions at such sessions would be based on perceived need, not on fault or inadequacy. In this way, decisions will give a boost to individuals' spirit as well as their progress. Each student's 'diet' of disciplines could be adjusted in full cognisance of all those responsible for his or her future. The reasons would be discussed and understood, and the adjustments supported by all concerned. Depending on the number of students, and providing there was a competent coordinator/administrator present, I believe most changes of direction or emphasis could be agreed and organised there and then.

Departments are made up of people. No hierarchy is inferred. On the contrary, if the organisation as a whole is to fulfil its intended function, each specialist has a definitive role to play. In a school of singing a specialist teacher must surely ask, 'How can I best do my job?' and 'How can it best contribute?' They broaden their own perspective and the usefulness and impact of their work by seeing how best it contributes to the aims of the whole of which they are a part. Equally, they will want to gauge what impact the school as a whole has on their ability to do good work. In what ways does it currently help or hinder their work?

Participating in a Vision

By far the most powerful force of attraction in organisations and in our individual lives is *meaning*.[7]

In the training of a singer, the merit of the different disciplines can only be judged by their contribution to the well-being of the student. As much as a school of singing can only be motivated by the love of singing itself, beautiful or truly healthy singing issues from the throat of a person, from their heart and soul. The more thorough the training, the more this is true.

I will come to the matters of 'consensus' and ethics in Part IV. Meanwhile, it is obvious that if we are going to participate in a vision, or a mission, we must agree on the idea behind it. This will reflect what we are dealing with: the 'bringing up' of a singer or a number of singers.

Seeing this vision and what it entails, however clearly, is not enough. For its materialisation it must be rooted in mutual aspirations, something that all are seeking, a shared dream and a strong desire to live it.

Teamwork

Living the vision implies a future, and this will need to be developed and refashioned between those who share it as they go along. A vision that is well grounded in the future, as far as that is possible, feeds the requisite awareness. Awareness illuminates and reinforces the vision. Achievement will come through shared clarity, not restraints. Participants in a lived vision acquire a collective intelligence which can only be to the benefit of all concerned.

Since no-one possesses the whole truth, teachers' shared sense of purpose must allow for collaboration and collective responsibility. After all, what I do may affect what my colleague does, and vice versa. It may help or hinder. The members of an organisation mutually influence and support each other.

Instead of taking total responsibility – or none – teachers can discuss what is needed, from whom, for instance to move a shared pupil on, or facilitate their participation. The achievement is shared and mutually endorsed, and the work, in which everyone is seen to participate, is more likely to be validated in the eyes of the student. Not bearing all the responsibility but being valued as part of a team for what you do best, can be more satisfying than going it alone.

Margaret Wheatley, in *Leadership and the New Science*, says,

> To make a system stronger, we need to create stronger relationships ... If a system is suffering, this indicates that it lacks sufficient access to itself. It might be lacking information, it might have lost clarity about who it is, it might have troubled relationships, it might be ignoring those who have valuable insights.[8]

The holistic perspective helps us to keep present and alert, to observe influences and work with them. By weighing up causes and effects, an organisation can anticipate future complications. Collaboration can make it much easier to find, consider, take on board and implement relevant new material or practices, stimulate its work and keep its vision alive.

Self-determination

Private teachers are often isolated in what they are endeavouring to do. Even when they join a conservatoire they can feel out of place or cut off from the action. They may just enter the building, give a lesson or a class and then leave. They may have little sense of how their expertise contributes, or it may not seem to be valued, especially if it is seen as something optional. In any case, they can feel, as students sometimes do, that they are merely a cog in a machine. They may have little say in what goes on.

Where this applies, it is a deplorable state of affairs. When teachers work in relative isolation they are limited in what they can offer a pupil. There is a boundary between them and their colleagues, and by extension between disciplines. Any adjustments for a pupil's growth are made mainly within the teacher's private and personal domain without due reference to the bigger educational picture.

I'm not suggesting that such teachers are stick-in-the-muds. I have met many at conferences who are conscientiously updating their knowledge base and experiencing new ways of working through workshops. But there is a world of difference between working on one's own and working with a group of people with a shared purpose that generates creative work across disciplines.

I personally have experienced the loneliness both of private teaching and being a member of an institution. But I have also had the privilege of working closely with colleagues of different complementary disciplines who share similar values in their approach to singers' development. The satisfaction gained by such collaborative work can be shared by all involved. This book could not have been written without this very positive experience.

Personal involvement in an organisation, in the sense of making a contribution, can instil a feeling both of belonging and of ownership. Belonging to a body in which we can grow because it is itself about growth. Ownership because our input is integral. The security and freedom that this provides makes it easier to open up to potentials.

In so far as we influence our pupils we are participating in their development. The influence is not only in the knowledge that we try to impart, but more importantly in how we do that. Whatever else the phrase 'Physician, heal thyself' may mean, it suggests that our ability to help others heal, or become whole, depends on our own fitness.[9] Fitness, of course, in the sense of having knowledge, experience and practical skills, but also in our attitude, as expressed in our actions, towards the idea of our own and another's individuation.

It is doubtful that we can help anyone else to achieve fitness if we have no sense of what fitness means, or no urge to achieve it ourselves. Our ability to help lies in our understanding of what benefits wholeness may bring, and in our grasp of the means whereby it can be gained. We cannot dictate or prescribe others' growth, only nourish it. We can only do this to the degree to which we are prepared to accompany them into their unknown. And of course we must respect students as maturing adults. In as much as teaching singing and learning to sing comprise processes of growth, the work is necessarily in a state of continuous change for both teacher and pupil.

> There is a path through change that leads to greater independence and resiliency. We dance along this path by maintaining a coherent identity and by honouring everybody's need for self-determination.[10]

We need to learn from one another, not in the sense of copying but in order to learn what's possible. 'Another's success encourages us to continue our own search for treasure'.[11]

> 'We see the world through who we are ... We refer to this self to determine what's important for us to notice'. This is not selfishness, but in the true holistic spirit of participation, '"self" includes awareness of those others it must relate to as part of its system'.[12]

PART IV
The Enshrining of Values

CHAPTER 20

Education

It is worth considering 'education' as applied to the particular needs of singers. Education in general seems broadly to be of two different types. One consists of amassing or being fed information. It may or may not have anything to do with what a person is interested in, and be only coincidentally to do with what a person is good at. The other consists of drawing out a person's potential – usually, but not always, applied to something that the individual wants to do and in which he or she shows promise. Examinations, or assessments of success, are based in the first type on what a person knows mentally, and in the second on what they can do or be.

Singing is experience

Descriptions of singing, however vivid or detailed, have little if anything to do with its experience. While good singing requires both knowledge and intelligence, and one can assume that a keen student will want to seek all relevant theoretical knowledge, it is nevertheless fundamentally a highly physical and also emotion-orientated activity. As trainers, tutors and organisers, therefore, we do well to distinguish between learning *about* singing, *about* voice or *about* vocal music, and learning *to* sing. Possessing all the theory and information available counts for very little if it is not incorporated in such a way that it materialises in practice.

I imagine that it is clear to most teachers, coaches and conductors that singing is nothing if not practical and expressive. Knowing what an appoggiatura is in theory is of no more use to a singer than knowing what an arabesque is in theory to a ballerina. It is abundantly clear that, whether we are referring to the rudiments of music, to rhythm, to the expression of meaning or emotion, to musical conventions, to presentation or communication, or to the voice *per se,* the work of becoming a singer, of achieving these ends, is, rather than an intellectual or academic pursuit, an experiential and personal one. Treating subjects theoretically or in isolation in the expectation that their practical relevance will be realised as soon as the singer begins to perform, that they will magically mesh together as and when applied, is a long-held but misguided notion. Time and time again it results in conflicting objectives and failure. The relevance of the different elements that make up a performance must be explored in a thoroughly practical manner. Their complementary nature must be experienced before it can be properly understood and put to use.

Given basic musical theory as a minimum entrance requirement, the subjects that are traditionally academic can, and I believe should, be learned practically. Performance practice, harmony and counterpoint, and even history can all be learned more usefully and effectively by being incorporated in practical work projects, whether in the course of musical coaching or in workshops from which all singers of all years can benefit and gain mutual clarification.

Carefully planned, such putting-into-practice sessions, together with dedicated recitals of songs and operatic excerpts, can help singers to gain historical perspective, experiencing first-hand how musical styles have developed, while exploring their peculiarities and nuances in different languages. The singing can be done by those sufficiently advanced vocally, say those in their third year, and be based on their current repertoire or standard repertoire. Gaps in the historical progression can be filled in with audio or audio-visual examples.

Harmony and counterpoint have so much to do with style and expression that, for a performer and interpreter, they only make sense when practised.

As for reading music, its benefits are debated. Many notable singers have done well without the ability. People often find learning to do it a confusing chore. An enjoyable, although by no means foolproof, way is associating intervals with already well-known tunes. The solfège system, at least the fixed 'doh' version, from what I have experienced of it in my students, is often more trouble than it's worth.

No doubt I was lucky in this respect, having first learnt to listen for and appreciate the harmonic and contrapuntal structures of music while singing the soprano line of various styles of music as a boy. Tuning was of the essence, and I learnt to read music through aural alignments both linear and vertical. While soloists might be said to have it easy because mainly they sing the 'tune', they often nevertheless suffer musically from a kind of harmonic disorientation. A judicious amount of madrigal singing or close-harmony (one per part) might be enjoyed to this end.

In the practical exploration of styles, it is important to remember our singing voice definitions. This applies particularly to the singing of styles generally regarded as pre- or post- bel canto, in which the singer might misguidedly inhibit or distort the voice for the sake of style, thus losing the integrity of the very instrument that enables them to recreate it.

Perhaps the problems of modern education lie mainly in the fact that

> We often underestimate our capacity to get the message through our senses – we try to analyse an impression before we fully experience it. Dalcroze ... deplored the school syllabus, in which music lessons caused children to '... read what they cannot understand, and write down what they have never learned or felt.' He believed the experience of the world must precede knowledge.[1]

Alan Watts says,

> Working rightly, the brain is the highest form of 'instinctual wisdom.'... The self-conscious brain ... is a disorder, and manifests itself in the acute feeling of separation between 'I' and my experience.[2]

Abbott Chrisman, acknowledging his debt to Dalcroze, refers to,

> ... a collective tendency to separate the sensory, mental, kinaesthetic, emotional, intellectual, and spiritual aspects of experience ... It's only when we attempt to analyse and structure experience that we make these separations that are essentially artificial.[3]

Rather than an analytical putting together of the above facets – the reductionist approach – there needs to be a process of sensory building up or balancing and of embodied expressive and aural awareness. It is the interrelatedness of music and movement, not their juxtaposition, which is the stuff of our work. This is what gives great singing its continuity or flow. It is also what makes it personal.

Potential

> The most basic of all needs is the need to actualize one's potentialities. Abraham Maslow[4]

Inextricably bound up with the need to know by experience, is the fact that we are dealing with individuals' potential. If, from the perspective of advanced training, a prospective student singer's potential is perceived in sufficient measure, the subsequent training will be one of releasing, developing and honing what effectively is already there. No amount of theorising or acumen can take the place of this all-involving experiential process.

It is often thought that a singer is in need of learning rudiments, and knowledge about what they are trying to do, when in reality it is the instrument which is at fault. A legato or a crescendo has to happen in order to exist. The requisite skills are there in potential and might be clearly imagined, a singer may know how something should go, or what they want to do interpretatively, but be unable to do it with any physical ease. Clever singers and techniques can 'get around' difficulties, or contrive what should by rights arise freely and naturally. That these singers or their techniques are deemed to be better than others is surely an illusion: in neither case has the singer's potential been realised. In neither case is the musical or emotional expression true. Deepak Chopra says, 'We have to move from the age of knowledge to the age of wisdom. If we radically shift our education to the unfolding of our potential, we will see a new world'.[5]

Authenticity

Education is a way of helping people to be what they are. Releasing, drawing out, fostering, nurturing, developing – these are all educational epithets. Through these means the student realises their talent and becomes empowered.

Part of the difficulty for a singer in adopting a holistic (complete and healthy) approach is the very thing that makes singing effective: authenticity. As Jung put it of people in general, 'the more conscious he becomes of his individuality, the more pronounced will be his difference from other subjects and the less he will come up to common expectations'.[6] We could take heart by observing that all the best singers are clearly individuals.

But we should also be careful to distinguish between 'individual' in the sense merely of being different, and 'authentic' in the sense of being oneself, and having a sense of integrity. This is more than being mentally aware. It is beyond feeling competent.

To achieve this status a singer, like an actor, needs to reach a point where their *body* and *voice* know themselves. 'Locking ourselves into a primarily conceptual framework interferes with our body's ability to function in its most vital way'.[7] An unbalanced voice is like an unbalanced mind – not aware of itself. Instead of facilitating efficient life it does the opposite.

Pupil-centred

There has been much talk in recent years of student-centred education. To my mind it is regrettable that this has had to become an issue. It would be illuminating to discover what an educational establishment is up to if it is *not* centred around its students? I suspect that the issue is actually about the disparity between individuals' needs, which are invariably to do with potentialisation, and schools' inability to cater for them.

If 'pupil-centred' means simply that a student has a choice in what subjects he or she studies, this seems only fair and just, at least from a certain age and with suitable advice to hand. But if it amounts to the student dictating the terms of the work and not necessarily co-operating in a suitable manner with those trying to help, one should ask why. What is lacking? On whose part? In any case, allowing the student to run the show makes a mockery of the whole concept of formal education.

Perhaps it is the formality, and by extension the educational 'levelling', which is at fault. One symptom of this is the increasing difficulty for singers to obtain work unless they have gained a recognised conservatory qualification. This has created a double bind. Many conservatories are unable to meet the needs of a trainee singer, at least as outlined in this book. Instead, students are obliged to study for a largely academic degree.

It is of course easier to organise a degree course and see twenty students through it than to cater for the needs of twenty individuals. But the fact is, a degree is of no use whatsoever to a casting director or conductor, and even less use to an audience who want to hear good singing and see a good performance.

Someone who has chosen to train to become a professional soloist would be well advised to obtain opinions from a number of unbiased professionals in the field as to their suitability, and get information 'from the horse's mouth' about what the profession requires by way of a comprehensive training and education. Before applying for a place at any school that purports to train professionals, they should ascertain exactly what it has to offer.

My observation is that not all suitable candidates for a degree course are suitable candidates for the profession – and that not all schools can provide what is required. If a school does provide a thorough training, the student should be safe in its hands. If not, the prospective student should beware. To complicate the issue, there are outstanding pupils who succeed whatever the quality or content of their education.

Responsibility

All of this raises the question of responsibility. The easiest answer is to say that it is shared. But few people see it that way. Typically, students think it is up to the institution to train them or give them what they want. Equally, the powers-that-be will relinquish responsibility if a student is deemed to be 'not up to the mark'. A head of department once referred to such students as 'natural wastage'!

In any case, the responsibility does not lie in turning out singers in the abstract, so many a year, so many courses completed with so many certificates to prove it. Nor does it lie in producing entertainers – performers who can do certain things, satisfy certain criteria with their voices.

To call a singer's job mere entertainment is to trivialise it. Some might think that a brilliant degree is superior to deeply moving singing. Others, the commercially minded, will treat singers as a commodity. All these avoid what is actually at stake.

The issue is broader and deeper. It begins with asking what those concerned with a singer's education (including the singer him- or herself) are actually dealing with. The answer is twofold: the singer as a person, and the singer's performance. How the singer *is* affects their performance – how authentic it is, how deep it goes and so on. The quality of a performance depends on the singer; not only on their aesthetic sense, but on how released their abilities, how free and responsive their instrument, how grounded, and so on.

If education is about realising potential, it is the responsibility of educational organisations to create the conditions conducive to this process. What they cannot do is the learning itself. Given conditions – situations, mechanisms, processes, exercises and so forth – students have the chance and the means of 'coming out', of making the most of themselves. But this is their responsibility.

Students must be helped to understand and believe that their singing comes from within themselves. It is not some kind of dress, or anything that anyone can give them. Descriptions of singing are not it, because words and measures don't of themselves give life.

Play

The things that are alive in singing – quality, art, communication – are not quantifiable. This is why play is such an important instrument of growth. Play is pre-wired behaviour which generates the experience that is a prerequisite for learning. Pre-set patterns of learning, modules, boxes to tick, etc., favour an outside-in approach, resulting in, at best, a colourful or extravagant costume. Creative, productive play, since it brings unplanned advantages, demands time, energy and risk-taking. The organisation can provide the circumstances and the time, the student must raise the energy and take the risks.

Studies that blindly waste time getting to 'know' a subject intellectually, to explain it, measure it and formulate it, end with the student being little the wiser on the practical-being-feeling level. Ironically, we often miss the obvious because we are intent upon analysing something before we do it. The essential experience and knowledge that accrues through doing, and the authenticity, trustworthiness and security that result, cannot be attained through the intellect.

'The biggest impediments to realizing the successes of which we dream are the limitations programmed into the subconscious'.[8] Play can go a long way towards short-circuiting this inhibitive programming.

Standards

With respect, audiences can be gullible. I believe they are often influenced by hype. Many seem to be easily 'wowed' – by a novel production, by loud high notes, or by the sheer fame of a singer. And yet, music and stories that are intrinsically beautiful or moving are likely to survive or even override the most crass production. If performers owe anything to their audience they owe the best that they can give. Furthermore, those responsible for artistic standards have a duty to inform and educate their audience.

When I say I think standards of singing are falling, I am referring to all the components of an artistic and meaningful performance. Responsible music schools share these considerations. They know that to promote great singing, the budding singers they are fostering need the instrument to satisfy the demands of great music.

Schools of singing do not have to live up to standards so much as create them. In creating high standards they and their charges are valuing the works that will be presented. In raising their game, singers pay due respect to colleagues with whom they expect to make music, and ultimately to their audience whose lives it is in their hands to transform.

Being Professional

All these considerations – being responsible and having standards – are the stuff of being professional. Good singing can be immeasurably satisfying to both the singer and those for whom they are singing. However, the singing world can be a tough place to be, especially if you want to do good work. From unscrupulous promoters, through bitchy rivalry and demeaning conditions, to disillusioned or disaffected colleagues, and peanuts for pay, the business is fraught with abuse and discouragement. A sensitive artist needs a thick skin!

A singer must be strong enough to maintain their integrity in the face of difficulties or indifference. They gain respect by husbanding their resources and not giving way to unreasonable demands. It is evident that many producers, directors and conductors have little understanding of what it means to be a singer – what is needed to sustain good work day after day. They can only benefit from being educated! A thoroughly well trained singer will be an attractive, dependable and versatile artist – with considerable bargaining power.

I cannot emphasise strongly enough how important it is for would-be professional artists to practise being professional right from the start of their training. From punctuality to preparation of material, from keeping fit to pacing work, from cultivating the art of singing to the consideration of colleagues.

How to manage a career, with all its ramifications, should be continually discussed – in groups, with tutors and visiting professionals – so that when the time comes to test the water it does not freeze or scald. How to deal with agents, how to network and advertise productively, how to prepare material and make the most of rehearsals, how to work with colleagues – all should be discussed and practised or simulated so that the issues become familiar and undaunting.

By encouraging performing of some kind from the start, a well-directed course will not only help potential singers to overcome their nerves but will foster each singer's uniqueness. It will prepare a singer for performance and auditions long before these become serious issues. Education should enable a singer to be independent in the sense of knowing what they need in order to support and sustain their career.

Teachers

Teachers must lead by example. If they are regularly late or, as I've come across a surprising number of times, don't turn up for classes or rehearsals, or if they do not take care of themselves, the message is clear – it doesn't matter. There should be no place for indifference, aloofness or self-serving, any more than there can be a place for incompetence. Lack of care is not only denial of responsibility but a betrayal of trust and a violation of expectations. A pupil needs affirmation and encouragement. The constant putting down of pupils that still prevails in many schools is an act of aggression.

Perhaps it is humility that marks out the best teachers. I don't mean being submissive, self-effacing, unambitious. Humility is the quality of recognising and acknowledging the truth. It gives strength – and brings it under control. It is the spirit in which something is given that imbues it with meaning and value.

The Search for Meaning

The work of re-discovering someone's singing voice is a humbling task. It is, in effect, searching for meaning. We should ask not only, 'Is this singing clear, direct, potent and expressive?' but 'What is this voice (itself) saying?' and 'What is it able to say?' Above all, 'Is this voice yet the voice (the whole/healthy voice) of this person?'

Finding our voice – metaphorically – is something we all need to do in order to express the meaning of our life. In literally finding our singing voice we tap into something that is able to express the depths of our humanity; this is why singing is so universally compelling. The opportunity to fully unlock the human singing voice is granted to very few. The message of this book is, in general terms, that we should not treat this privilege lightly, for its true satisfaction lies not so much in our own motivation as in the rare ability and opportunity to move the souls of others.

CHAPTER 21

Pupils

In human beings courage is necessary to make *being* and *becoming* possible. An assertion of the self, a commitment, is essential if the self is to have any reality.[1]

Rollo May

Selection

The world of professional singing is highly competitive. The way trainees are selected, therefore, needs more thorough consideration than it usually gets. It may be relatively easy to say that one singer has greater vocal or musical talent than another. It's more difficult to judge potential on a broader basis. And as any selection board would probably say, it is well-nigh impossible to judge whether a young singer has got what it takes to sustain a career as a professional soloist.

Furthermore, not all selectors assess candidates with the long term in mind. Some may be preoccupied with casting next year's opera. Some select candidates who look as though they can undertake the course rather than who are specially talented. I was horrified to be told by a head of department that places needed to be filled, and it therefore didn't matter if some students were 'sub-standard'. Didn't matter to whom?

Some adjudicators are prejudiced regarding voice or personality. I have 'rescued' a number of students who were pushed out of conservatories because they were considered 'difficult', when in fact they were either strong characters (great for the profession) who could stick up for themselves, or had 'problems' of a personal nature (solvable with time and suitable care) which were blocking their progress. These talented youngsters were not mouldable. If they were required to fit, why, one might ask, were they taken on in the first place? By way of mediation, adjudicating committees should be enlarged, with professors from departments other than singing, and even with some of the advanced students present.

I have often wondered how the suitability of a candidate can be judged through the singing of a couple of arias and sitting a simple theory paper. Of course, it can't. In Appendix 2a I have listed what I think should be the basic application requirements considering the demands of a high level course.

The next step – meeting the candidate – is crucial. A five-minute audition cannot possibly be adequate. They are, after all, going to dedicate the next few years of their life, at great financial cost, to equipping themselves for a tough, if rewarding, career. This is their dream. The question is, are they cut out for the real thing? Are they, in the first place, fit to embark on a demanding multi-disciplinary course?

How can such fitness be tested out?

1 Many questions might be asked an applicant. Why do they want to do this? Strong motivation is a must. What do they imagine are the demands of the profession? (Is the candidate in cloud cuckoo land?) What do they think about the course content, about hard work, keeping fit, opening up, having fun and working with colleagues – and a hundred other questions that will give clues to this young person's attitude and personality. Their own questions might be illuminating.
2 A thorough medical examination should be obligatory, and any history of drug abuse or physical or psychological trauma noted.
3 One-to-one work (such a crucial aspect of any course) could profitably be tried with tutors of different disciplines.
4 Interaction and working in a group needs to be tested too. This could be done in workshops of one kind or another. They might be carried out with teachers of different disciplines, with the assistance of pupils who are already in the school and who would benefit from their participation. Conducted over several days, secondary responses and reactions as well as first ones can be assessed.
5 Students could then be accepted provisionally for one term to see how they respond to a sustained version of the course. Some conditions, like getting fit, would be applied. This would

give them the opportunity to 'suss out' the school, and, to some extent, test their vocation. Candidates would only pay for this term if they proceeded beyond it. Such a thorough testing would be fair to all parties. It would benefit the individual, the established students, the school as a whole (and its reputation), and, not least, the profession.

6 Auditions, interviews and workshops should be videoed, so that there is something against which to measure real progress in all areas of work.

Two further ingredients are needed in order to proceed: (a) an agreement (at least a tacit one) that the school will provide and implement the services it purports to offer, and that the student will take full advantage of them, and (b) actual will and commitment, both collective and individual. After all, the various parties are going to be dependent on one another for the success of a shared venture.

Discipline

Some people still associate the word 'discipline' with submission – obedience, being controlled (by some external body), being punished and so on. Others associate it with being hard or insensitive. But if we look at what is behind the beautiful coordination of muscles belonging to a dancer or an athlete, discipline begins to take on a very positive, constructive and desirable meaning. Discipline does require will, but it also requires motivation and organisation.

Even if singing did not entail the training of muscles, it would be hard to refute the idea that to become a good singer demands planned work, the coordination of subjects throughout an extensive curriculum, and a great deal of self-control.

So far in this book I have defined the singing voice, outlined what studies I think are necessary in order to become a good professional soloist, and looked at some of the pitfalls that commonly get in the way of progress. A 'classical' singer, even only a competent one, needs to have a strong, flexible instrument, a command of languages, and musicianship of a high order.

The singer who wants to become really good must be musically as well as vocally talented, an imaginative artist, an accomplished actor and a respectful communicator. They need to be able to prepare their material, manage their career, get on with employers, work productively with colleagues, and not be camera-shy.

A student must exercise *self*-discipline. Many students don't know how to organise themselves or plan their work. Five years might seem plenty of time, but realistically and given so many unknowns inherent in a complex process there is no time to waste. Not being prepared (in all senses) for what lies ahead can adversely affect the work of all concerned. In professional terms this is not acceptable.

It is important to acquire good working habits from the start. If this means learning how to learn and how to conserve one's energy, so be it. Working habits impact on our performance generally.

One of the reasons for adopting the holistic perspective is that isolated subjects can seem of little, or else exaggerated, importance until they are laid out together. Having an overview enables us to see and understand with clarity how and to what extent the various facets of the work affect one another.

Working on subjects with insufficient appreciation of their value is inefficient. Knowing what we want, by understanding how it fits or contributes, can bring focus, economy and intuition to our efforts to achieve it. Teachers can help students to gain clarity and perspective.

Learning to learn is not just a matter of planning and staying cool. Nor is it a question merely of acquiring learning techniques. We can learn by exploring the *means* of working together and the *means* of relating to our material. It is also a question of gaining the capacity to recognise environmental and other working conditions – contexts and settings for example – in which desired changes might occur, and the ability to react or respond sensitively to them.

Students who have the courage to extend their perceived limits see new possibilities. Teachers help by presenting their pupils with challenges suitable to their stage of progress – neither too easy nor overwhelming. Surrounded by caring experts and other young singers on the same quest, a singer will get plenty of help and encouragement in pursuing their individual process. The 'definitions' of the singing voice that we have been exploring can serve, as I've explained, for progress referencing.

Students do well to understand that exercising is to do as much as anything with attitude. When exercising, we practise an attitude towards our work, our progress and, above all, towards ourselves. Similarly, when we sing we are exercising an *attitude* towards ourselves, our colleagues, our audience and, of course, to the music and words we are serving.

Singers often practise too long at a time, as though more is always better. This is an exercise in wishful thinking. At best some consolidation is achieved, which of course can give a feeling of security. Practising needs to be specific. It is easy to aim for targets prematurely, goals need to be realistic, building on present competence, not over-stretching.

Singers often have a better idea of what they want to achieve in the long term than what they need to attend to in the short term. But it's the latter that counts, since the voice needs to find its freedom and grow in strength if the singing is really to improve. Quality of work, rather than quantity, should be the aim.

A student singer is often working in the dark – doesn't know how best to exercise and cannot hear well enough to be sure that they are on track. While there is much to be said for experimentation, a great deal of time is wasted in pointless study.

A lot of time and energy can be saved by learning to listen, enlightening our ears and our effort. This should be each singing student's continuous quest. It can also be done in groups, using our recognition criteria:

- Before a voice comes into its own, ways of working can be explored and observed by all, with the aim of determining the soundness (or otherwise) of an individual's **voice structure**.
- Does the **music** flow through the singer's voice, responding naturally to their musicality, or is the music or the singing contrived? If the latter, what is happening in the voice that demonstrates this?
- Then, when it comes to singing music and words, observers can ask their ears simple but pertinent questions about **identity**. Do the person and the voice 'fit', or do they seem to be at odds? Discuss.
- What is the singer **communicating** – emotionally, physically, intellectually? Is it clear, genuine, direct? Does it

match the words? Is what is expressed faithful to or at one with the music? What might need to be done to improve the communication? Discuss.

In some schools a new student is assigned a companion from among those who already 'know the ropes' and who can help them to make the most of their time and energy and of what's on offer. Getting to know fellow-students (across years) early on is vital if a student is going to feel at home and benefit from the community ethos.

An atmosphere in which individuality, risk-taking, enjoyment and co-operation are the norm can hasten students' ability to work effectively and with confidence. A positive attitude generates energy, a constructive one – especially if shared – makes things happen.

CHAPTER 22

Co-operation

> What the world now needs is not competition but organisation and co-operation; all belief in the utility of competition has become an anachronism ... the emotions connected with it are the emotions of hostility and ruthlessness. The conception of society as an organic whole is very difficult for those whose minds have been steeped in competitive ideas. Ethically, therefore, no less than economically, it is undesirable to teach the young to be competitive.
>
> Bertrand Russell (1872–1970)[1]

Russell was born a year after the publication of Darwin's *The Descent of Man,* in which the great evolutionary scientist, contrary to the belief of many,

> ... pointed out how, in numberless animal societies ... struggle is replaced by co-operation, and how the substitution results in the development of intellectual and moral faculties which secure the species the best conditions for survival. He intimated that in such cases the fittest are not the physically strongest, nor the cunningest, but those who learn to combine so as mutually to support each other.[2]

Capitalising on a Myth

It is unfortunate that nature films so often feature the bloody dramas of predacious attacks rather than the more peaceful nourishment of life. Peace and love are considered mundane – less newsworthy than violence, scandal and the bizarre. The imbalance feeds the myth that we must fight and compete for what we want. It's a sad quirk of human nature that so-called 'competition' and all the negativity that goes with it makes for popular television, and a 'celebrity' (who almost by definition is competing for the limelight), especially one in trouble, keeps the hounds baying for months.

The myth of competition prevails partly through, as Steve Davis puts it, 'intellectual laziness':

> How much simpler and easier it is to detect and describe stand-out examples of competition, than it is to find the subtle intricacies of mutual aid and support that flow unceasingly but unnoticed, just below the surface of every life.[3]

The good news is that there are many who, far from being intellectually lazy, are interested in the better, more positive side of humanity. Companies around the globe, for example, are realising the value of treating their personnel as equally important in the running and policy-making of their organisation. While competition tends to create aggression and resentment, the co-operative ethos, as well as paying dividends, promotes well-being and enjoyment.

Empty Competition

There is sufficient evidence in our field to show that competition is meaningless. First, singers are unique in what they have to offer artistically. If only this fact were recognised and acted upon, performances of singing might be more interesting and exciting. As we have seen, uniqueness is not so easy to foster or encourage. Nevertheless it should be a factor of the greatest influence in a singer's training. Second, the work of learning to sing is multi-disciplinary and *requires* co-operation between all those involved if it is to be maximally effective. Third, singers, like all musicians, have to work together for the success of a musical venture. Its success is theirs collectively. It is in their interests to support and encourage others' singing. Whether at school or on stage, teamwork in the cause of creating 'a work of art' is beneficial all round.

When students' work is treated as though it must adhere to a standard or pre-determined model, to which everyone must conform, or a marked-out track along which everyone must proceed, they understandably feel threatened by those around them. How can they make their mark or be 'better' than the next person, or curry favour with those who might give them a good mark or a job? Vying for the limelight can entail nudging others out of it – or other unscrupulous behaviours. It can also make people cut corners in order to get there quicker.

Back in June 2007 I enjoyed reading an article by Stephen Moss about the violinist Ruth Palmer. Moss writes,

> The key thing in so competitive a world, she [Ruth Palmer] says, is to be a 'distinctive musical personality'. That may at first confuse promoters ... who can't pigeonhole you ... but it's the only way to build a long-term career.[4]

For Palmer, what was important was not being better but different. How much more so for a singer. Self-identity, as in the distinctive instrument, is the basis of this long-term career-building.

Advantages of Mutual Support

When the group is avowedly one of individuals helping each other to make the best of themselves by working with and supporting each other's individuality, we have the makings of seriously helpful group-learning dynamics. 'Who is better?' doesn't enter into the equation. If the purpose is to connect or reconnect participants with themselves, with each other, with their materials and skills, in their unique ways, everybody stands to better themselves. Individuals learn to 'do their thing' in relation to others doing theirs – working together creatively and effectively, while maintaining mutual respect. Interestingly, the word 'competence' comes from the same root as 'compete', but its sense is that of being fit, proper or qualified.

Solo singers make music in relation both to themselves and to their accompanist or music-making colleagues. They do this for the entertainment, edification or spiritual transformation of their audience. A singer who is there merely for their own glorification is indeed behaving like a selfish competitor. They gain nothing of value. Their audience loses out on what should be a life-enhancing experience.

The culture of co-operation and mutual support (many would call it instinct – since it appears that we are hard-wired to be sociable and communal beings) is first experienced in the family – a microcosm of the community at large. And it may be here that things begin to go wrong when they do. Genes, we now know, need the right environment or triggers to come into their own. A dysfunctional family will probably be a repressed one, or one in which individuals have to vie for affection or position. By contrast a happy family, like any loving relationship, will be one in which each individual is encouraged and empowered by the others.

Not Conformity

Sometimes people think of co-operation as passive conformity. Toeing the line in this sense can undermine individuality and even lead to inertia. The co-operation that I am talking about is the nurturing, investigating, growing and becoming which should be the stuff of any functional community. In helping others (whether it be teaching, learning together or singing for an audience) we give birth to ourselves. 'The stronger students helped the weaker and, in so doing, all became stronger. Their harmony was both surprising and beautiful to observe'.[5]

This mutual help completes the holistic cycle. We come into relation with ourselves (with the help of others) – exploring, training, realising our potential; and in so doing we are enabled to relate with others and be of service to *them*. This is a creative process – what living is about, a 'bringing forth' so that all can flourish. There is no place for aggression, inertia or even complacency.

Meaning

In learning to sing, and in the activity of singing, people connect through inner realisations, values, behaviours and motivations. These shared patterns of behaviour are an essential requirement for the generation of meaning and well-being. This is why the work and the process has to be *with* Nature, rather than the imposition of a way of singing which is at odds with Nature. Our disconnection from the natural muddies meaning or removes it altogether. Wellness does not come about through pressure, anxiety and resentment – the bedfellows of competition – which simply squander the energy that would be better spent on disseminating and enjoying good health.

We can be human only together. Well-being begets well-being, and this is as much a practice as an attitude. But it goes deeper. The psychiatrist Anthony Storr, in *The School of Genius,* writes about the maturing of personality:

> If by personality we mean a man's 'distinctive personal character' we are obliged to recognize that we can only conceive of such an entity in terms of contrasting it with other

personal characters ... A man in isolation is a collective man, a man without individuality.[6]

Talent

Talent is of little use if it is squandered, 'snapped up' too soon, finds itself in the wrong hands, or is not supported and encouraged. Of the many parables of Jesus Christ that I learned early in life, one that impressed me most seems apt in this moment:

> ***The Sower***
>
> 'Hearken; Behold, there went out a sower to sow:
>
> And it came to pass, as he sowed, some fell by the wayside, and the fowls of the air came and devoured it up.
>
> And some fell on stony ground, where it had not much earth; and immediately it sprang up, because it had no depth of earth:
>
> But when the sun was up, it was scorched; and because it had no root, it withered away.
>
> And some fell among thorns, and the thorns grew up, and choked it, and it yielded no fruit.
>
> And other fell on good ground, and did yield fruit that sprang up and increased; and brought forth, some thirty, and some sixty, some an hundred.
>
> And he said unto them, He that hath ears to hear, let him hear'. Mark 4: 3–9 [7]

Here, the seed and its fate refer of course to 'the Word of God'. However, the parable is so nicely applicable to what happens or doesn't happen to God-given talent, that I hope I will be forgiven for the misappropriation.

Another aspect of the nurturing of a singer's talent might be mentioned in relation to group-work. Without cultural roots the learning of music is liable to be little better than competent reproduction. In the absence of a deeply rooted cultural upbringing, individuals might benefit from the school group acting as a cultural family or 'melting pot'. Ideas and experiences, and knowledge of a cultural nature, might be shared in discussion and in practical ways.

Furthermore, students from different countries might enlighten each other about the roots of their own musical heritage. This exercise could be broadened, brought alive and underpinned by group visits to galleries, museums and concert halls. Members of the group might take it in turns to plan pertinent projects or specific objectives around such visits, which could then be creatively and enjoyably shared by all students. Two or three such projects might be presented each term, perhaps in the context of 'performing experience' (see Chapter 13).

Further advantages of working together

Working together, students have a better chance of broadening their knowledge and horizons. Competition and possessiveness can inhibit growth and expansion. Open discussions – about voice, the singer's art, the world of music – and appraisals of performances, can help singers to open up and develop what they have, and should be an organised part of a regular, healthy educational diet.

Many of the difficulties and worries of becoming a singer – which, for a student in subjective isolation, can seem insuperable – are common to all, and might be alleviated or lightened when shared. Being confined to the peer group is not realistic in terms of the world at large, so some groups can benefit from being mixed across years. Older students can support younger ones.

We learn to learn together. Children do it naturally and unselfconsciously through play and observation. As adult students we can still observe responses and reactions in others, and receive constructive feedback. We are all in much the same position – of working things out, undergoing a process, aiming to do well and so forth. But we often cannot see ourselves in the way others can. And our business is to be seen and heard – by others.

So it's important to overcome our inhibitions and capitalise on growing self-awareness. Our individual discoveries may or may not be of use to someone else, but anyone who has undergone group therapy will know that it is surprising how many 'unspoken' difficulties, anxieties and experiences we share with others. Bringing them out in the open can help someone, or even the whole group. Co-operation depends on mutual trust, and this may take time to develop. It is clear to me that many students are simply not granted the time, let alone the caring conditions, that they need. They stand to remain alienated from themselves and others for the rest of their lives.

While competitors might study one another's 'form', I suspect that they rarely listen to each other. Wiser students become more objective through cultivating acceptance, patience and compassion, and by sharing experiences and listening to one another. Further, through a process of participation and validation, they might even transcend objectivity and thereby raise each other's game.

Co-operating in the relating/creating sense – whether this is in a one-to-one situation, between departments, in class, or within the organisation as a whole – will help to give young singers the confidence to negotiate their position and their practice when it comes to the hard realities of what at present is a world of skewed values.

Respect

Mutual respect practically defines civilised society. It's more or less the same as treating others how you would like to be treated yourself. Unlike toleration (of others' differences, for example) or even admiration (which is sometimes the face of envy), respect is constructive. It sees others as being made of the same stuff as ourselves, and it looks for their good.

> Once we are committed to the holistic path, we are ever learning to honour all parts of ourselves, to honour others, and to honour spirit and nature. This is the path ... of relationship. And this honouring of respectful relationship is, almost by definition, the antidote to addiction and alienation.[8]

Getting away from it all

Stanislavski talked of the 'close and nervous atmosphere of the stage that always spoils peaceful relations' when 'close and friendly relations are necessary for true co-operation in art'. He had a solution – meeting in nature, 'common work on the soil', fresh air, 'the light of the sun', which he thought 'would aid in the creation of unison' among the students of his Studio. All this, of course, comprised an extracurricular summer project. 'This summer life in the lap of nature was not in vain. It ... brought the actors ... very close to each other'.[9] Stanislavski's purpose lay in getting his pupils away from the rarefied atmosphere of high art and getting them to connect in more mundane circumstances.

The social cohesion that singing students' work can engender, and the fun derived from it – through dancing, languages, outings and so on – I consider important for the generation of a healthy working ethos. While it may not be possible to 'work on the soil', extracurricular group activities which require a certain amount of shared organisation, teamwork and creativity – football, music camps and the like – are almost bound to be beneficial to students who need to work and develop together.

There are aspects of the singer's personal life which might also call for mutual support. I am referring to three in particular, more important than most singers seem to think:

1) The hydration of the body's system as a whole beneficially affects the voice. Drinking water needs to be a regular habit. Students can help each other to acquire and stick to this essential good health habit.
2) Given our modern, technological culture, attention to posture needs continual practice. Posture affects the efficient use of the body and affects its health in general. For singers, crucially, it affects breathing and the position of the larynx. Naturally, singers want to be healthy and sing well, but they might need encouragement to hold their heads high on a regular basis.
3) The need for healthy speech. Normal speaking is done on a partially collapsed singing voice – not a good thing to practise! Speaking healthily requires effort in the sense of sustained animation– more along the lines of singing in fact. For anyone not used to it, this increased aliveness can entail a change of vocal identity that might, at least to start with, be embarrassing among friends and family. But they, together with colleagues, are the very people who are best placed to applaud your efforts to be more clearly articulate.

Co-operation, born of mutual respect and the joy of creating, can bring home to individuals not only the worth of their work but their own intrinsic value. From this, goodwill naturally unfolds. The emphasis can shift from 'who is best?' to 'what is the best we can give?'

CHAPTER 23

Excellence

I have often wondered what in our context people actually mean by excellence. Even 'advanced' is baffling. So-called 'centres of excellence' and 'advanced courses' don't necessarily make us any the wiser. If a school is designed for excellence, or a course is described as 'advanced', we might assume that those who are taken on as students are thought capable of attaining excellence or working in an 'advanced' way. But this is a nebulous idea. Excellence as a crowning of every singer's training and education seems to be an elusive concept.

Masterclasses

Fifty years ago a 'masterclass' was conducted by a universally recognised Master, someone distant by today's standards, but nonetheless worthy of respect. Their greatest asset was arguably their insight – the fruit of the explorations and experiences that made them a great artist and interpreter.

Nowadays, any professional singer, or teacher who is sufficiently well known in his or her circle, can conduct a masterclasses. No qualifications are needed. I have witnessed some that, in terms at least of vocal knowledge, were frankly amateurish. In others the 'Master' appeared to be 'masterful', but did not need to be because the standard of participants was modest, and it was easy to improve on what they were doing. Equally, there have been experienced teachers or practitioners who, surprisingly, have been at a loss as to what to say or do. Either way, the Master has been applauded, and the pupil armed with something to add to their CV.

Singers' programme notes with lists of tutors can raise expectations. But when the singer opens his or her mouth you find yourself looking at the list again and wondering if you've got the right singer. Were the 'masters' incompetent or was the pupil not ready to benefit from their expertise? I think it takes two masters to make a good masterclass.

Certainly what is common to many masterclasses is an absence of excellence in the results. My contention is not that we have lost interest in excellence – the exquisite, the deeply moving, the truly transcending work of art – but that we have lost sight of the means of reaching it. If we do come across it in singing, it's by chance – and we marvel – but excellence remains the exception rather than the rule.

Barriers to Excellence

Elisabeth Schwarzkopf was a prolific conductor of masterclasses. Vespasiano says, 'she could be less than patient and even somewhat harsh particularly with singers who were vocally immature, technically insecure or musically unprepared'. He then quotes Renée Fleming as saying of her own experience with Schwarzkopf, 'Interpretatively it was phenomenal, it was the vocal side of things that was hard'.[1] In many cases that I have observed, 'masters', in dealing with 'interpretation' (often based, it must be said, on their own vocal quirks or proclivities), have demanded something for which the student voice has not been ready. The expectations have been unreasonable. An approximation has then been simulated, or an imitation attempted, neither of which has fitted or 'belonged to' the singer. Or else the singer has been made to look foolish.

There are three basic reasons why excellence is so rarely achieved:

1 Lack of vocal foundation. In this case artistic refinement and true mastery are unachievable. How can a student be prepared for a masterclass if he or she is 'vocally immature' or 'technically insecure'?

2 Insufficient time devoted to the finer details of the art during singers training and education. In many instances where excellence might have been attained, as soon as the singer is, to put it crudely, 'a marketable commodity', they are whisked off to market.

3 Insufficient knowledge of what excellence is and how to achieve it. This may be the result of chronic underestimation of what the human singing voice is capable of.

Students of singing who complete their course are rarely ready for advanced work, if by advanced we mean of a high artistic order. Judging by many 'final recitals', most are nowhere near fulfilling their vocal and performing potential. I should add in passing that the so-called 'master's degree' is usually not indicative of mastery in any practical sense.

If conditions or expertise have been lacking in a singer's training centre, or there are holes in the curriculum, or they have been misled as to their suitability in the first place, it is hardly their fault – but a tragic deceit and waste all the same.

Without skill, and the knowledge to accompany it, singing can deteriorate into what Husler and Rodd-Marling describe as 'intuitive-intellectualism', which 'nearly always leads to a helpless and unhealthy "naturalism"'. They characterise 'naturalism', as making music 'with greater or lesser passion on an instrument afflicted with all, or at least a great number, of the deficiencies of the normal vocal organ'.[2] This type of vocalism is common among enthusiastic amateurs, seems to be the norm among pop singers, and is sometimes labelled 'speech-level' singing. 'Classical' singers resort to it through frustration or ignorance.

Raising the Game

While the cultivation of excellence is primarily up to the singer, there are two sides to the excellence equation – what is going on within the singer, and positive external influences. The singer needs to be prepared in body and outlook, aware of their progress and cognisant of what comprises the basis of excellence. They need to seek out high-level instruction or coaching at the right time, having already immersed themselves in excellence in all its forms: in London at the Royal Ballet, for example, at the Victoria and Albert Museum, or the Wigmore Hall.

Foundations of Excellence

Excellence is not something optional or stuck onto the top of training, like cherries on a cake, but the continuation of the deepening and refining processes that have been underway for years – *singing built and refined on sure foundations.* Given suitable conditions, suitable promise – which crucially includes a positive attitude – and a foundational training, students at a school devoted to the art of beautiful singing are making a sound investment in their future and, indeed, the future of singing.

Excellence is not a fixed point or level. It is rather a state of being or development that makes for ever-changing expressivity, artistry and communication. Now is the time to capitalise on what true masters of style and interpretation have to offer.

The approach road needs to have been sound all along. This is where the interdisciplinary work – its openness, cross-checking and integration – really counts. All the skills have been introduced to each other, are making sense of each other, co-ordinating without fuss, and leading smoothly and solidly into the sphere of professional performance. By this stage, a high degree of empowerment, confidence and authenticity should be in place. Creativity, once felt as risky or threatening, has now become a compelling aim and exciting force.

Pre-requisites for forging ahead are:

a) The voice must have been freed to such a degree that its inherent musical and expressive skills are responsive and there is no longer a felt need for manipulation.
b) A high level of language proficiency must have been reached.
c) Similarly, a high degree of musicianship must have been incorporated.
d) The body must be free of constraint and, like the voice, in a responsive state.
e) The student must have grown sufficiently in maturity to want to become an artist ready to assume the responsibilities of a communicator.

Excellence in our field is a question not of accurate reproduction or any kind of glitter, but of appropriate response to the singer's performance material. The outcome of this intelligent and empathic relationship is enjoyment derived from its properties of liberation and order.

As this equal, respectful relationship (between singer and material) is realised, only the tiniest of details of music and language are likely to need correcting. Since the training has facilitated the expression of mind, body, emotion and spirit combined, the aspects of the singer's performance that can now be considered are subtleties of communication and vocal artistry. Questions of style, meaning and interpretation can be explored and implemented with imaginative and spontaneous ease.

The natural oneness of instrument and performer makes for the ease and potency of a singer's performance. In this respect a singer has it easier than other instrumentalists. The performer is made up of feelings, imagination, understanding, memory and so on; their voice merely reflects what is going on in these 'inner departments'. A large part of being a vocal artist is, therefore, the appositeness of departmental activity. This is a question of comprehension of material and its preparation – familiar processes by this stage of advanced training and education.

Articulation

As the singer and voice draw closer together, new sensitivities arise and old ones are sharpened. These bring with them 'new powers of articulation, thus we acquire new powers of creation. Sensitivity, therefore, holds the key ... to the understanding of ourselves'.[3]

Of my list of 'pre-requisites' above, the most crucial is the first (vocal response), if only because true excellence, as the bel canto school knew only too well, is possible only with the 'mixed voice'. Let me remind the reader that this combining of the stretching and tensing processes depends on the finest and most complex 'part' of the voice – the 'edge mechanism' (as described in Chapter 2), which at every pitch equally is a physiological bridge between the two tonal poles. It is not for nothing that excellence can only be arrived at after long training, for this defining fusional element is usually the most difficult to arouse and sustain.

This intricate 'edge mechanism', having been patiently approached from day one – in the best studios at least – but coming into its own relatively late, is easily weakened or blunted by thickening or weighting the sound or by any unduly effortful singing. The mixed voice needs to be practised until it is sufficiently robust and sufficiently appreciated. From then on, excellence needs to be 'continually sought out', 'taken care of', practiced and indeed 'savoured'.

There is great reward in the seeking and savouring of this miraculous pinnacle of artistic and expressive activity, since it makes for flow, precision, tonal stability, a colourful palette, ease of dynamic variation, as well as the articulation of pitches and the conveyance of feelings – all the excellent things in fact that a budding artist might desire – with a minimum of effort and a negligible expenditure of breath.

Integration

The definition of integration that is most apt just now is the psychological one: 'the combination of the diverse elements of perception etc., in a personality'.[4] Apt because we are talking about the combining of perceptions – musical, theatrical, aesthetic, intellectual, tonal, etc. – that might at first glance seem diverse and are certainly varied, and which together inform and create the 'singing personality'. Conversely, the individual personality is brought to bear on these various perceptions. This is how we can describe someone as a fine singer according to certain specific indicators (see Chapters 3–6) and at the same time experience their singing as quite unique. The perceptions listed, and others besides, have been sharpening and informing one another within the singer for several years so that, when the instrument is itself sufficiently integrated, dynamic, artistic interchange can begin to occur between the various elements without fuss or even bidding.

Creativity

> '… systems (not least organisms) are individuated by creative, interpenetrative interfaces rather than by limiting boundaries.' 'What we thought of as boundaries and limits become zones of interchange.' 'Imagine yourself as having an interface between intellect and body. The interface is where things really happen.'[5]

Although a singer needs to be intelligent to understand, organise or modify material from an intellectual standpoint, creativity is not a question of rational or conscious ingenuity. It emerges from many layers of mind, many zones of interchange (by means of those interpenetrative interfaces) that run between the conscious and unconscious mind. It is as well that this is so. Even if the various 'ingredients' of our creation could be deliberately mixed, the processes of the heart cannot be expressed in any rational way. Isadora Duncan said of her dancing, 'If I could tell you what it meant, there would be no point in dancing it'.

> Bateson suggests that she means, 'This is a particular sort of partly unconscious message. Let us engage in this particular sort of partly unconscious communication,' or 'This is a message about the interface between conscious and unconscious.' Skill, he says, always carries this message.[6]

We underestimate the singing voice's capacity to express the inexpressible. Singing is metaphorical as well as verbal, and needs to be appreciated as such. Duncan also said somewhere, 'The dancer's body is simply the luminous manifestation of the soul'. Some have described the singing voice as the voice of the soul; I would qualify this by saying that what the voice can articulate of the soul depends upon its degree of freedom. The singing voice is also the voice of mystery – human mystery. Such things can be revealed or witnessed, but not named. They can be allowed or released, as in Duncan's dancing, but not explained or demonstrated.

Transcendence

Perhaps it is our desire to name and explain everything that keeps us at 'the controls'. Whatever the reason, not giving the singing voice its freedom, not trusting it, cuts us off from its true creative and illuminating nature. We cannot 'nurture or take sustenance from a spirit that remains unspoken'.[7] It is only when the voice loses its self-consciousness (is restored to its natural self) that it can act as the conduit through which the soul can speak. Then we discover new things in ourselves. Herein lies the fruit of the creative spirit and its power of transcendence.

Technique or Balance?

Before we move on to 'craftsmanship', let me expand a little on 'letting go', for 'no craft will tolerate tied hands'.

Whenever two things are out of balance, neither is free, and there is undue strain. There are two ways of dealing with unbalanced forces in the singing voice: either by restoring the balance, and so automatically alleviating strain and releasing instrumental and expressive possibilities, or by means of compensation, which at best will reduce the strain and its limiting effects.

Techniques often amount to replacing one imbalance with another. The strain is lifted because the imbalance has shifted elsewhere, but the improvement in holistic terms (where any imbalance affects the efficiency of the whole) is illusory. Sooner or later, the new imbalance is betrayed in some other area of the singer's performance. Strain sets in once more.

To complicate matters, techniques can be practised to the point at which they are no longer felt as awkward or limiting in themselves. Some techniques make things easier for some people, or, according to taste, help them to produce an aesthetically interesting or pleasing effect. This result might be called 'better' singing, but applied techniques of this sort can dislocate singers from their own freedom, identity and fulfilment.

Young singers are faced with time-pressures to 'produce', to achieve specific objectives, to compete and so on, as though these things were measurable marks of progress.

> If you choose to participate in the rat-race and cut-throat competition, only strife will follow; and the shattering of peace within. If you think that you cannot avoid the rat-race and competition, it simply means that you are not ready to choose a way of life that leads to the integrated self.[8]

The alternative, however, may not be immediately attractive – five years of scrupulous and wide-ranging daily training, which seems at first to produce very little, and doesn't favour competition. Improvements are noticed here and there but don't necessarily amount to the kind of results that are hoped for, until eventually they become productive, not through quantitative accumulation but through qualitative combination. Meanwhile, there can be an unsettling change of identity, until the singer and voice begin to recognise each other, a feeling of losing control until it is replaced by something more grounded, and a growing sense of vulnerability, until vulnerability is perceived as a strength.

In a school in which the work is tailor-made to the individual, and there is all-round support, where it is normal not to be working to unrealistic deadlines, nor measuring progress by reckoning who is more accurate, quicker, louder, more glamorous – in a school where conditions favour poise and pleasure as well as fitness and hard work, students might relax and, with their sleeves rolled up, simply concentrate on one enjoyable mindful step at a time.

Those wonderful vocal folds, which each of us possesses, reveal between their functional extremes an unimaginably varied palette of colours. The balanced strength of these extremes is also responsible for a voice's stability, resilience and longevity. The tool that monitors and sustains this critical balance is the ear, which has, if the training has proceeded well, resumed its natural function. The singer's skill lies in matching singing to voice, learning to make the most of it while respecting its natural limits. This is a facet of excellence which through constant guidance and vigilance has to be learned. Many singers falter or fail because they are unable to balance or husband their resources.

Craft

Like any creative artist who values depth and meaning above superficial effect, a singer needs to be a craftsman or craftswoman. In our imaginary school, students have been doing what craftsmen do: getting to know their materials and engaging with them. Music, physical expression, language and languages, performance skills and so on, have all been explored, developed, interrelated and enjoyed through daily play, experimentation, risk-taking, observation and meticulous hard work.

In singing, our materials are also our tools. We use them not by manipulation but by incorporating them, becoming aware of how they potentialise one another. For example, the singing instrument is fired by emotion, but also facilitates its expression.

The small but potent centre of musical and expressive events is both the singer's route to self-discovery and the channel through which their innermost feelings can be shared with others. The holistic achievement is manifest in the singer's ability to benefit from and capitalise on this two-way communication – a simultaneous flowing inwards to the self and outwards to the other, the listener.

This is the present-in-action that is achieved through balance, the drawing-in even as we breathe out, a dynamic state of flux between memory and imagination. With this active presence the listener's attention is captured and they are drawn into the singer's inner experience. This is the holistic quality of participation – of shared depth and meaning, achieved through an intimate acquaintance with the materials to hand.

One might imagine that being present would make the singer too conscious of what they have to do. If it were a matter of projecting the voice, articulating the words, 'engineering' marks of expression, or demonstrating emotion, the singer might try to do things self-consciously in order to perform. Their attention would wander from one tricky moment to the next. But a singer who has devoted years to intensive work in all 'departments', and experienced their interdependence, will have discovered that the controls they were used to exerting over the voice were antithetical to creativity. They will not try to be 'technical' or 'perfect', but will focus on more important things: shapes and emphases, fullness and fineness, sweeping lines and delicately turned details, dynamic ebbing and flowing – gestures of the sure craftsman.

Beautiful singing is only made possible when all facets are free to become one – to integrate. When the singing voice is whole, all its facets, rolled into one, respond in concert to the complex makeup of our on-going intentions. Thanks to its incredible design, this coalescence is manifest in a single sung tone, emanating from the tiniest imaginable source. Thus we get a large return for a relatively small effort.

Imagination

What is there then for the singer to do? What actually triggers this all-in-one phenomenon, clearly and unselfconsciously? What amalgamates the singer's material and conveys its continually changing sense with such ease and economical clarity? It is the imagination, which 'has the power to assemble the elements of our experience into coherent, lively wholes: it has a gift'.[9] In singing, the stuff of our musical and expressive intentions combines as though it consisted of mixable fluids – constantly changing in relative proportions – to which the voice in its highly sensitive way instantly responds. Put another way, what triggers the voice to sing is what calls it forth: joy or sadness, music, poetry, drama, or simply the desire to communicate. All these set it going by means of imagination without our conscious interference.

Those who are used to the idea that singing is achieved technically, are often also those who neglect imagination. So much of our technologically-driven modern life is presented on a plate or flung in our face, little is left to imagine. Touch a screen and there it is. But imagination is fertile because it searches, reaches out in all directions, and is free to roam. Technique, dogma and rigid rules all dim imagination's light or dampen its delight in adventure.

Luckily, singers have plenty of evocative and inspiring material to play with. Performing and presentation classes lend themselves to creative imagination. Clowning too! Literature provides a mine of stimulating material. A singer's aural imagination must be cultivated along with musical perception. There is no better way to cultivate aural imagination and musical perception than by being physically alive and aware.

Musical and expressive qualities need to be embodied. This is especially true for vocal musicians. With a largely practical curriculum, a student learns to respond to a score through the body, which is after all the music-making instrument. Singers need to be true masters of vocalising before their music can fully benefit from imagination.

But beware: 'There is nothing more dreadful than imagination without taste…' Goethe.[10]

Appreciation and Sensitivity

Both imagination and the generation of excellence, in the sense of quality, can be aided by studying the properties and characteristics of beautifully crafted objects or performances. In architecture, dance, theatre, sculpture, painting and poetry we can learn about rhythm, structure, unity, simplicity, vividness, authority, economy of means, sensitivity, delicacy, clarity, grace, texture, timbre, elegance, emphasis, sensuousness, flow, grandeur, suspense, brilliance, exoticism, subtlety, shading, precision, proportion, contrast, depth, agility, and so on. Curiosity begins the quest for quality, and marvelling begins to inspire and stimulate our imagination.

Imagination, bearing on other art objects or experiences, seems to initiate a process of osmosis, whereby they become a part of our inner life and experience. In this way, when it comes to singing, there is a fund of 'embodied' images, memories, impressions and qualities ready to be drawn upon and imaginatively mixed.

Observing and contemplating other arts through the senses of sight, sound and touch, we learn to discern what is 'good'. Observing nature in its form, movement and colour, its intimacy and intricacy, is another way. It is the coming together of various characteristics that brings quality. The recent London Olympics amply demonstrated this in the relationship of efficiency with strength with timing with elegance.

Maturity

A singer does not have to strive for excellence. Nor does it just come about; there is no guarantee built into the vocal folds. Excellence may be the fruit of desire, but desire on its own is not enough. It is the person who *cares* that gets to see real quality and work with it. Love of their material makes a performer want to make the most of it. It is to be expected that a school for beautiful singing, with its caring ethos, will deepen that love.

Maturity on the part of an organisation is reflected in the co-operative and 'relational' nature of its approach, and in the cultivation of a professional attitude from the outset. In operating a flexible curriculum and timetable, it recognises the need of the individual to individuate as a moral imperative. The singer, through their commitment, curiosity, desire to learn, practice and perseverance, can mature naturally. No longer separated from their material and its realisation, the individuated person and the fully-fledged performer have become one and the same. 'In inner development, mastery and power accrue only to that artist who is worthy of his art'.[11]

It is important to understand that the process has not been one of taking something on, as in acquiring skills or a suitable persona, but rather of transformation, the results of which accord with the definitions in Part I. Through restoring the voice's *natural singing structure* we release its innate skills. The singer can make *beautiful music,* having the instrument designed as though for the purpose. Any 'mixing and matching' of skills is no longer the province of artfulness but the natural consequence of the *genuine expressivity* of the singer. Emotion, instead of being self-consciously discharged, is expressed, because what converts it into sound is free. The singer has the economy of means and the authority of genuine confidence to keep it simple, and no longer needs to flaunt expertise. The ego is no longer an impediment to sharing: 'The work of the artist can only come to its powers in the world when it moves beyond the self as a gift.'[12] The mature artist assumes their role of *communicator.*

Having reached a level at which singing and artistry feed maturity and vice versa, the singer is at the beginning of a further process of 'maturation in communication'. This process involves both the singer and audience in greater depths of emotional expression and meaning:

> The artist appeals ... to that in us which is a gift and not an acquisition – and, therefore, more permanently enduring. He speaks to our capacity for delight and wonder, to the sense of mystery surrounding our lives; to our sense of pity, and beauty, and pain; to the latent feeling of fellowship with all creation – to the subtle but invincible conviction of solidarity that knits together the loneliness of innumerable hearts, to the solidarity ... which binds together all humanity.[13]

CHAPTER 24

Measures of Progress

In the field of singers' training, as elsewhere in education, assessment is a contentious issue.

How a student's progress is measured (in any field) must surely depend on a) what he or she is trying to achieve and b) what constitutes progress to that end. So much seems obvious. Unfortunately, in terms of performing skills at least, neither of these criteria is very helpful, let alone self-explanatory. Making courses more academic, and therefore more theoretically explicit, is to my mind a misrepresentation of both the ends and the means.

As I see it, a would-be professional vocal soloist has four interwoven objectives:

1. The releasing and developing of the instrument;
2. Learning how to make music with it;
3. Finding an individual voice, metaphorically as well as literally;
4. Learning how to communicate as an artist.

These objectives are peculiar to the vocal artist and are all fundamentally experiential.

The types of work enumerated in Part II are what I consider necessary for the attainment of these objectives, given suitable conditions and sufficient musical and vocal talent in the first place.

Considering the diversity of skills required, one might assume that they could be tested as discrete subjects (like geography, French and chemistry in school). But for the singer they must be complementary, and seen and heard to be so – each having a bearing on the efficacy of the others.

Testing the various components separately is unrealistic. What counts is not that they are all present and correct and deserving of so many points each, but how they impact on one another. If we say 'he's good musically, but vocally weak', we forget that his music-making depends on his instrument; the only way to judge progress on both counts is on how voice and music interact. There has to be a way of recognising mutual influence and interrelationship between 'parts'. This is one area in which traditional examining fails to be a genuine indicator of progress.

There is another, perhaps more insidious since it is based on deception. That is the one in which students are given overall points. The more points received the better the student is deemed to be – the implication being that one student is better than another. Or the more points gained, the better he or she is reckoned to have done in that year.

It is often difficult to know exactly on what bases yearly points are awarded, but clearly it is not always on genuine progress. Illustration 24.1 gives an inkling of the incomprehensibility of some systems. Three students, A, B and C, are accepted for a course. At the start A is considered 'better than average', B 'average' and C 'good enough'. The arrows indicate the amount of progress made by each individual, according to the original estimation of ability, thus meriting places 1, 2 and 3. The points are those given according to which student is judged (by some other estimation) the 'best', 'second best' and 'third best' at the end of each year.

It will be clear that at the end of the first year C, according to his ability, has improved more than A, but A has nevertheless been awarded more points because he has been judged to be 'better', or, by some distortion of

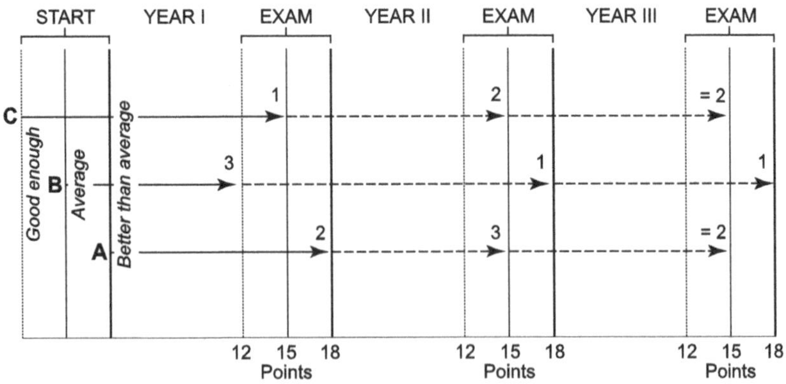

24.1 Points or Progress?

judgment, to have progressed further. While this illustration is simplistic, the incomprehensibility and therefore the injustice that this model represents is obvious.

We could speculate on what might have happened, what might have been felt by the various parties, if, for example, student A had been marked down at the end of his first year for having in reality made less progress than C. Or how C might feel having improved so much only to be awarded 15 points.

Such conjectures, however, are as trivial and meaningless as the criteria upon which the students' performances have been appraised. In this model there is no way of telling whether a student fulfils their promise. A standard is being applied which fails to recognise individuality, in two crucial ways:

1 The student's training and educational requirements and process must be particular to him, because of his personal characteristics and propensities
2 If the student has been taken on as an embryonic artist, the results, all along, are bound to be unique.

There is one occasion on which students' ability can reasonably be measured by some standard, and that is at the point of selection, when a panel must determine, within certain parameters, whether a candidate is up to the level required for undertaking the course in the first place. As I have already suggested, it is only fair to all concerned if this selection process is much more rigorous than it generally is.

In order to dilute the influence of prejudice, and to broaden the terms of reference, opinions as to the suitability of candidates need to be obtained from representatives of all the main departments that will contribute to the students' nurturing and development. For future reference, audio-visual footage is imperative.

Students must often wonder what they have to do to come top of the class, whether it is what they do or what they don't do that counts. Does accuracy count for more than communication or originality, vocal quality for more than intelligibility? Or is it the other way round? Should so many points be given for this 'skill' and so many for that? What happens in the end when most of a person's skills are considered good but some are not? What about creativity, originality, inventiveness, intuition, etc., which as yet lie outside theoretical or scientific measurement and could be thought of as a matter of opinion?

Frankly, trying to standardise progress is unrealistic and therefore unfair and a waste of time. Appraisal of this kind of personal developmental work should begin – and indeed end – with the person concerned. When it comes to singing, a standard can only be an abstract notion, nebulously alluding to an indeterminate product.

The question then remains: how do you measure individuation? Again, our four definitions can help, since they come together as the work in general gains balance and coordination. It is important to remember that the process of *becoming* follows an individual route which, although it might be enlivened and advanced in various ways with methods or techniques known to be helpful within a discipline, cannot be predetermined. There cannot be one way for all, only that particular person's way. The individual's singing voice is just that; with the aid of the teacher's drawing-out skills, and the pupil's participation, it has to be found. Any measurement or weighing up must accord with a process of discovery that cannot be mapped out ahead of the journey.

The challenge is that:

1. We are dealing with the progress of an individual: his or her individual process.
2. The performing artist is a composite of interrelated skills, not measurable separately but only for how well they potentialise and relate to one another.
3. These skills tend to develop at different rates.

The process must therefore be open-ended. Of any move, we should always be able to ask, 'is this paving the way for new development?' Making music is facilitated as the voice's skills come into their own, not before. This is why theory can be so unhelpful – even counterproductive.

Having to produce something specific, at a specific time, preoccupies the singer in such a way that it inhibits growth – in particular flexibility and openness to new skills and new experiences, which must be able to be incorporated for further development. Continuity is essential.

A fair appraisal will allow for the fact that an individual's true quality (and therefore 'identity') in sound has to be revealed before it can be truly appreciated. The colours unique to the singer's vocal palette will come to light through the developing interaction between imagination and instrument. Artistry and authenticity also emerge. There cannot be specific times or lengths of time for the realisation of these unpredictable qualities. Time and energy can be served profitably by allotting more to a constituent that is slow in developing and less to another that seems to be forging ahead – until, that is, they are able to pull together in a more productive way. Progress would then be acknowledged accordingly.

The constituents of progress are a complex mix, the true efficacy of which can only be measured through sensitivity and a holistic paradigm. If there are any quantities involved they are only measurable in terms of relative proportions – like the composition of a picture. Singers need time to grow into their skills laterally as well as linearly – checking and cross-checking the developing 'parts' (or disciplines) against the emerging whole. Constant monitoring, whereby the proportions of ingredients might be opportunely adjusted, is more useful than examining which can arrest progress through unrealistic performance objectives.

At one end of the appreciation spectrum we must attend to the inception of the singing sound, from which we can gain so much information about vocal health and the student's approach. What level or type of energy is the student employing? Is the whole voice there (in terms of structure) from the onset of the first tone? Does the voice move as though inevitably from note to note, or is it being 'helped along' in some way? How agile is the voice?

What makes for agility (in structural terms, the action of the 'closers') fits very well with the concept of vocal centring and with the articulation of words. If the words cannot be clearly enunciated, the voice is not centred, is off balance. A voice with its natural agility will not sound fat or cumbersome. On the contrary, agility being an essential constituent of what concentrates the tone at that tiny core, it is responsible for the voice's clarity and directness.

At the other end of the appreciation spectrum is the song, grasped musically and meaningfully as a whole. These extremes will eventually be complementary. Meanwhile, they can be so far apart that they seem incompatible. What brings out the innate skills of the singing voice is meticulous hard training. What brings the song into being is how well these skills serve. What needs to be examined in detail is the progress of skill development combined with skill serving.

This is why the developmental process must be gradual. Too much 'information' too soon, too much confusing of issues, is counterproductive. Conventional examinations can muddy the appreciation of progress to the extent of putting it in doubt. Furthermore, repertoire can have a negative effect. It is a common experience that a young singer's performance of repertoire says more about what they cannot do than what they can. This is discouraging. It looks as though the student is at fault when in fact it is the task they have been set. It may be obvious on the surface what is lacking, but the solution rarely reaches beyond the symptoms to the instrumental causes. The singer will try harder, with only superficial benefit. To assess where the singer has got to, the repertoire must be suitable, not the other way around.

If there is any order of priorities in this process, it has to be the development of the singer's voice (or instrument) first. It is not just a question of the coming together of the various physical-physiological strands, but of how the person is, what they bring, what they have experienced, what they feel, what they fear, what they hope for.

The energy that a singer brings to their work, their mental approach, and their general health both physical and emotional, all affect progress. Dealing with these very real aspects of the young singer's make-up is fundamental. Emotional blocks create physical or physiological blocks, and vice versa, sometimes locking the singer into a vicious circle. These are sensitive and crucial issues, the effects of which cannot be adequately gauged by conventional examinations.

Any fair system of evaluation will factor in an individual's personal growth. Similarly a singer's ability to be expressive, their ease or spontaneity of delivery, confidence to take risks (as distinct from 'playing safe'), originality as against conformity, along with 'entertainment value' and performance professionalism, must all sooner or later be noted.

I do not believe that formal modes of examination are fair. They almost always judge results on spurious or subjective criteria, and are inherently ill-equipped to measure real-time, real-person progress. Worse, because of the vocal distortion or unbalancing that is often required in order to meet required standards (imagined or otherwise), they often have the effect of inhibiting progress and obscuring what is truly valuable. They encourage imitation and rule-following, empty virtuosity and meaningless competition.

When a student is ready to begin singing, providing the training has been carried out in a logical, holistic fashion, the performance will be less about vocal 'technique' or musical literacy, and more about expression and communication.

A guide for suitable performing repertoire is that it should not over-tax the singer's voice, but rather help it to improve. To be realistic and productive in expressive and communicative terms, performances need to be given in the presence of an audience, comprising not only peers but students from other years as well as representatives from each of the main disciplines – many performance skills will be coming together.

This crucial work can be openly discussed around various specific issues – meaning conveyed, dramatic qualities, clarity of text, imagination, intention, presentation, and so on – so that the singer gets a true impression of their impact on listeners. The various tutors can use their knowledge to analyse balance and, where desirable, technical matters. In this way it can be discovered and understood by everyone present, including the teachers, how the various elements combine to make a meaningful, artistic performance – or in what respects they do not. What are fair expectations in each individual singer's case can be gauged from day-to-day observations as well as the initial audition and its audio-visual footage.

One could reasonably expect that this exercise would reinforce and support the singers' on-going work, draw them closer to each other in their enlightenment, and be duly encouraging. Better than exams would be regular feedback sessions, such as I experienced with Toastmasters International public speaking club. Although there were experienced members as well as beginners like myself, there were no 'instructors' as such. But there were plenty of tried and tested objective indicators of progress, as well as the opportunity to receive subjective impressions (anonymously) and kindly advice from all members. We were never ever made to feel incompetent, or failures. We were praised for our individuality, originality and humour, and encouraged every step of the way. I had never been in a group that was more supportive or confidence-building. Such a spirit of mutual support is what I would like to see in all areas of a singing school.

A Teacher's View

People often ask me which singers I like. They want to know what I think is good singing. After all, listeners respond to different stimuli. Some like to be impressed by big or rapid high notes, some are not bothered about words, requiring only what they experience as beauty of tone. Others demand musical fidelity before emotional expression. Some people, among them even serious critics, are 'taken in' by struggle or artifice. Can it really be good singing if the singer's words cannot be made out, or the tone is monochromatic or constantly loud? By way of reply I usually say, 'Think of all the qualities you like in singing. Then find a singer who has these'.

It has been said that unless we know what is behind a craft we cannot judge it. I would apply this to any serious criticism of anyone's singing. As a teacher I have to be careful to distinguish what I like (subjectively) and what is good or healthy (objectively). Unfortunately, what we like, or what gives us pleasure or excitement in some way, is not necessarily 'good' in the sense of healthy.

Everyone likes praise, and many people are keen to show their appreciation. Singers need to be encouraged. In a school of singing it is vitally important that singers are exposed to criticism that is well-founded, well-balanced, and constructive. Our task is to build, not to accumulate, so what is offered to a student must also be timely – something they are ready to take on board.

I hope this book will stimulate a much greater expectation of the singing voice, as well as giving adequate bases for a more objective and constructive criticism of singing.

Other Critics

Singers are often egged on by well-meaning admirers from within their institution and from well-wishers without. They are advised by people who are not qualified to advise them about the state of their voice and what they need to do to improve. While they like to be praised, students are often only too aware of what they see or feel as their 'inadequacies'. They need to know from people with a well-informed and balanced view what can reasonably be expected of them, and what at this stage will most benefit their development.

The relative merits of students, judged as they usually are from within the school, are nothing to go by. They can, through their very relativity, give a false impression of what a good professional standard is all about. How things are or seem to be can depend on who is looking at them and from what angle. Agents, conductors, singing teachers, coaches, fellow singers all have their point of view – and their taste. They don't all always see eye to eye. Who is the singer to please?

Even the market does not depend on healthy singing. An entrepreneur may not have high standards, or care about wholeness, but sees an opportunity to stage an event, and persuades promoters who may have even less idea about such things. Singers who are not ready, but willing to take insultingly low fees, are often booked for such events. A recording producer may judge how good an artist is by how many records they sell. A conductor may be obsessed with accuracy but have no ear for quality. Audiences are easily impressed with aspects of a singer's performance which are less than healthily achieved. Rarely is it perceived how much better a performance would be if the singer were ready in a finished sense. None of these people, upon whom artists depend for their careers, will necessarily know how to take care of them. Worse, a singer is commonly viewed as a dispensable commodity.

One might then ask if being a 'good' (or whole) singer really matters? Isn't the job a bit of a lottery anyway? Writing as a singing teacher, I believe that my most important task is to help each individual free and develop his or her natural voice. I have explained what I mean by natural, and described how I think this task can best be approached. I cannot in all conscience allow myself to be swayed by objectives or pressures that have nothing to do with this quest, or that threaten to undermine it. And I certainly cannot be influenced by uninformed opinion. Singers too must learn to be discerning and stand on their own two feet.

If the reasons that I have already given for this are not sufficiently cogent, let me draw your attention again to the subtitle of this book. When I told one person that it was 'Personal and Performance Values in Training', he knew instinctively that these were somehow interchangeable – of mutual benefit and interest. This book attempts to articulate the fact that what makes for the personal in singing makes also for articulate and potent performance. Personal is not the aim; singing is. Singing is personal. The liberated singing voice is the liberated performer.

The Main Critic

Young singers must study the singing of other singers, whether 'great' or not, their peers included, and learn to be critical in an objective and constructive way. This can be done in private listening, open analyses of internal school recitals, and group analysis of singing heard by the class outside the school. As importantly, would-be professionals must study the music of great song and opera composers in some depth and detail, with the purpose of ascertaining what is required musically and vocally of a great singer – why, in other words, it is so essential to unlock their talent, and why the mere imitation of those who have gone before will not suffice.

Our best, most knowledgeable critic, in art as in life, is ourselves. The holistic process that I have outlined encourages self-discovery, self-acting, self-knowledge or awareness, self-examination and self-affirmation. This is achieved by the individual singer (with the help and encouragement of those around) through curiosity and exploration, as well as hard work and the pursuit of excellence. The whole personal approach needs to be underpinned by an ethos of caring, openness and co-operation. Just as the work, both individual and collective, values depth and detail, so can the process culminate in the realisation of self-worth, and manifest in self-motivation, self-possession and self-reliance. Only the individual can discover and appreciate these things within themselves. This is both the quest and the empowering quality of individuation – the progress and the measure.

CHAPTER 25

Consensus

A new school of singing – one of a high order – would be based on a vision of excellence shared by all those concerned with setting it up. Such a vision would necessarily centre on an agreement about what is meant by good (healthy) singing. Clarification of this matter would then provide a basis for determining how to make the school most fruitful.

Starting from scratch, while providing the best chance of recruiting staff with a similar vision, would have its problems. It would be an act of faith on the part of all concerned. In some ways an established institution might be better placed for implementing innovative ideas. Much that would be needed, for example organizational tools, personnel for the everyday running of the place and expertise in various teaching spheres, would already be available. Established institutions are often universally respected and therefore have the weight and influence needed to bring about widespread change.

The main problem, as I see it, would be changing minds and hearts. By this I mean seeing things from a different perspective. About 15 years ago the word 'holistic' was whispered at a rare meeting of singing teachers at a prestigious school. The idea was immediately dismissed. Perhaps it smacked of 'new age' or – God forbid – 'alternative'. This was not the first time I had come across such a reaction when an unfamiliar or potentially uncomfortable matter was broached at a meeting, threatening to rock the teachers' boat. Resistance to change is a defence against feeling insecure or embarrassed.

I have come across a number of teachers at institutions who would like to see improvements both to their own conditions and to the treatment of their students. Many of them suffered as students themselves from well-meaning but inadequate and inhibiting musical establishments. So I believe that many hearts *are* in the right place. And it is in individual hearts that change is conceived.

Hearts were probably in the right place when the great institutions of music were first established. However, as time goes on there is a danger that original ideas and procedures lose their justification. It's not just that people's outlooks change as society changes: practical circumstances change too, and there is a desire and need to assimilate information and update attitudes and practices. In Britain we see this in other long-established institutions. The efficiency and effectiveness of the NHS, the Government, the penal system, the Church, and educational establishments in general, have all come under scrutiny in recent years

While voice science, until recently at least, has favoured a reductionist approach, and the education of singers has likewise been disjointed or even arbitrary in many quarters, the sheer common sense and desirability of a 'whole' approach to the training of singers must have often been at the back of teachers' minds. There is sufficient documentation to show that something of the sort was in the minds and practice of the Old Italian School. Husler's classic *Singing*, published in 1965, makes the logic as well as the efficacy of vocal wholeness abundantly clear. I have been offering a broader picture simply to show (in the holistic view) what I believe is needed to achieve this today.

There are of course dangers. Changes are sometimes made for the sake of change, as when a new CEO feels the need to make his or her mark. They are sometimes made to appease funding bodies who don't understand the requirements of what they are funding.

Also, it is one thing to update practices considered to be ineffective or redundant, but quite another to replace the best practices of the past with new-fangled ones based on the latest technology or information, or to lose sight of what Janice Chapman calls the 'heritage of artistry on which the profession relies'.[1]

But the opposite also happens, when people within an institution merely perpetuate the long-established ways of doing things that they have grown up with. They sometimes make token 'modernisations' but nothing substantially improves. Change or innovation implies dissatisfaction with the status quo – which is seen as tried and tested – and venturing into the relatively unknown – which of course has *not* been tried or tested. Better the devil you know!

There are reasons why 'institutional' has come to mean 'regimented' or 'unimaginative' and why 'the Establishment', in exercising its authority or influence, is seen as resisting change.[2]

What we are after

An untenable assumption sometimes made by singing teachers and endorsed by institutions is that 'we are all after the same thing'. I have always taken this 'thing' to mean 'good singing', so I nod my head in comradely wishful-thinking. Who can gainsay such a statement?

But isn't this just another way of avoiding the slippery ground beneath attempts to explain what this 'thing' is and how it can be reached? It is hard to believe there is so much 'sameness' of objective when we consider how many different 'techniques' of singing are on the market. Harder still when they appear to conflict, and unbelievable when we see that different techniques concentrate on different aspects of a voice to the exclusion of others.

It is a matter of moral as well as artistic concern how the employment of techniques refutes the claim to freedom, limiting voices to the requirements of a style rather than providing them with a choice. Worse, the teaching of different 'types' of singing invariably begins not with a free voice but with one that is already deficient.

Particular styles of singing are usually created by their originator, by making the most of restricted freedom or a strongly individual voice production. This is then copied. This is why classical singers whose voices are in some way fixed, sound at best like poor imitations of their more free brethren. We hear not the true classical style, which for all its various conventions requires unconstrained lucidity, but a simulated sound, which passes for classical voice but which, because of its fixedness, renders the music clumsy and the emotional expression self-conscious and ambiguous.

Does it matter that there are so many 'ways' of singing? Well, yes, for teachers at a singing school. Otherwise, 'anything goes' will eventually morph into 'anything-at-all goes'.

How can it be that in one studio a singer is taught to hold his ribs out, while in another he is taught to pull them in? How can it be that while one student is urged to increase her breath capacity another is bidden to concentrate on exhalation. Contradictions abound around 'registers', 'support', 'falsetto', 'resonance', 'placement' – any of the jargon that is commonly applied to singing.

Chapman is right to state that 'Pedagogy based on physiology/anatomy/function/acoustics and provable scientific information is essential in the 21st century'.[3] But this basis can at best be a rough guide. Much is still unproven which may or may not be of value. What about the myriad variations of condition and needs between individuals?

How does it all hang together scientifically when there are so many gaps in the knowledge. These will only be filled in when the natural (not the normal) voice is examined as a whole. It might then be discovered that some current 'findings' were not so well-proven. Meanwhile, is not the incomplete theory encouraging a new kind of scientifically-orientated technique?

For all the 'knowledge' that has proliferated in the last 20 or 30 years, there are more ways of singing and of teaching voice than ever. Some, I'm afraid, are based on titbits of 'science'. I have observed colleagues grasping with one hand at uncoordinated bits of information, and with the other at surviving pieces of past practice. Neither together nor separately do these straws add up to a reliable basis for sound practice. Worse, their incoherence makes a mockery of science and dishonours the past. It adds to the feeling that consensus about what singing is and what is required to achieve it seem an impossible dream.

Let us accept that the singing voice is a natural phenomenon, which in most people needs singing teachers to unlock it and get it working again, and that the 'thing' we are all aiming for is 'the best that a voice can do'. We can take a step forward by replacing the rather stale question 'what is the best way to achieve this?' with 'what do we perceive to be possible?'

Let us not put limits on our pupils, but rather remain open to discovering and bringing out their possibilities. This exploratory attitude was, I believe, what motivated the Old Italian School. Why should we not do the same?

> Could you but hear one of these enervating performances executed with all the devices of art, you might think it a chorus of Sirens, not of men; and you would be astounded by the singers' facility ...[4]

No, not something from bel canto times, but a description of singing made more than 500 years before! This shows us that opinions, even appreciative ones, are not something we can rely upon. At least the singers of the late 16th century were not convinced that such Sirens told the whole story! I cannot resist completing this delightful quotation:

> ... with which indeed neither that of the parrot or nightingale, nor of whatever else there may be that is more remarkable in this kind, can compare.

Individuation

Singers change as they open up, as they grow – we all do. This should not mean becoming an imitation, or becoming someone else. These are reasons why people have difficulty singing in the first place.

The bel canto quest was not to create a new technique of singing. Rather, they believed that the human voice had more to it – as exemplified by the 'natural singers' whom they sought out and studied – than had hitherto been realised. They wanted to explore the 'whole' voice, and find ways of restoring this wholeness in those who showed talent but had not yet fulfilled their potential.

The Old School did not try to make the voice faster, higher and stronger, let alone more beautiful. Rather, I believe the composers of the time knew intuitively that the voice was more capable, musically and emotionally, than it was being given credit for. The Renaissance polyphonic style mould was limiting. If they were right, opening up the voice to its natural capacity would serve their own imaginations and their desire to develop their art. They were not disappointed! And they got beauty into the bargain.

The difficulties that opening up a voice presents may lie in the very thing that makes the idea exciting; neither teacher nor pupil know exactly where it will lead, how it will turn out. The danger with depending on a scientific model (even if it were complete) is that it leaves no room for the unpredictable, the inconsistent, the individual.

Chapman continues, 'In the past singing teaching was transmitted through intuitive, experiential and experimental methodology based on subjective sensations, often using unrealistic imagery. But prior to the development of the fibre-optics and endoscopy, this was all that was available'. Chapman has been a leading light in the British Voice Association, and made it her business, like Miller before her, to keep abreast of research, to contribute to it, to share it and to incorporate it in her practice where appropriate. It is indeed to be hoped that in the future science will play a more guiding and underpinning role in the development of voices generally.

Meanwhile, I don't think that Chapman means to imply that intuition, experience and experimentation have lost their importance. In fact I would say that finding and developing voices, whether our own or someone else's, is as dependent on intuition as the act of singing itself is. Yes, 'subjective sensations' can be very misleading, especially where relevant information is lacking. Nevertheless, even the best singing is experienced subjectively; it is never entirely rational.

As for 'imagery' – it is simply a tool. Like 'placing', its efficacy depends on the individual imagination. Its usefulness can be gauged by the result. While teachers must be able to visualise the anatomy and physiology involved, as accurately and knowledgably as possible, it is of no use unless they have a way of knowing to what extent it is working. What is required is more objectivity, particularly on the part of the teacher, and suitable participation from both parties.

Chapman points out that 'students have access to current information via the internet, are doing their own research, and are demanding more from teachers'. She says that 'teachers need to catch up and keep up'. Indeed, singing teachers need to be ahead of the game. But to renounce the very real and fruitful human qualities of intuition and imagination in favour of a relatively rational or abstract scientific model would be as perilous as abandoning the ideals of bel canto; the baby would go out with the bathwater – and perish in the cold!

There is no way that students can attempt to apply scientific considerations without it resulting in some kind of conscious physical fixing. Students need a teacher they can trust. Consensus among singing teachers at the top schools is urgently needed to give teaching at this level legitimacy. There needs to be a recognisable, authoritative and sound basis to the work. Establishments that teach classical voice need to agree with regard to vocal physiology – that is, correct natural functioning. Adhering to the various qualities that characterise the free singing voice would ensure that emerging outcomes make sense of each other – that the various facets of the singer's art are not in conflict. Let me be clear: I am not talking about teachers' individual ways of teaching, only about what it is based on and what its purpose is.

A good start would be to collate all the advice, technical and otherwise, and see if it hangs together. Things that truly potentialise, complement and reinforce each other can be seen to be helpful. Things that do not are probably best discarded.

The holistic paradigm shows us that no skill is more important than another, so none can be an objective in itself. This view can go a long way to avoiding conflict of interests or mixed objectives in the work. With our four definitions as a collective guide, the question could then be put, 'Is the work (whatever aspect of it) contributing to the realisation of these ways (all of them) of defining and recognising the singing voice, or is it causing confusion?'

Surely, we are trying to find the 'good' in each and every student. Whether in the form of vocal physiology or the ability to communicate, this 'good' must be observed and affirmed by the knowledgeable teacher. The student should neither be submissive nor take charge of the work, but needs to participate because the training process is a two-sided affair. The teacher is dependent upon the student's willingness and ability to take part in the exploration. The student, in turn, is dependent on the teacher for guidance and feedback.

Theoretical and visual 'knowledge about the voice' can give the impression that the task of learning to sing is the same for each and every singer. You follow the instructions that go with the plans. In reality, getting to the various 'parts' of very differently configured voices depends on a certain amount of experimentation as well as intuition. Above all, the process is experiential; That will never change. The results, overall and in detail, can only be arrived at and objectively comprehended by a perceptive and knowing ear.

So long as there is no agreed basis for the training and education of singers, there can be little or no faith in it. So, we have isolated teachers, a lack of coordination between departments, and poor outcomes generally. Everybody suffers, from the pupil, who is surely the focus of our attention, to the profession that we represent, to the audience for whom we all labour.

I remember somebody pointing out that you can always learn something from a teacher, however bad he or she might be! It is also the case that however good we think we are, we cannot know it all. We need the work of others to complement our own work, we need the knowledge and experience of others to fill in the gaps in our own, we are dependent on others to help us on our way. Conversely, if we *do* know a lot, or have something special to offer, we can help others and, by extension, the general cause, by sharing it.

Goldberg, in *The Intuitive Edge*, puts it very nicely: 'Each of us is a cell in the collective brain'.[5] This is a humbling thought, but it also implies that each of us is necessary; our individual behaviour and its impact on what is going on around us counts. This is why openness and co-operation, by enabling us to learn from each other, can help us to progress. This is not just a matter of gathering and pooling information, as valuable as that may be; it affects the value and meaning of what we are doing.

I have been described as a 'scientific teacher', because I am interested in the science and can explain certain aspects of singing scientifically, yet I have also been accused of being 'anti-science'! Perhaps this is because I do not subscribe to the idea that science is where 'all the answers' lie. In my teaching I am neither for science nor against it. If someone asks me what is a good exercise for such and such a (described) problem, I say – in all honesty – I don't know until I hear it applied.

Problems, while looking similar in kind, belong to an individual. They are invariably different in make-up – multi-layered, differently configured, and so on. Each voice has a different 'history', and while we are unlikely to have to go far into this, the problems have developed or been dug in over time. This is why I am wary of methods and techniques that fail to search conscientiously for the roots of individuals' problems. Pat answers don't exist – only many variable ways of drawing out a voice and restoring it to freedom.

While it is true that different teachers are good for different pupils, we should beware of this being just because different pupils fit different techniques. If the singing voice is a natural phenomenon there is only its freedom to aim for, not a way of singing. Rather than wrangling over which techniques or methods are best, consensus needs to be built on objectivity and participation without any vested personal interest in the outcome.

Collective wisdom will come, in other words, from a collective commitment to the good.

In the course of writing this book I keep coming back to the bases of this 'good', the bottom line: the singer and his or her voice. If improvements are to be made to the lot of trainee singers, our consensus-building dialogue and learning will have to be not only about what we are doing and how best to do it, but also and primarily, *for whom* we are doing it.

Anything that takes our focus as teachers and educators away from the singer – his or her natural voice, individuality and potential – is an abnegation of responsibility. Objectives, such as singing higher, faster or louder, or being the next Pavarotti, or getting high marks or becoming a star – all of these become false objectives once we give the singing voice its due credit, and honour the individual.

Such false objectives contribute, I believe, to the lowering of standards. They prevent concentrating the attention and energy where it needs to be in order to generate good results. I come across much talent which I judge to have needlessly gone to waste because aims were misplaced – and on countless occasions I have heard singers whose voices are well-schooled or technically proficient but are not free. Saddest of all, I have come across voices that have lost their naturalness through the imposition of someone else's idea of 'how to do it'.

I have also met numbers of teachers who are not free to do their best, either because there is an unrealistically timed agenda, or there is insufficient support from other departments or from the top. Teachers who want to change things for the better often feel powerless to do anything about it. We need to pull together.

CHAPTER 26

Leading the Way

The difference between the possible and the impossible is merely the measure of man's determination.[1]

A need for improvements in the quality of teaching and singing is recognised and desired. Nevertheless one wonders in whose hands lies the power to change anything. Among singing teachers, who should be the most qualified to press for improvements, there is at present too little agreement about what is 'good'. Perhaps preoccupied with defending or protecting our own pitch, we carry little collective or credible weight.

Charles Dickens, winding up his commentary on Darwin's theory of evolution referred to:

> Timid persons, who purposely cultivate a certain inertia of mind and who love to cling to their preconceived ideas, fearing to look at such a mighty subject from an unauthorized and unwonted point of view.[2]

Singers are often confused by pedagogical discrepancies, and cannot know what a good training is before they experience it first-hand. Teachers and students might legitimately lobby for better conditions, but neither has the power to instigate the kinds of innovations that the 'mighty subject' of training and educating singers calls for. Speaking out can bring disapproval or alienation. On the other hand, not speaking out can give silent consent to other peoples' power games.

Leadership

In a refreshingly candid and apposite article called 'Connecting Conversations: The Changing Voice of the Artist', written in 2003, Peter Renshaw said,

> At present, too many higher arts education institutions continue to hide behind hierarchical management structures that rest on outmoded assumptions and fail to respond to change and innovation. Often dominated by inflexible forms of line-management, in which departmental tribalism and parochial power politics prevail, little attempt is made to create a trusting environment in which shared leadership and authority are encouraged throughout an institution.[3]

For relevant changes to come about, power, in the sense of say and agency – together with the responsibility that goes with it – needs to be more evenly distributed.

Contemporary models of management are beginning to capitalise on what a friend of mine describes as 'shared system leadership so all sectors can work closely together in a coordinated way'. This makes for 'a more integrated approach to leadership across boundaries'.[4]

Meaningful development or progress entails bottom-up as well as top-down influence, intra- as well as inter-departmental dialogue and education. Everyone is part of the whole, and therefore has by definition something of value to contribute to its health.

> Leading … is there to enrich, to nurture, to release human possibilities, to inspire people to believe that they matter and that they have something of value to say.[5]

The best leaders are not necessarily those with charisma, authority or bags of self-esteem, but those who actively encourage genuine debate and collaborative solutions. Open-minded, aware, searching, sharing and appreciative, they are *enablers*. They are curious:

> Anyone who is not curious is not asking questions and, mostly, those who are not asking questions are those who do not wish to challenge the status quo and have a vested interest in not doing so.[6]

A growing thirst for fairness, transparency and personal empowerment, as well as efficiency in the work-place has made leadership a hot topic. Dictatorial or prescriptive ways, secretive and irresponsible ways are no longer acceptable and are being challenged. More democratic, humane and soulful models have been researched and are beginning to be implemented.

> It is possible for organisations to learn to change because 'deep down, we are all learners' ... When we give up the illusion that the world is created out of separate, unrelated forces ... we can build 'learning organisations' ... when people continually expand their capacity to create the results they truly desire.[7]

The above relates to a book by Peter Senge called *The Fifth Discipline*, which deals with 'approaches ... for developing core learning capabilities: fostering aspirations, developing reflective conversations and understanding complexity'.

According to Wikipedia, the fifth discipline, Systems Thinking, integrates the first four. These are:

1. Personal Mastery – the fostering of personal motivation to continually learn how our actions affect our world. Continually clarifying and deepening our personal vision, energy focus, patience, and objectivity with regard to reality.
2. Mental Models – dealing with the influence of assumptions and generalisations on how we see the world and how we act.
3. Building Shared Vision – unearthing shared pictures of the future that foster genuine commitment and enrolment rather than compliance.
4. Team Learning – starting with dialogue, the capacity of members of a team to suspend assumptions and enter into genuine thinking together.
5. Systems Thinking – needs the integration of the other disciplines to realise its potential.[8]

It is clear from what I have observed in institutions and conferences, and discussed with colleagues, that the way forward is, as Renshaw puts it, 'through engaging in a "conversation" that respects differences, sees commonalities and crosses boundaries ... an institutional conversation that embodies such qualities as trust, active listening, openness, humility, integrity and empathy'.[9]

As well as shared leadership this is a matter of individual empowerment. A workforce or organisation, in which each person is valued and has a voice which is listened to, is happier, more creative and more productive. Individuals united in a creative purpose have a sense of belonging and pride in what they are doing. They want it to work, and are more ready to invest themselves in it. Such is the wisdom that comes from active objective commitment without any vested personal interest in the outcome. The question is not, 'who is right?' but 'what is best for our mission?'

Accountability

As I see it, the institution needs to be as accountable to its employees as they need to be to it, and as voice trainers and other 'enablers' need to be to their charges. Schools are also accountable, of course, to their governors and to the public sector. Up until now, this has meant 'quantifiable performance indicators', as Renshaw calls them. He says,

> The danger is that the present system can be too controlling and debilitating. Within this culture of compliance it is only too easy for arts organisations to become disconnected from the heart of their artistic life. Knowledge, understanding, skills and professional attitudes form the bedrock of learning in higher education, but the ways in which they are defined and acquired can easily be undermined by the perceived expectations of Quality Assurance and performance management. An organic approach to development that depends partly on the fostering of an institutional conversation, does not fit comfortably within a mechanistic system of controlling and managing knowledge.[10]

And while

> Explicit knowledge can be clearly articulated, codified, quantified, replicated and transferred from one context to another ... tacit knowledge which is more intuitive, reflexive and learned in very particular situations ... is intangible, less observable, more complex and more difficult to detach from the person who created it or from the context in which it is located ... much of the energy, immediacy, spontaneity and creativity central to artistic processes are rooted in a form of life in which knowledge and awareness are more implicit than explicit. Finding ways of managing the apparent paradox between Quality and quality, and between explicit and tacit knowledge, is critical to the future work of higher arts education institutions. Conversations involving artists and teachers are

> absolutely essential if the integrity of artistic engagement is not to be destroyed.[11]

The message is loud and clear if the future of 'classical' singing is to be secured.

Possibilities

In what ways and to what extent are established schools open to possibilities? To what extent are they held back by Quality Assurance, or even by fossilisation? Sometimes leaders lose touch. They go blathering on about things they no longer know much about. Or there's plenty of talking and precious little walking! Sometimes a conservatoire is much like a conservatory – 'where plants are arranged in a pleasing manner ... a building for the cultivation and exhibition of plants under controlled conditions'.[12] The institutional model can be a closed circle in which those who have undergone a certain type of institutional programme go on to be teachers and managers of it. Sometimes 'managing' seems to be the raison d'être.

We can and should learn from the past. We cannot and should not hang onto it wholesale as though there were no future. But, unless we no longer value our magnificent classical music inheritance, modernisation (if that is the word) can be neither a matter of rejecting nor of replacing the past.

Innovation can be a judicious improving on yesterday's practice in the light of what we know today, together with an examination of what contribution the singing voice can make to compositional developments and 'portfolio careers' (performer/teacher/director/composer – after those innovative members of the Camerata of Florence). Any reassessing must surely be a question of what is possible without sacrificing the singing instrument and its innate qualities. Are these objectives compatible? I think 'yes', providing all reassessment examines the relationship between the singer and their performance, and makes this the basis of any changes.

Talent and standards

The oldest musical institution in Britain, the Royal Academy of Music (founded 1822) 'aims to enrich musical culture through the training and education of the most talented students to the highest standards'.[13]

Perhaps we should enquire what 'the most talented' refers to. Is it 'of the current applicants', or are there specific criteria or qualities which all candidates are expected to meet? What happens if there are not sufficient 'talents' to fill the available places? What does 'the highest standards' mean? Do these words infer some kind of fait accompli, a comparison with the past or with what we see and hear around us, or could an institution be aiming always to *raise* standards?

'Talent' and 'standards' are abstract terms. Let us return to the singer, and discover anew what talent is – what quality and excellence means in each and every individual. Let us be more accountable to him or her. Only then can we determine what contribution he or she can make to the enrichment of musical culture.

Valuing the Genuine

If singing is not genuine or natural, we might say that it is affected, fake, not entirely honest. Singers who are always doing something to affect their singing never sing easily or naturally, or authentically.

Given such a precious gift as the singing instrument, it is arrogant to suggest that we can somehow contrive it, or that one contrivance is better than another. Such a stance presumes an implied unnaturalness of the singing voice and provides an excuse for those who wish to manipulate it to their liking. Furthermore, the supposed unnaturalness supports the idea that music making is necessarily a matter of reproduction. In this case, true engagement (of the singer) is superfluous or a distraction, and real communication goes by the board.

Listening to someone whose singing is both effortless and beautiful, we can but marvel. Learning to sing can be a daunting enough prospect for young singers, without thinking they have to emulate someone else. They need to be disabused of this idea and learn early on that they are on a personal quest, the result of which will be something quite unique.

Responsibility

The responsibility of high-level schools of singing is not only to espouse excellence, but to demonstrate by open and accountable means how this can best be achieved, and to lead the way in excellent teaching. The aim should be to release individuals' voices so that they can communicate and make music as unique performers.

Perhaps it is not so strange that among those who have studied at a high level, many come away imitating what they think or have been taught is good singing, both in sound and in what is sometimes erroneously called 'style'. After all, a school of classical singing must teach its students how to sing baroque, classical and romantic opera, lieder of various countries and eras as well as 20th and 21st century music. What often seems to be forgotten is that, whatever the music, whatever the style (some contemporary music excepted) it has to be sung. The various 'ways' are passed on regardless of the intelligence and creativity of the newly emerging singer, and the uniqueness of his or her voice and talents.

A big strength of the singing voice, and indeed its advantage over all other voices, is its versatility. So long as it remains balanced it remains versatile: no need to limit it in any way.

Imitation is often sanctioned simply because of the sounds we have got used to, but the idea that if you imitate a certain style the voice will sing 'correctly' is a dangerous one; nothing could be further from the truth. Many voices have fallen by the wayside because of this naïve attitude. The voice (the instrument) comes first – then the singing – and only after that the style.

Too often singers learn to sing certain types of music before they can sing in any 'whole' sense. It is worse when they specialise prematurely – perhaps because their voice seems to lend itself particularly well to a certain style. The diverting of energy away from the search for a deeper, more engaged singing into the confining demands of a limited style or way of vocalising effectively curtails the singer's growth. 'Inhibiting growth processes is also debilitating in that growth is a process that not only expends energy but is also required to produce energy'.[14]

Authenticity

The classification of genres brings with it rules and conventions, the strict observance of which tends to preoccupy the artist to such an extent that, instead of facilitating a fine performance, they impede freedom to perceive and explore the subject-matter, to make it their own and enjoy it both as a singer and an interpreter. Sacrificing vocal and personal authenticity in an attempt to be stylistically authentic, nothing of excellence is gained. We should remember that many rules and conventions only came into being long after the respective works of art were born.

The accepted way of doing things has often originated from a particular individual. Once an artist is pronounced 'great', everything about him or her is admirable and deemed worthy of imitation. Schwarzkopf (lieder), Callas (bel canto repertoire), Pierre Bernac (French song), Peter Pears (Britten), all put their mark on their respective specialties, only to be followed by a host of imitators. As Ruskin put it: 'mere imitation is mere deception'.

Masterclasses would be notorious for their encouragement of imitation if the master's way were ever questioned from a physiological standpoint. It should never be a matter of 'this is how to do it', but always 'let's see how you can best do it'. This allows for growth and imagination as well as current limitations. Ability increases as the voice develops. Attempting to satisfy musical or expressive expedients in a vocally un-physiological way is an abuse of the instrument. The horse is bound to suffer if the cart is put before it.

The predetermined end-product almost invariably results in a mechanical and academic performance – it is the fruit of calculation and empty of aesthetic value. Training should enable the singer to be creative and bring their own personality to bear. This is achieved not by some external influence but through self-knowledge.

Both imitation and reproduction are abnegations of the responsibility to be real, to be natural, and thereby to appeal to the real and the natural in others. It is the schizophrenic result of the subject-object dualism which separates the singer from his or her material, and alienates listeners or at best leaves them unsatisfied or in ignorant admiration.

Remember, the healthy voice is derived from the healthy singer and vice versa. As the singer's capacity for wholeness is realised the quality of their performance grows exponentially.

Valuing Health

Of all the responsibilities that singing schools have, health has surely to be their top priority. Not only is health – or wholeness – basic to the singer's progress, sound singing boosts the health of the singer. Musical culture in general can only benefit from the generative nature of this relationship.

We tend to think that we are in good health unless we are obviously unwell. But this good health is often only what enables us to get through

– a kind of benign survival mode. If we want something more lively or exciting we seek some pleasurable stimulant, like strong exercise, partying or such like. When illness does come, we treat the symptoms. Indeed, health care in general seems to concentrate mainly on cure rather than prevention.

Sometimes prevention seems too much like hard work, or is misconstrued as some kind of deprivation. Many people don't bother to find out how well they *could* be, and therefore how much better their quality of life. We settle for what seems to be 'workable' or painless, knowing that when we feel less than OK there's usually a remedy in the form of a treat or a treatment. However, we are not only not taking preventive measures, we are not helping ourselves to function optimally. A malfunctioning voice is often not detected until the singer has a serious problem and needs to visit a clinic. Once cured of the immediate symptoms, the singer is only back where they were before the problem manifested.

Many everyday preventative measures are obvious: make sure your immune system is as good as can be, avoid draughts, keep hydrated, take care of your posture and speaking voice, and so on. Singing itself is highly therapeutic, even before we sing well. But for singers of any standard, prevention of illness is just a start, a prerequisite for the pursuit of specific vocal health.

There was a time when a laryngologist pronounced a person's voice as normal, and by implication healthy, even if that person couldn't sing. Singing was deemed to be something extra. But the reason why normal people cannot sing, or why they land in the clinic, is more often than not precisely because their voice – the normal one – is not the healthy one. It is vulnerable to abuse and strain in ways that the singing voice is not.

Normal people who depend on their speaking voice to any great extent often need help to be effective. Sometimes this is in the form of voice lessons. It is beginning to be realised that, starting with children, voices generally need to be taken care of. Speaking with as much of the singing voice operational as possible – actors might take note – is not only more healthy than 'normal healthy', but more rich and effective in communicative properties, such as clarity, colour and carrying power, and more durable too. When singing it's the same, only more so.[15]

Potential

Once again we are looking at the question of potential. Rather than substituting one voice for another, and rather than 'healing' as such, we are concerned with the 'original possibility'. Individuals achieve this through developing new and 'more constructive patterns of healthy behaviour; enhancement of emotional sensitivity; greater control of one's life: These are the primary and secondary outcomes of all effective health education'. In each person these benefits are 'reflected in his or her ability to reach previously unattainable goals'.[16] Healthy behaviour comes first; the results are outcomes rather than goals.

By cultivating healthy patterns of behaviour, singers bring about the systemic health of their original instrument. 'General health' is only a precondition for being able to adequately undergo the rigorous process of liberating the singing voice. Crucially, it includes emotional well-being. Opening up the voice can be disturbing. Suppressing emotions often causes physical blocks. Except in children, who as yet have no reason to hold back their feelings, ecstatic joy and deep anguish are rarely voiced. Training digs to the source of these things.

So, in the singing school there are two fitnesses that need differentiating: general and specific. Neither is optional. General fitness is basic and must be on-going; it underpins specific vocal training work. This highly specialised work differs little from workouts at the gym, where energy is expended as specific muscles and muscle-groups are worked on.[17]

Since lack of physical and emotional fitness are more common obstacles to progress than seems to be generally realised, a school of singing needs to be able to advise its students collectively and individually, and be in a position to help them constructively. Some music schools, I understand, make no provision for psychological help for their students. In my opinion there should be, at the very least, a counsellor on hand to help students who are finding it difficult to cope. With a caring ethos in place, constant liaison between departments and a spirit of co-operation among students, it should be possible for everyone to feel morally supported and encouraged.

Singers need to know how to take care of themselves. It may not occur to them that they need to take special care of their hearing, their teeth, their weight, their sleep, their stress, their diet, their digestion, their hygiene and so on. They may well need advice about the influences of hormones on their voice, and the adverse effects of drugs and alcohol. Such personal matters have not always been addressed at home. It is therefore incumbent on a school staffed by people who understand their importance to the trainee and the performer to advise its students and to lead by example.

I have included in The Work (Part II) subjects related to health from which every student of singing can benefit. I would make these compulsory. For example, meditation or mindfulness is a great day starter. It helps with awareness and focusing attention, and to lift a person's mood and alleviate anxiety. Alexander Technique educates the body to be optimally efficient.

Individuals may have other physical, emotional and vocal fitness requirements. There are many therapies and disciplines from which they might find something suitable. Apart from Psychotherapy there are Meridian Tapping Techniques for the relief of negative emotions and pain, or relational techniques through, for example, Circling (or InterSubjective Meditation). Reiki aims to eliminate a physical disease through its emotional coordinate. Yoga is generally a good mind-body-spirit practice, and Feldenkreis, which I have personally experienced, is an amazing body coordinator. Some students need vigorous exercise, or might benefit most from a form of martial art.

Teachers in the different departments are likely to spot individuals' needs and, in consultation with their colleagues, be able to advise pupils. A school would do well to have visiting exercise and therapy practitioners, or at least know whom to consult. They should be in a position to negotiate discounts for external sessions.

To embrace life and access feelings on a deep level – that is the training of the voice and the singer's education. To be in both the condition and the position to express and communicate those feelings – that is the singer's health and the singer's privileged occupation.

CHAPTER 27

Ethical Matters

The healthy voice is the 'whole' voice. The whole voice is the singing voice. A singer, like any musician, needs his or her instrument to be in tip top order. Not because it then has the whole gamut of required skills, numerically speaking – though that would be logical enough – but because, unlike in any other instrument, all the skills required are intrinsic to it. They are what makes the voice whole.

In an unbalanced voice, different possible configurations of imbalance result in gains and losses. The gains in each case are illusory. I am not talking about temporary effects, which are, and should remain, just that. But any skill that the singer might prize or specialise in, and train specially for, can only be achieved in its most comfortable, most effective and most beautiful form if it happily works in concert with all the other attributes of the singing voice of which by nature it is an integral part. With a constant bias towards one particular skill, the voice's other skills will be marginalised and can only be accessed incompletely. The complete singing voice on the other hand, while being a musical instrument *par excellence,* allows for the continuous intermixing and remixing of all the singer's expressive intentions.

It would be an entirely different matter if the voice were a machine. We might then fiddle with it and adjust it to our hearts content. Indeed, because of its astonishing resilience the human voice can withstand a good deal of wilful manipulation and distortion. It is unlikely, however, that such tinkering would ever bring contentment to the heart. For, like the heart, the singing voice is an organ designed to respond with the greatest sensitivity to what is essentially the stuff of singing.

We might sum this up broadly in two words: self-expression and communication. These are two sides of the same coin – we want to be able to express our feelings (or those of our character), and we want to share them or to be understood. With the singing voice up and running we have the wherewithal to communicate feelings truthfully and tellingly. Our performance resonates with the audience.

Values

One can no more put a price on singing than one can put a price on the person who is doing it. This is why the market, which values anything that sells, can be so misleading, and distract us from delving into the essence of what is truly excellent. It is why performers go along with what is marketable, why talent is so often flaunted and squandered before it's developed and secured. This is why attempts are made to create ways and means of producing different effects. But as we have seen, such specialisations yield a paucity of skills, and are shallow and short on emotional truth.

The whole voice is more expressively effective and affecting on every level because of its correlation with the whole of the singer. By the same token it has the greatest range of vocal effects (in one person) of any voice. Diversification is its province, both within a style and over a range of them. Classical singers have always benefited from such flexibility. Nowadays I would say it is imperative. Specialist fields are narrow, their markets limited. With a healthy voice the singer is not tied to any one 'way' of singing, or a particular style, or a passing fashion.

Action in the sphere of teaching is deliberate. While it may be motivated by a genuine desire for a good outcome, it is moral in as much as we consciously weigh up its pros and cons and consider its consequences. A sense of the 'ethical' comes through being awake to the consequences of our actions – what effect they have on the singer's voice, and therefore on the singer and their ability to perform. The ethical and the aesthetic are mutually engendering.

Institutions, as the embodiment of reason and knowledge, often mean well. But that doesn't always mean that they do well by their students. They may take credit for the successful ones, but they don't always take responsibility for those who struggle. 'Good will' and 'meaning well' do not of themselves generate genuine interest or a healthy spirit. On their own they are morally deficient.

Teaching is a kind of loving. It is through love that we bring out the best in ourselves and nourish the best in others. It is through love that seeds of understanding and belonging are sown. What makes good teaching is how – in what spirit and with what intent – it is done. Recognising value in others opens ways to positive interrelationships, co-operation and goodwill.

In our modern times, the industrialisation of the music profession leans heavily towards entertainment, which requires only instrumental values to succeed commercially. It is generally believed that these can be satisfied from the outside – by action based on instructions. Even the teaching of singing in some quarters has been organised on a commercial basis with this outside-in approach.

Perhaps more people should be asking, 'Are schools turning out stereotypical pop stars, chorus lines, early music specialists and opera singers, or are they enabling young people to become whole beings in sound?' So, not, 'Does this voice serve?' but 'Is this voice this person's voice?'

Let us once more review the four 'definitions' I suggested in Part I by way of identifying the singing voice:

- a physiologically sound structure;
- musical facility;
- individuality of sound and character;
- depth and ease of communication.

These defining qualities are common to all liberated singing voices. Through a dedicated and thorough process of training and education, a voice can regain its innate potential and thereby reveal its owner's unique identity. Through this process the singer's full capacity for vocal and personal communication, music-making and artistry can also be discovered. Economy in terms of means and energy, vocal resilience and longevity all come with this package. In addition to its instrumental values therefore we must acknowledge and honour the *intrinsic* values of this voice and the work that goes into its development.

If more evidence of such value were needed, we only have to consider the singing voice in terms of health. It is healthy to be able to use the body in such an extensively expressive way, and through it to voice, both metaphorically and literally, ourselves and our feelings. Good health is also derived from using the whole extent of the breathing apparatus – the effect this has on posture and the functional dynamics of the throat, and by extension on our overall fitness.

Recognising the singing voice as a complex whole, with so many attributes beyond those allied to entertainment, singing teachers as well as medical practitioners should assume their responsibility to heal malfunctioning vocal organs, instead of compartmentalising or fragmenting them. I am not talking about the cure of pathological or medical symptoms, or about something the measure of which is merely its serviceability or marketability. I am talking about the regeneration and development of a powerful human phenomenon, the functional health and natural capacities of which can only be measured by its wholeness and unique combination of attributes. The neglect of this healing process, or the deliberate distortion of a voice – for whatever reason – is reprehensible. While it is true that adults may choose how they use (or abuse) their voices, it is vocal misuse, or imbalance that usually lands them in the clinic seeking a cure. Can the deliberate unbalancing of a voice (a person) ever be justified?

As a singer's vocal capacity is realised, so their true sound comes to light, and they deepen to their own being and thence into their performance. We as voice trainers, educators and organisations have a moral obligation to those in our charge, as well as to their audiences. While as professionals we must be fully cognizant of the profession at large and its demands, we should not be cowed by the market or swayed in our purpose by its fickleness, pretentiousness or false messages. Nor can we afford to be complacent with regard to a gullible public. On the contrary, we need to educate and position ourselves to raise the profile of both the teaching and singing professions. Above all, we must be constantly aware that with each and every student we are assisting in the empowerment of a human being, in the freeing of a spirit and its voice.

When asked by the pianist Eric Himy for advice for upcoming musicians, the great Earl Wild said, 'Seek the truth in Art and within, without compromise. It is not always enough to be honest and so I think not only seek the truth in what you do but seek YOUR truth.'[1]

The penultimate word goes to someone whose ideas, after nearly a century of sterile debate in educational circles, are patiently awaiting realisation – the great philosopher, psychologist and educational reformer, John Dewey, who wrote:

> There is an old saying to the effect that it is not enough for a man to be good; he must be good for something. The something for which a man must be good is capacity to live as a social member so that what he gets from living with others balances with what he contributes. What he gets and gives as a human being, a being with desires, emotions, and ideas, is not external possessions, but a widening and deepening of conscious life – a more intense, disciplined, and expanding realization of meanings. What he materially receives and gives is at most opportunities and means for the evolution of conscious life. Otherwise, it is neither giving nor taking, but a shifting about of the position of things in space, like the stirring of water and sand with a stick. Discipline, culture, social efficiency, personal refinement, improvement of character are but phases of the growth of capacity nobly to share in such a balanced experience. And education is not a mere means to such a life. Education is such a life. To maintain capacity for such education is the essence of morals. For conscious life is a continual beginning afresh.[2]

The future of singing lies, I believe, in our ability to perceive the relevance of vocalisation to being human. The natural singing voice has its roots in our very existence. The fact that we normally have to labour to regenerate it shows us how disconnected we generally are from those roots.

In a world that is discovering the value of 'connecting', it seems timely to enquire with all diligence what it is that the singing voice can uniquely say for us, that begs to be heard and that merits our single-minded dedication.

APPENDIX 1

A few random repertoire sources

Pupils having such differing individual needs at different stages of their development, it can be difficult to find the 'right' piece at the right moment. The intention here is merely to identify some material, in no particular order of difficulty, which may be useful and suitable in the early stages of singing.

Carefully selected repertoire should first and foremost, by means of suitable inspiration and stimulation, enhance the individual's voice. It should neither inhibit the singer nor simply consolidate a technique.

Things singers need to remember:

a) Prepare thoroughly what can be done without singing, particularly the words and the rhythm, so that the singing is triggered by emotion and is not hesitant. Once embraced, this elemental approach is much easier than it may at first seem. It is much more rewarding than trying to do everything at once.

b) Because of a), singing in one's own language can be helpful to begin with, but from a purely vocal point of view Italian is probably best.

c) Until the voice gains overall natural stamina, quicker tempi and pieces with an easily felt pulse are more beneficial than slow, drawn-out ones. Short phrases are easier than long.

General

Folk Songs: from the culture of the individual singer

Odd phrases from almost any opera, including some *recitativo secco*

Vocalises by Vaccai

Songs from the Shows (it is important that singers use the vocal freedom they have gained so far, and not mimic other singers)

English

Elizabethan Songs: *An Elizabethan Song Book*, ed. W. H. Auden, C. Kallman and N. Greenberg, Faber & Faber, 1957

Songs from Shakespeare's plays and popular songs of his time

Songs from *The Beggar's Opera* by John Gay

Some delightful settings of Shakespeare by Thomas Arne

Songs by Purcell

North American

Songs by North American composers such as Ned Rorem, Charles Ives and Lee Holby

Songs by Cole Porter and Irving Berlin (it is important that singers use the vocal freedom they have gained so far, and not mimic other singers)

Italian

An endless supply of *Arie Antiche Italiane.* In addition to the time-honoured Parisotti volumes, I have found the *La Flora* volumes useful, and some collections published by Alfred Publishing Co. Inc. and edited by John Glenn Paton: refreshing

The series *Grandi Operisti per Giovani Cantanti*, compiled by voice and edited by Ricordi, have proved useful and enjoyable.

'L'ho perduta, me meschina!' Barbarina's aria from Mozart's *Le Nozze di Figaro* (perhaps on hands and knees!)

Songs to Italian texts by Tosti

Composizioni da Camera by Donizetti or Bellini

Songs by Rossini

A wealth of material from the works of George Frederick Handel

German

Lieder by Mozart

Arias from Mozart's *Bastien und Bastienne*

Lieder by Haydn: I recommend the volume of *Lieder für Gesang und Klavier*, published by G. Henle Verlag

Eight Early Songs by Anton von Webern

Lieder by Arnold Schoenberg – e.g. *4 Deutsche Volkslieder* or from *The Book of the Hanging Gardens and other Songs*, published by Dover Publications

French

Arias from operas by Gluck (in their French versions)

Arias from operettas by Offenbach – e.g. *Le Fifre Enchanté*

Songs by Ravel – e.g. *Cinq Mélodies Populaires Grecques*

Songs by Eric Satie – e.g. *Quatre Petites Mélodies*

Songs by Camille Chaminade

Huit Chansons Polonaises (with Polish) by Francis Poulenc

Spanish

13 Canciones Españolas Antiguas arranged by Federico Garcia Lorca

Various songs in various languages by Fernando Sor (many with guitar accompaniment)

Spanish Songs by Fernando J. Obradors, Enrique Granados, Eduardo Toldra

40 Songs in Spanish, French and English by Isaac Albéniz, collected under the title *Integral de l'obra per a veu i piano* published by Tritó, Barcelona

South American

Songs by Carlos Guastavino – e.g. *12 Canciones Populares*

Songs by Heitor Villa-Lobos – e.g. *6 Modinhas e Canções*

Portuguese

Modinhas Luso-Brasileiras

Songs by Francisco de Lacerda

Nove Canções de António Ramos Rosa by António Pinho Vargas

Russian

Sechs Romanzen (with German and English) for bass voice by Dmitri Schostakovitsch

Romanzen und Monologe (with German) for low voice by Dmitri Schostakovitsch

Songs by Stravinsky – e.g. 'Pribaoutki' (with French), *8 Short Songs* for medium voice (and piano) or *Berceuses du Chat* (4 songs for low voice) or *Trois Histoires pour Enfants* (3 children's songs with French and English)

For those who are happy to sing Russian songs in English there are volumes by Boosey & Hawkes and the *Complete Songs for Voice and Piano* by Rachmaninoff published by Dover

APPENDIX 2A

Curriculum

Please refer to appendix 2b for further information

ENTRANCE REQUIREMENTS	CURRICULUM	YEAR I	YEAR II	YEAR III
• **Voice:** Obvious talent	(a) Voice	10 - 30 minutes voice training twice daily depending on individual → (at least four days per week)	Beginning singing when ready	45 minutes, 3 times weekly
• **Musicality** Obvious talent or feel for music	(b) Rhythm { Dancing	45 minutes 2 or 3 days a week (plus occasional evening special) →	→	60 minutes, twice weekly
	{ Drumming / Body music }	30 or 45 minutes 2 or 3 times weekly }	Optional or where needed	
• **Musicianship**	(c) Eurythmics	As alternative to drumming/body music where required - 45 minutes twice weekly	Where required	
• **Aural** • **Harmony & counterpoint all at least Grade 7** (Associated board of the Royal Schools of Music) or equivalent	(d) Listening (Harmony/Counterpoint/History/Style)	1. Based on vocal repertoire/style → 2. Individual or group assignment Material analysed in class → 60 minutes (3 x weekly) →	→	Private study / workshops →
	(e) Improvisation	45 minutes (twice weekly) →	→	60 minutes per week
• **2nd Study Instrument** 1* at least Grade 5 (ABRSM)	(f) 2nd Study instrument (concentrating on musicianship)	45 minutes (twice weekly) →	→	
	(g) Coaching			Singing Coaching proper begins: 30-45 minutes daily, depending on student's capacity
• **History** 3*	(h) Audition class		One each month for those sufficiently advanced	All student's audition at outset of year then once each month depending of capacity
• **Language** A feeling for language	(i) Clowning	60 minutes first thing Monday morning →	→	
• **Languages** 4* One of German, French or (preferably) Italian in addition to native tongue	(j) Performance ('Acts')	60 minutes twice weekly (individual & duos) →	→	Singing every 2 weeks
	(k) Alexander Technique 5*	30 minutes daily depending on need →	→	Less frequently depending on need
	(l) Language (Text)	45 minutes, 3 times per week →	Specific texts related to current repertoire →	→
	(m) Physical expression (Acting)	Begin term 2 or 3 60 minutes, 4 times weekly →	→	Tied with (g), (h) and (j)
• **Fitness** 2*	(n) Stage craft	Begin term 2 or 3 60 minutes weekly →	→	
	(o) Presentation	60 minutes per week →	→	With reference to (h) and (j) →
	(p) Languages (Foreign)	2 of German, French, Italian 45 minutes twice weekly each language →	→	Add third language
	(q) Meditation	10-15 minutes each day, Tuesday-Friday (before classes begin) →	→	→
	(r) Outings/Aesthetics etc	At least 3 outings to be arranged per term (followed up by class) →	→	Optional
	(s) Fitness	STUDENTS EXPECTED TO KEEP GENERALLY FIT THROUGHOUT COURSE →	→	→

1* Blown instruments (apart from flute) are not compatible with singing. Violin and viola sometimes adversely affect posture.

2* Candidates should be natural weight. Medical/surgical history should be checked for anything that might adversely affect hard training.

3* Candidates should have an historical perspective with regard to different styles and their chief representatives.

4* A good working knowledge of ENGLISH should be obligatory in English speaking countries.

5* Alexander technique will help students to monitor their body's efficiency throughout the course.

APPENDIX 2B

Hours

The Work – Hours (in minutes)

Department	YEARS 1 & 2					YEAR 3					YEARS 4 & 5				
	M	T	W	T	F	M	T	W	T	F	M	T	W	T	F
Voice Training	30	30	30	30	30	30	30	30	30	30	45	-	45	-	45
2nd Instrument	45	-	45	-	-	Self arranged					Self arranged				
Dancing	45	-	45	-	45	-	60	-	-	60	-	60	-	60	-
Drum/Eurythmics	-	45	-	45	-	-	-	-	-	-	-	-	-	-	-
Improvisation	-	45	-	45	-	-	60	-	60	-	-	-	-	-	-
Physical Expression	60	60	-	60	60	60	60	60	60	60	Rehearsals/Workshops				
Stage Craft	-	-	60	-	-	-	-	-	-	-	-	-	-	-	-
Presentation	-	-	-	-	60	-	60	-	60	-	Performances				
Clowning	60	-	-	-	-	60	-	-	-	-	Optional				
Meditation	-	15	15	15	15	-	15	15	15	15	15	15	15	15	15
Alexander Technique	30	30	30	30	30	30	-	-	30	-	Optional				
Perform ('Acts')	-	60	-	60	-	Singing fortnightly					Audition workshops				
Literacy/Texts	45	-	45	-	45	60	-	60	-	60	Rehearsals/Workshops				
Foreign Languages	45	45	-	45	45	45	45	-	45	45	60	-	60	-	60
Listening etc	-	60	60	-	60	Private study/Workshops					Private study/Workshops				
Coaching	-	-	-	-	-	30	45	30	45	30	60	30	60	30	60

Nota Bene: Apart from Voice Training, these 16 subjects have not been listed in any order of priority.

Endnotes

PART I ~ The Singing Voice

Chapter 1 ~ Defining and Identifying the Singing Voice

1 The word lyric(al), as used in Latin countries, usually refers to operatic music, but sometimes, as in the Portuguese, it denotes lyrical song, or classical music that is lyrically expressive. Lyric(al) is in fact more apt than 'classical' since it's more in tune with the character and qualities of the human singing voice.

Chapter 2 ~ The Holistic Perspective

1 Skolimowski, Henryk (1994) *The Participatory Mind – A New Theory of Knowledge and of the Universe,* London: Arkana (Penguin Books Ltd.), p. 181.
2 Ibid. p. 141.
3 Johnson, Will (1993) *Balance of Body, Balance of Mind – a Rolfer's vision of Buddhist practice in the West,* Atlanta: Humanics Trade Paperbacks, p. 90.
4 Skolimowski, Henryk (1994) *The Participatory Mind,* p. 213.
5 Ibid. p. 5.
6 Read, D. and Stoll, W. (1998) 'Healthy Behaviour – the implications of a holistic paradigm of thinking through bodymind research', International Electronic Journal of Health education (1998) – quoted at head of article.
7 Capra, Fritjof (1976) 'Modern Physics and Eastern Mysticism', The Journal of Transpersonal Psychology (ATP) 8, 1 (Winter 1976): 26.
8 Skolimowski, Henryk (1994) *The Participatory Mind,* p. 151.
9 Ibid. p. 141.
10 Read, D. and Stoll, W. (1998) 'Healthy Behaviour' – see endnote 2.6.
11 Ibid. p. 3.
12 Johnson, Will (1993) *Balance of Body, Balance of Mind,* p. 9.
13 Ibid. p. 21.
14 Ibid. p. 38 and 40.
15 Husler, Frederick and Rodd-Marling, Yvonne (1976) *Singing – The Physical Nature of the Vocal Organ* (revised edition), London: Hutchinson, p. 3.
16 Johnson, Will (1993) *Balance of Body, Balance of Mind,* p. 49.
17 Husler, Frederick and Rodd-Marling, Yvonne (1976) *Singing,* p. 3.
18 Harrison, Peter T. (2006) *The Human Nature of the Singing Voice – exploring a holistic basis for sound teaching and learning,* Edinburgh: Dunedin Academic Press Ltd.
19 Rogers, Carl R. (1980) *A Way of Being,* Boston: Houghton Mifflin Company, p. 114.
20 Maslow, Abraham (1973) *The Farther Reaches of Human Nature,* Harmondsworth, p. 59

– quoted by Storr, Anthony (1988) *The School of Genius*, London: André Deutsch Ltd., p. 200.

21 Chopra, Deepak (2010) *The Soul of Leadership*, U.S.A. Harmony Books (2011 edition by Rider, an imprint of Ebury Publishing), p. 89.

Chapter 3 ~ Physical Structure (Anatomy and Physiology)

1 As much as we are obliged to use them, terms such as 'parts', 'structure' and 'mechanism' are neither strictly accurate nor helpful when talking about something organic, if by them we mean discrete parts, fixed structures or mechanical mechanisms. The structures we are dealing with here are muscle systems. They are not independent; they depend for their effective activity on their elastic, interactive relations with each other.

2 Piaget, Jean (1973) *Einfuhrung in die genetische Erkenntnistheorie*, Frankfurt: Suhrkamp. (English translation New York: Columbia University Press, 1970) – quoted by Blaukopf, Kurt (1982); translated by David Marinelli. *Musical Life in a Changing Society*, Munich: R. Piper & Co. Verlag. (translated by David Marinelli: revised and enlarged English-language edition, Amadeus Press 1992) p. 16.

3 Harrison, Peter T. (2006), *The Human Nature of the Singing Voice* – mainly chapters 2, 3 and 4.

4 Husler, Frederick and Rodd-Marling, Yvonne (1976) *Singing*, p. 6.

5 Ibid. p. 7.

6 Ibid. Chapter IV.

7 Ibid. pages 37–38.

8 Ibid. p. 12.

9 Ibid. p. 17.

10 Ibid. p. 17.

11 Ibid. p. 21–22.

12 Ibid. pp. 23–24.

13 Harrison, Peter T. (2006) *The Human Nature of the Singing Voice* chapter 5.

14 Reid, Cornelius L. (1983) *A Dictionary of Vocal Terminology & Analysis* (reprint edition), Huntsville: Recital publications p. 394.

15 Ibid. p. 394.

16 Ibid. p. 345.

Chapter 4 ~ Beautiful Singing (Bel Canto)

1 Source: Pieter van der Stölk, one time pupil of Frederick Husler and a great voice teacher.

2 Negus, V. E. (1949 reprinted 1962) *The Comparative Anatomy and Physiology of the Larynx*, New York, Hafner Publishing Company, Inc., p 199.

Note: With evolution the human vocal folds became less sharp-edged than those of our arboreal ancestors. They may therefore be less efficient in respect of the need for increased strength in arms and chest. By the same token our vocalisation is less shrill. This makes the human larynx, in regard to human expression, all the more fascinating.

3 Herbert-Caesari, E. (1958) *Tradition and Gigli*, London, Robert Hale Ltd., pp. 26–27. Note: E. Herbert-Caesari was a pupil of Ricardo Daviesi, one of the greatest Sistine Chapel singers of the 19th Century.

4 Denis Arnold (1984) *The New Oxford Companion to Music* Vol.2, Oxford University Press, p. 1196.

5 John Potter (2009) *Tenor – History of a Voice*, Yale University Press, p. 13.

6 Herbert-Caesari, E (1958) *Tradition and Gigli*, p. 27.
7 Ibid. pp. 31–2.
8 Ibid. p. 32.
9 Ibid. p. 54.
10 Ibid. p. 69.
11 Harnoncourt, Nikolaus (1982) *Musik als Klangrede*, Salzburg and Wien, Residenz Verlag. (1988) *Baroque Music Today: Music as Speech*, Amadeus Press (Translation), p. 129.
12 Parish, C. and Ohl, John F. (1953) *Masterpieces of Music Before 1750*, London, Faber and Faber Ltd., p. 124.
13 Harnoncourt, Nikolaus (1982) *Baroque Music Today: Music as Speech*, p. 130.
14 Ibid. p. 130.
15 Husler, Frederick and Rodd-Marling, Yvonne (1976) *Singing*, p. 47.
16 Robert Donington (1978) *A Performer's Guide to Baroque Music*, London, Faber and Faber Ltd., p. 53.
17 Ibid. p. 49.
18 Celletti, Rodolfo (1991) *A History of Bel Canto*, Oxford University Press (Translation), p. 107.
19 Reid, Cornelius (1983) *A Dictionary of Vocal Terminology & Analysis*, p. 188.
20 Husler, F. and Rodd-Marling, Y. (1976) *Singing*, p. 84.
21 Reid, Cornelius (1983) *A Dictionary of Vocal Terminology & Analysis*, p. 206.
22 Husler, F. and Rodd-Marling, Y. (1976) *Singing*, p. 64.
23 Titze, Ingo R. (Editor) (1993) *Vocal Fold Physiology: Frontiers in Basic Science*, Singular Publishing Group, Inc., San Diego, p. 1.

Chapter 5 ~ Individual Identity

1 Maria Callas, whose teacher, Elvira de Hidalgo, was supposedly a teacher of the Old Italian School, said herself that this schooling no longer existed.
2 Elizabeth Schwarzkopf is supposed to have said, 'We have a long way to go to reach the standards set by the great singers of yesteryear'.
3 Jessye Norman may have said, 'a pigeon hole is only satisfactory to a pigeon'. In neither case have I been able to trace the relevant interview. This quote was mentioned by Martha Kearney on the BBC Radio (July 31, 2009), but it may have come from Patrick Watson's interview with Norman in 1989.
4 Johnson, Will (1993) *Balance of Mind, Balance of Body*, p. 24.
5 Ibid. p. 41.
6 Ibid. p. 42.
7 Skolimowski, Henryk (1994) *The Participatory Mind*, p. 226.
8 Fromm, Eric (1978) *To Have or To Be*, London, Jonathan Cape ltd., p. 94.
9 Husler, F. and Rodd-Marling, Y. (1976) *Singing*, p. 21 (quoting K. Goerttler).
10 Storr, Anthony (1988) *The School of Genius*, London, André Deutsch Ltd., p. 201 (quoting Abraham Maslow).
11 Prochnik, George (2010) *In Pursuit of Silence*, U.S.A. Doubleday, p. 252.
12 Taylor, Gordon Rattray (1972) *Rethink: A Paraprimitive Solution*, London, Martin Secker & Warburg Ltd., p. 142.
13 Stevens, Anthony (1982 repr. 1990) *Archetype: A Natural History of the Self*, London, Routledge, p. 293 (quoting Carl G. Jung: CW 17, para. 296).

Chapter 7 ~ False Perspectives and Misperceptions

1 Midgette, Anne (November 2005) 'The End of the Great Big American Voice', an article in the *New York Times* (Arts) p.1 www.nytimes.com/2005/11/13/arts/music.

2 Shapiro, Yehuda (July 2008) 'Voci Verdiane', an article in *Opera*, London, Rhinegold Publishing, p. 778.

3 Ibid. p. 778.

4 Holroyd, Michael (ed.) (1979) *The Genius of Shaw*, New York, Holt, Rinehart and Winston, pp. 71–72 (an article entitled 'The Music Critic' by Charles Osborne, in which he also says, 'Shaw castigated Verdi for having, so he claimed, ruined the baritone voice by writing only for the upper fifth of its compass'!).

5 Quoted by Albert Innaurato (1996) in programme notes to the Testament CD release of Eileen Farrell: *Opera Arias and Songs*.

6 Midgette, Anne (November 2005) The End of the Great Big American Voice, p. 2.

7 Husler, Frederick and Rodd-Marling, Yvonne (1976) *Singing*, p. 42.

8 Manuel Garcia Jnr. (1805–1906). It is the author's opinion that, although well-intended, the invention of Garcia's laryngoscope in 1854 marks the beginning of a decline in aural perception.

9 Midgette, Anne (November 2005) 'The End of the Great Big American Voice'. p. 2.

10 For example, from Placido Domingo's Operalia:

Pretty Yende from South Africa – winner (2011)
Guang Yang from China – winner (1997)

and from the BBC Cardiff Singer of the World:

Nicole Cabell from the U.S.A – winner (2005)
Anja Harteros from Germany – winner (1999)
Dmitri Horovstovsky from Russia – winner (1989)
Bryn Terfel from Wales – song prize (1989)

11 Reid, Cornelius (1983) *A Dictionary of Vocal Terminology and Analysis*, p197. See also 'covering' 77–82, and 'Lowered Larynx', pp. 195–197.

12 The British Voice Association: www.britishvoiceassociation.org.uk

13 Vocalises, such as those by Vaccai and Concone 'have little pedagogic value…they center on the art of singing and rarely address themselves to a specific problem'. Reid, Cornelius (1983) *A Dictionary of Vocal Terminology and Analysis*, p. 411.

14 www.britishvoiceassociation.org.uk.

15 Ibid.

16 *Communicating Voice* (Vol. 13: Issue 1 – Summer 2012), p. 15.

PART II ~ The Work

Chapter 9 ~ Voice

1 Chapman, Janice L. (15th July, 2010), Plenary Lecture 'Choice for Voice' Conference, British Voice Association at the Royal Academy of Music, London.

2 How to Sing Bel Canto I – YouTube.

Chapter 10 ~ Music (singing)

1 The Associated Board of the Royal Schools of Music: www.abrsm.org/exams.

2 Dewey, John (1934), *Art as Experience*, New York, The Berkley Publishing Group (Perigree trade paperback edition 2005), p. 153.

3 Rée, Jonathan (1999) *I See a Voice: Language, Deafness & the Senses – a Philosophical History*, London, Harper Collins, p. 133.
4 Husler, F. and Rodd-Marling, Y. (1976) *Singing*, p. 108.
5 Schnebly-Black, Julia and Moore, Stephen F. (1997) *The Rhythm Inside: Connecting Body, Mind and Spirit Through Music* (Music CD included), Oregon, Rudra Press, Back Cover.
6 Ibid. p. 34.
7 Ibid. p. 29.

Chapter 11 ~ Physical Expression (Acting)

1 Rée, Jonathan (1999) *I See a Voice* London, Harper Collins, p. 133.
2 Marshall, Lorna (2001) *The Body Speaks: Performance and Expression*, London, Methuen p. 27. (A second,revised edition was published in 2008).
3 Ibid. p. 27.
4 Stanislavski, Constantin (1924) *My Life in Art* (Trans. by J. J.Robbins), Great Britain, Geoffrey Bles Ltd. (repr. Methuen Drama 1991), p. 562.

Chapter 12 ~ Language (Text)

1 Contrary to the view, in some circles, that they 'don't need classical voice training', actors only ever trained their voices for the same reasons as singers – to be able to use their voices more expressively and so that they carried. Vocal expressivity and carrying power are the results of health or wholeness. The healthy voice is the singing voice. Anything less than this voice is by definition less healthy as well as less effective.
2 Fischer-Diskau, Dietrich (1968) *Texte Deutscher Lieder*, Munich, Deutscher Taschenbuch Verlag GmbH & Co. / (1976) *The Fischer-Diskau Book of Lieder*, (with English translations by George Bird and Richard Stokes), London, Gollanz, p. 28.
3 Tomatis, Alfred A. (1992) *The Conscious Ear – My Life of Transformation Through Listening*, New York, Station Hill Press, p. 89.
4 Lois Philips (1979) *Lieder Line by Line – and Word for Word*, London, Gerald Duckworth & Co. Ltd.
5 Harrison, Peter T. (2006), *The Human nature of the Singing Voice*, Chapter 19 (Being Fully Prepared) pp. 194–206.
6 The Stúdio, to which I was appointed Director of Vocal Studies, refers to the Estúdio de Ópera do Porto (2001–2006).
7 Arden, Paul (2003) *It's not how Good you Are, It's how Good you want to Be*, London, Phaidon Press Limited, p. 51 – Einstein quote.
8 Schnebly-Black, J and Moore, Stephen F (1997) *The Rhythm Inside* p. 75.

Chapter 14 ~ Supporting Cast

1 Schnebly-Black, J. and Moore, Stephen F. (1997) *The Rhythm Inside*, p. 81.
2 Ibid. p. 4.
3 Ostwald, David F. (2005) *Acting for Singers*, New York, Oxford University Press Inc., p. 49.
4 Schnebly-Black, J. and Moore, Stephen F. (1997) *The Rhythm Inside*, p. 85.
5 Wade, Graham (1991) 'A Conversation with George Hadjinikos', European Guitar Teachers Association (UK), p. 3. The full quotation: 'The rudiments are abstract notions that were conceived in order to find a way of writing music, while the roots of music stem from our inner being and correspond accordingly to the laws of nature'.

http://www.egta.co.uk/content/hadjinikos
6 Schnebly-Black, J and Moore, Stephen F. (1997) *The Rhythm Inside*, p. 81.
7 Ibid. p. 83.
8 Johnson, Will (1993) *Balance of Body, Balance of Mind* p. 91.
9 Allen Ginsberg (1980) *Composed on the Tongue*, California, Grey Fox Press, pp. 111–112. Quoted by Lewis Hyde (2006) *The Gift*, Edinburgh, Books Ltd., p. 147.
10 Ristad, Eloise (1982) *A Soprano On Her Head*, Utah, Real People Press, p. 144.
11 Arden, Paul (2003) *It's not how Good you Are, It's how Good you want to Be*, p. 50.
12 Charlton, Noel G. (2008) *Understanding Gregory Bateson: Mind, Beauty and the Sacred Earth*, Albany, State University of New York Press, p.97 – quoting from a paper called 'The Message, "This is Play"' given by Bateson at the 1955 Macy Conference.
13 Edward de Bono (1991) *Handbook for the Positive Revolution*, London, Viking (Penguin Books Ltd.,), p. 70.
14 Feldenkrais, Moshe (1985) *The Potent Self*, New York: Harper and Row, chapter 13 – a survey of the many causes of bad posture.
15 There is no substitute for experience, and people have often found Alexander's writings difficult to comprehend, but there are at least two books that the reader might find both comprehensible and helpful:
1. Edward Maisel (ed) (1969), *The Alexander Technique: The Essential Writings of F. Matthias Alexander*, London, Thames and Hudson.
2. Various writers, Jerry Sontag (ed) (1996), *Curiosity Recaptured: Exploring Ways We Think and Move*, U.S.A., Mornum Time Press.
16 Chopra, Deepak (2004) *The Book of Secrets*, U.S.A., Harmony Books and London, Rider, p. 34.

PART III ~ Conditions

Chapter 16 ~ Environment and Attitude

1 Lipton, Bruce H. (2008) *The Biology of Belief: Unleashing the Power of Consciousness, Matter and Miracles*, U.S.A., Hay House, Inc., p. 37.
2 Stanislavski, Constantin (1924) *My Life in Art*, pp. 534–535.
3 Fritz Winckel (1967) *Music, Sound and Sensation* (English translation by Thomas Binkley of *Phänomene des musikalischen Hörens*, published by Max Hesses Verlag, 1960), p. 58.
4 Ibid. p. 65.

Chapter 17 ~ Ethos

1 'I saw the angel in the marble and carved until I set him free.' Michelangelo (1475–1564).
2 Dewey, John (1934) *Art as Experience*, p. 291.
3 Brazier, Caroline (2003) *Buddhist Psychology*, London, Constable and Robinson Ltd., p. 201.

Chapter 18 ~ Process

1 Charlton, Noel G. (2008) *Understanding Gregory Bateson: Mind, Beauty and the Sacred Earth*, Albany, The State University of New York Press, p. 183.
2 Ristad, Eloise (1982) *A Soprano on Her Head*, Utah, Real People Press, p. 81.

3 Feldenkrais, Moshe (1985) *The Potent Self*, p. 121.
4 Ibid. p. 121.
5 Quoted by Barbara Kent (1996) in *Curiosity Recaptured: Exploring Ways we Think and Move* (ed. Jerry Sontag), U.S.A., Mornum Time Press, p. 220.
6 Adapted from Ouspensky, P. D. (1978), *The Psychology of Man's Possible Evolution*, London, Routledge & Kegan Paul Ltd., pp. 43–44.
7 Wade, Graham (1991) 'A Conversation with George Hadjinikos', p. 3.
8 Maisel, Edward (1969) *The Alexander Technique*, p. 11.
9 Charlton, Noel G. (2008) *Understanding Gregory Bateson*, p. 182.

Chapter 19 ~ Systems and Organ-isation

1 William Shakespeare (1564–1616) *Othello*, Act III, iv 69.
2 Goodwin, Brian (2007) *Nature's Due: Healing Our Fragmented Culture*, Edinburgh, Floris Books, p. 46.
3 Goldberg, Philip (1983) *The Intuitive Edge: Understanding Intuition and Applying it in Everyday Life*, New York, Jeremy P. Tarcher/Perigree, p. 72.
4 Goodwin, Brian (2007) *Nature's Due*, p. 46 – I have made an analogy here with the 'healthy heart'.
5 Ball, Philip (2004) *Critical Mass: How One Thing Leads to Another*, UK, William Heinemann, p. 571.
6 Goldberg, Philip (1983) *The Intuitive Edge*, p. 162 – quoting Peter Senge, Director of the Centre for Organisational Learning at MIT Sloan School of Management.
7 Wheatley, Margaret J. (1999) *Leadership and the New Science: Discovering Order in a Chaotic World*, San Francisco, Berrett-Koehler Publishers, Inc., p. 132.
8 Ibid. p. 145.
9 Holy Bible, Luke 4, 23 (King James Version).
10 Wheatley, Margaret J. (1999) *Leadership and the New Science*, p. 89.
11 Ibid. p. 174.
12 Wheatley, Margaret, J (1999) *Leadership and the New Science*, p. 167.

PART IV ~ The Ehsnrining of Values

Chapter 20 ~ Education

1 Schnebly-Black, Julia and Moore, Stephen F. (1997) *The Rhythm Inside* p. 36.
2 Watts, Alan W. (1974 repr. 1985) *The Wisdom of Insecurity – A Message for an Age of Anxiety*, London: Rider and Company, p. 67.
3 Schnebly-Black, Julia and Moore, Stephen F. (1997) *The Rhythm Inside* p. 15.
4 Rattray Taylor, Gordon (1972) *Rethink – A Paraprimitive Solution*, London: Secker & Warburg, p.22 (From *Motivation and Personality* by Abraham Maslow).
5 Chopra, Deepak, quoted by Jane Taylor in her report 'New University dedicated to global transformation' for *Positive News*: Issue 70 Winter 2011, p. 5.
6 Stevens, Anthony (1982 repr. 1990) *Archetype*, London: Routledge, p. 293 – quoting C. Jung (CW 8, para 344).
7 Johnson, Will (1993) *Balance of Body, Balance of Mind*, p. 29.
8 Lipton, Bruce H. (2010, 10th edit.) *The Biology of Belief – Unleashing the Power of Consciousness*, Matter & Miracles, UK: Hay House, p. 139.

Chapter 21 ~ Pupils

1 John Lane (2006) *The Spirit of Silence – Making Way for Creativity*, Dartington: Green Books Ltd., p. 75 – quoting Rollo May.

Chapter 22 ~ Co-operation

1 Meighan Roland (Compiled) (1994) *The Freethinker's Guide to the Educational Universe – A Selection of Quotations on Education*, Nottingham: Educational Heretics Press, p. 88.
2 Steve Davis (2009), 'Rethinking the Theoretical Foundation of Evolution' (quoting Peter Kropotkin) – Science 2.0.
3 Ibid.
4 Quoted by Stephen Moss (03.05.07) 'The DIY Violinist', *Guardian* Arts Music.
5 Lipton, Bruce H. (2010, 10th edit.) *The Biology of Belief*, p. 16.
6 Storr, Anthony (1988) *The School of Genius*, p. 147
7 Holy Bible, Mark 4: 3–9 (Authorised Version).
8 Josephs-Serra, Mark (2000) *Sex, Spirit & Community*, Oxfordshire: Jon Carpenter Publishing, p. 58.
9 Stanislavski, Constantin (1924) *My Life in Art* (trans. J.J.Robbins), Great Britain, Geoffrey Bles Ltd. (repr. Methuen Drama 1991), pp. 538–539.

Chapter 23 ~ Excellence

1 From *The Expressive Voice* – Part II, posted by the Vespasiano Forum for Ayn Rand fans, April 2010.
2 Husler, Frederick, and Rodd-Marling, Yvonne (1976) *Singing: The Physical Nature of the Vocal Organ* (revised edition), London: Hutchinson p. 83.
3 Skolimowski, Henryk (1994) *The Participatory Mind – A New Theory of Knowledge and of the Universe*, London: Arkans, (Penguin Books Ltd.) p. 15.
4 *The Reader's Digest Oxford Wordfinder* – Editor, Sara Tulloch (1993): Oxford, Clarendon Press.
5 Charlton, Noel G. (2008) *Understanding Gregory Bateson*, Albany, The State University of New York Press, pp. 39, 140 and 206.
6 Ibid. p. 109.
7 Hyde, Lewis (2006) *The Gift – How the Creative Spirit Transforms the World*, Edinburgh, Canongate Books Ltd., p. 200.
8 Skolimowski, Henryk (1994) The Participatory Mind, p. 252.
9 Hyde, Lewis (2006) The Gift, p. 153.
10 Johann Wolfgang Goethe (1749–1832), whose poetry was set by Beethoven, Schubert, Schumann, Brahms, Wolf and Mahler amongst others, and who, among his many other accomplishments, wrote aesthetic criticism.
11 Buber, Martin and Friedman, Maurice (intro.) (1965) *The Knowledge of Man – Selected Essays by Martin Buber*, London: Allen and Unwin. p. 41.
12 Hyde, Lewis (2006) *The Gift*, p. 205.
13 Ibid. p. 155.

Chapter 25 ~ Consensus

1 Chapman, Janice L. (15th July 2010), Plenary Lecture, 'Choice for Voice' Conference, British Voice Association at the Royal Academy of Music, London.
2 *The Reader's Digest Oxford Wordfinder* – Ed. Sara Tulloch (1993): Oxford, clarendon Press.

3 Chapman, Janice L. (July 2010) 'Choice for Voice' Conference.

4 John of Salisbury (1120–1180) – from descriptions of twelfth century vocal techniques – quoted on the website of the new vocal group Capella Duriensis.

5 Goldberg, Philip (1983) *The Intuitive Edge: Understanding Intuition and Applying it in Everyday Life*, New York, Jeremy P. Tarcher/Perigree, p. 214.

Chapter 26 ~ Leading the Way

1 The author could not find the source of this saying.

2 Charles Dickens (1859–1895), from the closing paragraph of his major commentary on Charles Darwin which appeared (1860) in his own periodical called *All the Year Round*

3 Leadbeater, C. (1999), Living on Thin Air: The New Economy, London, Viking pp. 152–16). Referred to by Renshaw in Connecting Conversations, p. 11 – see below.

4 My friend, Nicholas Bradbury, recently appointed to the NHS Leadership Academy, in a letter.

5 Renshaw, Peter (2003), Connecting Conversations: The Changing Voice of the Artist (European League of Institutes of the Arts Teachers' Academy), p. 11.

6 Clark, Susan in an article about Tim Smit (Founder of the Eden Project) entitled 'Maverick Leadership' (Resurgence January/February 2011 No. 264). Other 'core qualities and values of a visionary leader' sited here are energy, passion, language, trust, relationship and community, in addition to curiosity.

7 Wikipedia on: Senge, Peter (1990) *The Fifth Discipline*, Doubleday Business.

8 Ibid.

9 Renshaw, Peter (2003), Connecting Conversations, p. 2.

10 Ibid. pp. 7–8.

11 Ibid. p. 8.

12 *Reader's Digest Oxford Wordfinder* – Ed. Sara Tulloch (1993) and The Free Dictionary by Farlex (Thesaurus 3).

13 From a mission statement of the Royal Academy of Music, London. A recent version reads to 'preserve and enrich national and international music culture' through 'the recruitment of the finest musicians….'

14 Lipton, Bruce H. (2010, 10th edition) *The Biology of Belief*, p. 116.

15 Singers who put on what they imagine to be a 'singer's voice' – particularly common amongst male singers – are not speaking naturally. They sometimes find themselves at the voice clinic because of symptoms arising from the distortion.

16 Read, D. and Stoll, W. (1998) *Healthy Behaviour*, p. 11.

17 For more on muscle training and fitness see Chapter 13 of my book *The Human Nature of the Singing Voice*.

Chapter 27 ~ Ethical Matters

1 From an interview between Judith Monk and the pianist Eric Himy found in *Musical Opinion* (May/June 2007: Issue No.1458).

2 Dewey, John (1916) *Democracy and Education – an introduction to the philosophy of education*, U.S.A., bln publishing (Classic Reprint 2010), pp. 217–218.

Bibliography

Arden, Paul (2003) *It's not how Good you Are, It's how Good you want to Be,* London, Phaidon Press Limited.

Arnold, Denis (1984) *The New Oxford Companion to Music* Vol. 2, Oxford University Press.

Ball, Philip (2004) *Critical Mass: How One Thing Leads to Another,* U.K., William Heinemann.

Blaukopf, Kurt (1982) *Musical Life in a Changing Society: Aspects of Music Sociology* (translated David Marinelli) – revised and enlarged English-language edition (1992) Amadeus Press.

Brazier, Caroline (2003) *Buddhist Psychology,* London, Constable and Robinson Ltd.

Buber, Martin (1965) and Friedman, Maurice (intro.) (1965) *The Knowledge of Man: Selected essays by Martin Buber,* London, Allen and Unwin.

Capra, Fritjof (1976) *Modern Physics and Eastern Mysticism* – The Journal of Transpersonal Psychology (ATP) 8, 1 (Winter 1976): 26

Celletti, Rodolfo (1991) *A History of Bel Canto,* Oxford University Press (translation).

Chapman, Janice (2010) Plenary Lecture 'Choice for Voice' Conference – British Voice Association at the Royal Academy of Music, London.

Charlton, Noel G. (2008) *Understanding Gregory Bateson: Mind, Beauty and the Sacred Earth,* Albany, State University of New York Press.

Chopra, Deepak (2010) *The Soul of Leadership,* U.S.A. Harmony Books (2011 edition by Rider, an imprint of Ebury Publishing.

Clark, Susan (2011) *Maverick Leadership,* Resurgence January/February 2011 No.264.

Davis, Steve (2009) *Rethinking the Theoretical Foundation of Evolution,* Science 2.0.

de Bono, Edward (1991) *Handbook for the Positive Revolution,* London, Viking (Penguin Books Ltd.).

Dewey, John (1934) *Art as Experience,* New York, The Berkley Publishing Group (Perigree trade paperback edition 2005).

Donington, Robert (1978) *A Performer's Guide to Baroque Music,* London, Faber and Faber, Ltd.

Feldenkrais, Moshe (1985) *The Potent Self,* New York, Harper and Row.

Fischer-Diskau, Dietrich (1968) *Texte Deutscher Lieder,* Munich, Deutscher Taschenbuch Verlag GmbH & Co./ (1976) *The Fischer-Diskau Book of Lieder* (English translation George Bird and Richard Stokes), London, Gollanz.

Fromm, Eric (1978) *To Have or to Be,* London, Jonathan Cape Ltd.

Ginsberg, Allen (1980) *Composed on the Tongue,* California, Grey Fox Press – quoted by Hyde, Lewis (2006) *The Gift,* Edinburgh, Canongate Books Ltd.

Goldberg, Philip (1983) *The Intuitive Edge: Understanding Intuition and Applying it in Everyday Life,* New York, Jeremy P. Tarcher/Perigree.

Goodwin, Brian (2007) *Nature's Due: Healing Our Fragmented Culture,* Edinburgh, Floris Books.

Gray, S.D. (1991) Basement membrane zone injury in voice nodules. In J.Gauffin and B. Hammarberg (eds.), Vocal Fold Physiology Conference (pp. 21-28) San Diego, CA: Singular Publishing Group, Inc.

Harnoncourt, Nikolaus (1982) *Musik als Klangrede,* Salzburg and Wien, residenz Verlag. (1988) *Baroque Music Today: Music as Speech,* Amadeus Press (translation).

Harrison, Peter T. (2006) *The Human Nature of the Singing Voice: exploring a holistic basis for sound teaching and learning,* Edinburgh, Dunedin Academic Press Ltd.

Herbert-Caesari, E. (1958) *Tradition and Gigli,* London, Robert Hale Ltd.

Hirano, M (1981) Structure of the vocal fold in normal and diseased states. Anatomical and Physical Study. *ASHA* Report, 11, 11-30

Holroyd, Michael (ed.) (1979) *The Genius of Shaw,* New York, Holt, Rinehart and Winston.

Husler Frederick and Rodd-Marling Yvonne (1976) *Singing: The Physical Nature of the Vocal Organ* (Revised edition), London, Hutchinson.

Hyde, Lewis (2006) *The Gift: How the Creative Spirit Transforms the World,* Edinburgh, Canongate Books Ltd.

Johnson, Will (1993) *Balance of Body – Balance of Mind: a Rolfer's Vision of Buddhist practice in the West,* Atlanta, Humanics Trade Paperbacks.

Josephs-Serra, Mark (2000) *Sex, Spirit & Community,* Oxfordshire, Jon Carpenter Publishing.

Lane, John (2006) *The Spirit of Silence: Making Way for Creativity,* Dartington, Green Books Ltd. – quoting Rollo May.

Lipton, Bruce H. (2008) *The Biology of Belief: Unleashing the Power of Consciousness, Matter and Miracles,* U.S.A., Hay House, Inc.

Maisel, Edward (ed.) (1969) *The Alexander Technique: The Essential Writings of F. Matthias Alexander,* London, Thames and Hudson.

Marshall, Lorna (2001) *The Body Speaks: Performance and Expression,* London, Methuen. (2008 second – revised – edition).

Maslow, Abraham (1973) *The Farther Reaches of Human Nature,* Harmondsworth – quoted by Storr, Anthony (1988) *The School of Genius,* London, André Deutsch Ltd.

Meighan, Roland (compiled) (1994) *The Freethinker's Guide to the Educational Universe: a selection of quotes on education,* Nottingham, Educational Heretics Press.

Midgette, Anne (2005) *The End of the Great Big American Voice,* The New York Times (Arts).

Monk, Judith (2007) Interview with Eric Himy, Musical Opinion (May/June 2007 : Issue No. 1458).

Moss, Stephen (2007) *The DIY Violinist,* Guardian Arts Music.

Negus, V.E. (1949 reprinted 1962) *The Comparative Anatomy and Physiology of the Larynx,* New York, Hafner Publishing Company, Inc.

Ostwald, David F. (2005) *Acting for Singers,* New York, Oxford University Press Inc.

Ouspensky, P. D. (1978) *The Psychology of Man's Possible Evolution,* London, Routledge & Kegan Paul Ltd.

Parish, C. and Ohl, John F. (1953) *Masterpieces of Music Before 1750,* London, Faber and Faber Ltd.

Philips, Lois (1979) *Lieder Line by Line – and Word for Word,* London, Gerald Duckworth & Co. Ltd.

Piaget, Jean (1973) *Einführung in die Genetische Erkenntnistheorie,* Frankfurt, Suhrkamp (English translation New York, Columbia University Press, 1970) – quoted by Blaukopf, Kurt (1982) *Musical Life in a Changing Society* (translated David Marinelli), Munich, R.

Piper & Co. Verlag.

Potter, John (2009) *Tenor – History of a Voice,* Yale University Press.

Prochnik, George (2010) *In Pursuit of Silence,* U.S.A., Doubleday.

Read, D. and Stoll, W. (1998) *Healthy Behaviour: the implications of a holistic paradigm of thinking through bodymind research,* International Electyronic Journal of Health Education (1998).

Rée, Jonathan (1999) *I See a Voice,* London, HarperCollins Publishers.

Reid, Cornelius L. (1983) *A Dictionary of Vocal Terminology & Analysis* (Reprint edition), Huntsville: Recital publications.

Renshaw, Peter (2003) *Connecting Conversations: The Changing Voice of the Artist,* European League of Institutes of the Arts Teachers' Academy (Institut del Teatre and Escola Massana, Barcelona).

Ristad, Eloise (1982) *A Soprano on Her Head,* Utah, Real People Press.

Rogers, Carl R. (1980) *A Way of Being,* Boston, Houghton Mifflin Company

Schnelby-Black, Julia and Moore, Stephen F. (1997) *The Rhythm Inside: Connecting Body, Mind and Spirit Through Music,* Oregon, Rudra Press.

Senge, Peter (1990) *The Fifth Discipline,* Wikipedia, Doubleday Business.

Shapiro, Yehuda (2008) *Voci Verdiane,* Opera magazine, London, Rhinegold Publishing.

Stanislavski, Constantin (1924) *My Life in Art* (translated J. J. Robbins), Great Britain, Geoffrey Bles Ltd. (reprinted Methuen Drama 1991).

Skolimowski, Henryk (1994) *The Participatory Mind: A New Theory of Knowledge and of the Universe,* London, Arkana (Penguin Books Ltd.).

Sontag, Jerry (ed.) (1996) *Curiosity Recaptured: Exploring Ways we Think and Move,* U.S.A., Mornum Time Press.

Stevens, Anthony (1982, repr. 1990) *Archetype: A Natural History of the Self,* London, Routledge.

Storr, Anthony (1988) *The School of Genius,* London, André Deutsch Ltd.

Taylor, Gordon Rattray (1972) *Rethink: A Paraprimitive Solution,* London, Martin Secker & Warburg Ltd.

Tirze, Ingo R. (ed.) (1993) *Vocal Fold Physiology: Frontiers in Basic Science,* San Diego, Singular Publishing Group.

Tomatis, Alfred A. (1992) *The Conscious Ear: My Life of Transformation Through Listening,* New York, Station Hill Press.

Tulloch, Sara (ed.) (1993) The Reader's Digest *Oxford Wordfinder,* Oxford, Clarendon Press.

Wade, Graham (1991) *A Conversation with George Hadjinikos,* European Guitar Teachers Association (UK).

Watts, Alan W. (1974 repr. 1985) *The Wisdom of Insecurity: A Message for an Age of Anxiety,* London, Rider and Company.

Wheatley, Margaret J. (1999) *Leadership and the New Science: Discovering order in a Chaotic World,* San Francisco, Berrett-Koehler Publishers Inc.

Winckel, Fritz (1967 revised) *Music, Sound and Sensation,* New York, Dover Publications, Inc., (1960) *Phänomene des musikalischen Hörens,* Max Hesses Verlag.